His Excellent Greatness

In the Lives of Ordinary People

Isabel Downe

innovo
PUBLISHING

Published by
Innovo Publishing, LLC
www.innovopublishing.com
1-888-546-2111

innovo
PUBLISHING

Providing Full-Service Publishing Services for
Christian Authors, Artists & Organizations: Hardbacks, Paperbacks,
eBooks, Audiobooks, Music & Film

HIS EXCELLENT GREATNESS
In the Lives of Ordinary People

Scripture quotes marked KJV taken from the King James Version of the Holy Bible. Scripture
quotes marked NASB taken from the NEW AMERICAN STANDARD BIBLE ®, Copyright ©
1960, 1962, 1963, 1968, 1971, 1972, 1973, 1975, 1977, 1995 by The Lockman Foundation. Used by
permission. Scripture taken from the New King James Version ®. Copyright © 1982 by Thomas
Nelson, Inc. Used by permission. All rights reserved. Scripture taken from the HOLY BIBLE,
NEW INTERNATIONAL VERSION. Copyright © 1973, 1978, 1984 International Bible Society.
Used by permission of Zondervan Publishers. Copyright © 1982 by Thomas Nelson, Inc.

Library of Congress Control Number: 2014947584
ISBN 13: 978-1-61314-236-3

Cover Design & Interior Layout: Innovo Publishing, LLC

Printed in the United States of America
U.S. Printing History

First Edition: August 2014

Dedicated to JESUS CHRIST, my Savior and Lord.

"Not to us, O LORD, not unto us, but to Your name give glory, because of Your mercy, because of Your truth"
(Psalm 115:1, NKJV).

Acknowledgments

First, I would like to acknowledge my Lord and Savior, Jesus Christ, Who called me to Himself. He reached way down, brought me up, and is in the process of making something beautiful out of my life. He then called me to write this book about Him many years ago, in order to "Praise Him according to His Excellent Greatness" (Psalm 150:2b, NASB). It is my heart's desire that in the writing of this book, He receives praises in ways my mind could never imagine.

I would like to thank my husband, who has been my staunch supporter through it all. I thank you, my dear one, for everything. As my mind reflects, it is unbelievable all that you have done to make this come about, not the least of which was being my computer "geek." Thank you, too, for the prayer support, and the love and concern when the days were so tough during times of illness. Thank you for believing in me and that it was God's will right from the start. I love you. Rewards in heaven!

I also want to offer my gratitude to our pastor at the time who has since gone to be with the Lord. It was a special day for me when he so enthusiastically endorsed this as being from the Lord and that I was just the one to do it.

An incredible thank you to each of you who shared your own special story of God's excellent greatness in your own life. Without your desire to give praise and honor to the King of kings, this book would not be what it is. My heart of gratitude goes to you.

And to you who contributed stories that you knew to be true but were not your own, my gratitude goes to you too. One of those is my oldest brother. I so appreciate all of the prayers, love, and support from all of my friends from the beginning to the end. You know who you are. If I dared list the names, I am sure I would leave someone off. To my loyal supporters here in Tennessee, around the United States, Asia, South Africa, Canada, the Philippines, or wherever you are, I thank you from the bottom of my heart.

A very special thank you goes to the one dear lady who introduced me to key people in accomplishing the completion of this work. And to another dear sister in Christ Jesus, I offer my thank you for doing the initial editing.

A special thanks to you, my special friend on the mission field, for getting my computer set up in a special way to make things easier for me. I would love to give your name, but I cannot due to your location. Thank you, too, for the suggestion to rewrite the book years ago. Here it is, my friend.

My deep appreciation goes to Bart Dahmer and his entire team at Innovo Publishing for their exemplary help and understanding. My special thanks to Innovo Senior Editor Darya Crockett who helped shape this book in such a professional manner.

May God our Father bless you all! This could not have been done without you.

"God's plan is to take ordinary

people with ordinary talents, do

extraordinary things through

them, and give glory to Himself."

—Adrianism[1]

---

[1] Adrian Rogers, *Adrianisms: The Wit and Wisdom of Adrian Rogers, Volume One* (Bartlett, TN: Love Worth Finding Ministries, 2007) 57.

Most of the names in this book have been changed to protect people's privacy.

Contents

Special Stories

Preface

This book contains stories I believe the Lord wants to use for His glory. This has been a long labor of love. After discovering that writing this book was a call from the Lord, He made it known to me that it was to be others' stories as well as ours. Many people from around the world were excited to share their personal stories. These stories have been accurately presented in love to the Lord Jesus Christ and for His glory.

Chapter 1

_____

The Early Years

The crape myrtles, cottonwoods, large oaks, maples, chinaberry trees, roses, and daffodils, along with other blossoming flowers and evergreen hedgerows, were all dressing up and showing off their splendor, with each one seemingly attempting to outshine the others in all the yards surrounding the house. A peach orchard, apple tree, and pecan tree all complemented the extended areas around the old Southern country home. Parts of it were old enough to be on the historic registry. It had a smoke house out back with the land sloping off and giving way to corrals and barns of all shapes and sizes. It was a working farm with herds of cattle and horses grazing and roaming through rolling pastures where hillsides gave way to wooded acreage, meadows, babbling brooks, springs, and creeks. The muscadine and blackberry bushes gave their thanks by producing luscious fruit. All of this, plus the Blue Ridge Mountains as a backdrop, reflected the beauty of a pastoral and idyllic scene of tranquility. Trained dogs worked the herds of cattle and assisted in keeping order in what looked to be a sea of serenity. It was a place where beautiful memories should be made.

It was in the deep South on this lovely old farm where I spent my formative years. After seventy-one years in our family, there is an unexplainable love for that land that runs through our veins just as surely as the life flow of blood runs through every living being. I still love that place, and there are good memories stored away in my mind. Unfortunately, ours was a very dysfunctional family; therefore, many of my memories from there are not so good. Gratefully, our great God takes even the broken pieces of lives, restores them, and uses them for good—for His glory and for our joy to be made full.

In Genesis, we are told the story of Joseph whose brothers sold him into slavery as a very young man. Many years later, they were reunited and the brothers were afraid that Joseph would avenge himself of their earlier evil perpetrated against him. He, who had experienced slavery and prison, by the grace of God, eventually held an esteemed and enviable position second only to Pharaoh in Egypt. Yet Joseph said to them, "Fear not . . . you thought evil against me, but God meant it for good." (Genesis 50:19–20, NASB). Genesis 45:5 says, "And now do not be grieved or angry with yourselves because you sold me here; for God sent me before you to preserve life" (NASB). It seems incomprehensible that our wonderful Lord looked down through time, saw the choices that would be made, and used them for good in the family of Jacob whose sons had done such a dastardly deed to one of his favorite sons. Not only was it for good, but it was lifesaving and life-changing good. Moreover, He avenged the life of Joseph, the once wrongly charged outcast, and raised his position from a slave to a prime minister second in line to Pharaoh of Egypt during a famine in the land. Our God, the Creator of the universe, very creatively uses any and all pieces of fabric (circumstance) to craft the mosaic of our lives. In His economy, He uses everything; there are no throwaways from God's perspective. If you happen to be banished, it's of your own doing. From God's position, He has a decided advantage with His view of things, forming a composite picture and accomplishing His purpose in each of our lives. Fortunately, He sees the beginning, the end, everything in between, and is able to piece it all together for good (Romans 8:28).

My mother was a heart patient and required bed rest most of the time as I grew up. Sadly, my earliest memories as a little girl are of my dad abusing my mother and me. He was clever in that although my siblings saw the outbursts of anger, rage, and bitterness toward us, he was careful not to let them, or anyone, see the really rough stuff that went on. As the years progressed, my dad became increasingly worse.

I can now thank the Lord for allowing those tough days for my mother and me because I am learning that God does take those times and turns them into something good. I surely cannot understand the mind of God in all of that, but God's Word says that He doesn't withhold any good gift from His children. Since I've grown older, I can certainly attest, in reflection, that He gave me one of the most wonderful gifts a young girl could ever have—my godly mother. She made sure we were in church, raised all of us to believe that Jesus is God, and taught us that the Bible is God's Word. The best part of all that is that she faithfully lived what she taught even in the midst of deep trouble. On the other hand, even though my daddy went to church for a short time, made a profession of faith, and was baptized in his early twenties after he and my mother were married, his life never indicated that he loved the Lord. There was no interest on his part in attending church, nor was there any fruit. Unfortunately, it was quite the opposite.

He did begin to watch some television pastors like Dr. Charles Stanley, and he enjoyed listening to him in his senior years. A couple of us children, along with others, shared the gospel message with him, and he always assured us that he was in good standing with the Lord; yet, his life never indicated it. Perhaps if men had welcomed my daddy into the church and assisted him in growing up in the grace and knowledge of our Lord and Savior Jesus Christ (2 Peter 3:18), our lives would have been different. Instead, another "religious" gentleman who lived nearby began visiting and teaching him things that were totally not biblical. My dad readily accepted those things, and they continued to change him.

We must remember that when the devil or any of his minions see a vulnerable place, they will surely attempt to tear away any truth and replace it with lies. An important lesson for each of us to remember is that if we say we are Christians, we are always representing Christ Jesus, so we need to make sure it is a positive representation. Unfortunately, in this, many of us have failed. I am grateful, however, to my dad for providing food and shelter for us. There was never a day that I lacked either of those.

Although he did not attend church, and my mother was unable to attend because of heart disease, thankfully, he usually did not prevent his children from attending. Somehow at that very young age, I had a love for the Lord that would set my little heart soaring. When my Sunday school teachers would tell us Bible stories and give us little pamphlets with Jesus' picture and a memory verse for the next Sunday, I could hardly wait to get home to tell my mother. When the car door would open in our driveway, my little feet would barely touch the ground until I got inside the house and ran to tell her. Probably because of that, and my mother's prayers, for many years it was my heart's desire to be in church every time the doors were open.

At about age eleven, during the invitation time at the end of the service, a lady who was sitting by me whom I had never seen before or since, leaned over and said to me, "Aren't you old enough to make this decision?" I slipped out past her into the aisle and walked down to the front of the church where the pastor met me. I made a decision to join the church and be baptized. For many years, it was my understanding that all was well with my soul. As much as I could understand at the time, that was what it took to become a Christian. I might add here, too, that I certainly always believed that Jesus was the Messiah, our Lord and Savior, Jesus Christ, the Bible was God's Word, and it was to be obeyed. However, when I attempted to read it, it was so difficult to understand that I received nothing from it. That's a good indication that we are not truly born again spiritually.

~ Author's Note ~

When we are truly born again, God opens our minds so that we are able to begin to understand His Word. The more we read and obey what we do understand, the more He opens our minds to understand even more. He is a complex, awesome, and holy God. We should attempt to dig out all the nuggets we can. That is how we grow spiritually. Although it wasn't something that preoccupied my mind back then, I did want to live right as a Christian.

However, as I grew older, and the temptations of other things in life became more readily available, that desire to live right by the standards I had been taught became more and more difficult to fulfill. Even though the things of God didn't occupy my mind so much anymore, it was still my belief that Jesus is God and all that the Bible says about Him is true. That never changed! In Romans 7:19, Paul said, "For the good that I want, I do not do, but I practice the very evil that I do not want" (Romans 7:19, NASB). Paul was already a believer at that time, but he was explaining that the only way we can live the right way is by inviting Jesus into our hearts. Then, the Holy Spirit immediately comes and resides in us, enables us, convicts us, instructs us, and teaches us. Therefore, if we are not believers, there is no hope until we turn to Him. Some preachers teach more of the wrath of God and the dos and don'ts of the Bible than they do the love of God and His grace, mercy, and forgiveness that accompanied and balanced the truth. Conversely, some teach about His love and grace and leave out the wrath of God. It needs to be balanced.

It was many years before I knew that mercy very simply means that God doesn't give us what we deserve, which is punishment for our sins, if we put our faith and trust in Him for salvation. Grace means God gives us what we don't deserve—forgiveness for our sins, salvation, and eternity in heaven with Him. Of course, the greatest way to understand His unconditional love is by looking at what Jesus did on the cross for us. The shedding of His blood became the covering for our sins, if we would accept it. He not only died on the cross for our sins, He took the punishment from God the Father upon Himself for each and every one of the sins of every person so that we would not have to receive the penalty of death for our sins. No one will ever be able to comprehend what He suffered. Then He willingly offered us eternity in heaven with Him *if* we will only surrender our lives to Him, accept His *free* gift of salvation to us by grace through faith (Ephesians 2:8), and live by His Word, the Bible. For those of us who have accepted Jesus Christ as our Savior, even when we sin, God does not impute our sins to our account; He imputes them to our Savior, Who has paid it all. Moreover, His work is finished! It is all so simple to me now. Sometimes I wonder to myself, *How could I have missed all that for so many years?* When I was younger, it was not that I didn't want to live for Jesus; I simply didn't understand how.

At the age of about eleven or twelve, the responsibilities of running the household were given to me since my mother was a heart invalid. As I grew into my teens, deep in my subconscious mind there was a huge need and desire to get away.

I just thought that if I were in control of my life, I could make it a utopia; somehow, I would build a perfect life for myself. At some point, while still living at home, it was my great pleasure to land a job as a secretary in a hotel located on the campus of a major university. My responsibilities included administrative work for the general manager, booking reservations of all types, booking social events, planning large conventions, and planning menus for bridal parties, wedding receptions, and bridge parties. Eventually, I was promoted to a position like a resident manager, which meant I had to be on call at strange hours, so I moved into the hotel. I loved working for the general manager, an older gentleman, who saw potential in me and gave me the opportunity to soar. I loved the people I worked with. I made friends, and we had fun together. The biggest problem was the job offered no more upward mobility for me. It was a wonderful position, and I enjoyed it immensely. It also gave me a lot of confidence and self-esteem to launch out into other positions. Soon, an urging inside called me to something more.

Chapter 2

———————

Taking the Next Step

At twenty-one, after surviving much in my home, after completing the education that I planned, and having already launched my career in the business world, I moved out of the family home to an apartment in the city about thirty miles from home. I lived there four nights out of the week and went back to be with my mother three nights a week for long weekends. Someone was hired to help with the household chores in my absence. When my mother needed more help, I would stay more nights with her.

Because I knew so few people in the area, and because I loved my job, initially work became my obsession. It came to my attention there was a beautiful and spacious old two-story house in a premier location in the city, and it had been turned into two big apartments. The choice apartment with the entry from the handsome front porch was available. The rooms were large and furnished elegantly with antiques and Persian rugs. Thankfully, because the space would accommodate us, two other young professional women joined me there.

Soon I had become friends with a salesperson who was a native of the city. It wasn't long before I began dating and attending social galas. The thought that I could turn my life into a utopia was finally becoming a reality. Our new apartment in the old house seemed to be a good place for me, and it also became the favorite place for many of my new friends to congregate after work. While not perfect, life was good for me. Church remained significant for a time but was becoming less and less essential for my life.

Money had become of great importance to me. Somewhere along the way, out of a desire for projecting a perfect image for both work and play, a huge interest grew for just the right clothes. At times, I took on contract jobs where I typed masters' students' theses or provided music for events. Since I had played the piano at church and moved on to the organ, I was invited on occasion to either sing or play the piano or organ for weddings, receptions, funerals, or other social/civic events. Once I played for a group attending a convention. Since it had been my privilege to represent my class in a beauty pageant at a small college I attended briefly, there was even an occasion for training a contestant for the state's beauty pageant. None of this was steady work. Looking back, if there was any glamour or glitter attached to anything, it would just be another necessary ingredient for building my perfect life. Any thoughts about Jesus Christ seemed to be getting more and more distant.

Chapter 3

Life-Changing Events

My mother's cardiologist decided that she should be transported to a medical college for observation and tests to see if there was anything they could do for her. She prayed about it, and felt it was the right thing to do, so everything was put into place. She would be transported the four hours by ambulance. My parents were friends with a family that owned a mortuary and ambulances. One of the owners actually drove the ambulance, and an aunt and I attended to her on way with two of my siblings following in a car.

Since my mother had told the cardiologist at the medical college she wanted to know everything, he told her there were some rather unusual findings, and therefore any further plans for surgery had been eliminated. He added that she would be dismissed to go home soon. Then he said, "I don't know how you lived to make the four-hour trip here by ambulance, but you won't live to make it back home." He was wrong!

It was eighteen months later when my mother began deteriorating and had to be hospitalized. This was such a dramatic turn from anything we had ever confronted before with Mother. She went into the ICU, and although they did everything they could for her, nothing seemed to be helping. She was only fifty-seven. Every day the cardiologists and other attending physicians would tell us she could not last more than a few hours.

One day she took my hand, looked me in the eyes, and said, "For years I have prayed that God would let me live to see my children grown. And He has answered that prayer. Recently, I began praying that he would let me live to see you married to a good man who would take good care of you. But He is not going to do that." To which I responded, "Oh you don't know that. You have gotten down really low like this before, and you have bounced back." But she gripped my hand really hard, incredibly so for one so ill, and said, "No, He is not going to let that happen. I won't be going home." She prayed this even when she knew that as quickly as she breathed her last breath, she would be in heaven with the Lord and never have to suffer again. Incredible! What a sacrificial heart! That is God's agape love through a mother. Soon after that conversation, she slipped into a coma. She was propped up under an oxygen tent where she labored to breathe day and night.

Three days later, my lovely mother went home to be with her Lord and Savior, Jesus Christ. Our family friend, who co-owned the mortuary, happened to be in the hospital at the time and learned of her death right away. He told me that he quickly went to her, and this is what he saw: "She had the most beautiful smile on her face, the room was lit up with an incredibly bright light, and there seemed to be a Presence there that I had never experienced before. Somehow I knew I was intruding, so I quickly backed out of the room and walked down the hall. After a few minutes, I returned and slowly pushed the door open again. Everything was as it normally would be, so I went in." What a blessing for me to know that Mother is in heaven with our Lord, and we will be together again one day. I really appreciate having been told that story. Although I certainly believed that she would be with the Lord, it was so comforting to really know in that time. She is in the Presence of Almighty God and she is safe! She walks on streets of gold, and she will never be sick again. How awesome is that! How good is our God.

Now, more than ever, the busyness of my life was used to fill the hole in my heart so the pain would not be so intense. My new friends were there for me during that time, but the tie to my home and family was eroded even further. Somehow though, after my mother's death, my life of socializing and working had lost its luster. There was nothing fulfilling in the long term. I would attend parties where I might be the center of attention with young men waiting to dance with me, and yet, I would feel so lonely I could cry. When I got home, frequently, I would lie in bed feeling that loneliness so acutely that I would weep. What was wrong with me? Looking around me it seemed that I had everything to fill a person's life, all the things a young woman could desire. But I had a void deep down inside my heart that never seemed to go away, no matter what I filled my life with at that time. I wanted everything I saw until I got it, only to find out that really wasn't very satisfying either. Something was still missing.

Chapter 4

More Change

Now, I didn't grow up dreaming about my Prince Charming like a lot of young women do, quite the opposite, in fact. However about a year and a half after my mom's death, I met and fell in love with a charming commercial pilot. Despite the fact that on our very first date we assured each other we were looking for a strictly platonic relationship, four months later, we were married! Whew! It wasn't love at first sight, but it was nipping at the heels. Finally, I had really found my perfect life. A husband was all I needed! I didn't know they were such wonderful creatures. From approximately the early age of eleven or twelve, my mother had taught me to cook from scratch, and I could hardly wait to try out my homemade biscuits on him, along with other dishes. It was too funny; he didn't know what they were! My mother-in-law had prepared him for life very well. He was very self-sufficient, but he thought that homemade biscuits were the ones bought in the store and baked at home. He was so impressed. Almost everything was bliss for the first few months of our marriage. Suddenly, we started to have disagreements. Actually, my husband called them high-level discussions. I must say that some of them were extremely high level, and they would last for a while.

Nevertheless, life went on. We both had our work. He was away so much because of his flying that when he had time off it was almost always during the week when I had to work. Weekends were extremely lonely times. Most everyone who flew with him was either still single, divorced, or getting a divorce. Not a pretty picture. He hated being away from home, and I hated him being away. In fact, while we were dating, he was home much more, but on the day we returned from our honeymoon, he was moved up to flying larger aircraft, and that required much longer trips, more time away from home. I wept when he left, and I wept when he returned.

Finally, after a couple of years of that, he made the decision to change careers. The company tried to entice him to stay, but he had made up his mind to leave and he did. I know he is a wonderful pilot. Let me take a moment here to caution any ladies who might insist their husbands make a career change. Make sure that you pray long and hard before you encourage your mate to make a drastic career change like that, especially if it was something they had set their hearts on from a very early age. It took a while for us to settle into a new way of life. It caused us years of frustration in some ways, until he was finally in the place God had for him to blossom and grow again. In reflection, he was always where God wanted him to be, as He was preparing him for the one place that lay ahead that he would truly enjoy. So before long, the luster of another new life for me began to wear thin.

His new position led us to make a move to a small town near the South Carolina beaches. That was a very painful move for me. It was fun to be able to enjoy the beautiful beaches of South Carolina and the lure of Charleston's historic past, the lovely gardens, and all the delightful seafood to please anyone's palate. After a couple of years there, a new opportunity was presented to my husband. This company was located in the mid-South. He accepted. Our second move was coming up.

Chapter 5

Terror in the Night

The time finally arrived for us to go on a house-hunting trip. After a very late arrival at the airport, and driving to our new location, we didn't get into bed until the wee hours of the morning. The next morning began with an eight o'clock appointment to meet someone about a place for us to live. At the end of the day, we were entertained at my husband's company party, in our honor, with some of the staff and their spouses. Just before midnight, we returned to our motel room for the evening. En route we noticed how hot and humid the night was, and we casually remarked about the lightning off in the distance. We were dog tired, so shortly after returning to our room, we fell into bed and immediately went to sleep, totally unaware that we were about to experience one of the most evil encounters a human being would ever be subjected to.

Little did we know that the biggest tornado in that state's history, and the third most destructive one in the nation at that time, was weaving a path toward us. "WE NEED TO GET DOWN BETWEEN THE BEDS; IT'S A TORNADO!" We had been sleeping soundly and those were the words that woke me from a deep sleep as my husband yelled at me. Suddenly, and simultaneously, before we could move, the steel door of the motel room was ripped off its hinges and flung past our bed in a U-shaped trajectory. The windows burst out, and debris of all shapes and sizes began flying into our room. A Walmart was located just across from the pool of the motel that our room overlooked. It was there when we went to bed, but it was totally blown away within the next few minutes. We were right in the path of the flying debris. Although my husband had attempted to warn us in time to get to the floor before the tornado hit, it didn't quite work out that way. At the initial onset, just after the door flew past, some of the debris hit me in the head and knocked me out. Somewhere in the midst of all that unbelievable horror, my very brave husband had thrown himself on top of my body to protect me. My next cognizant thought was the realization that he was dragging me down between the beds onto the floor by one of my arms. There we lay in what seemed to be a surreal, yet incredibly ghoulish, reality. We lay in a continual mounting heap of ruins and rubble, totally terrified of what would happen next. It seemed to be an interminable malevolent attack raging against us. It seemed like a war between heaven and hell, and we were caught on earth in the middle of it with no end in sight.

Afterward we learned that the force of the storm would later be characterized by experts as second only to a nuclear explosion. The noise was excruciatingly deafening. It sounded like numerous freight trains passing right through the room. Simultaneously, there were incessant hissing sounds, ear-crushing crashes of thunder in mighty crescendos, and continuous intensely bright lightning. It was almost like the middle of a sunshiny day, but with a peculiar aura. Later on we were informed that three or four tornados had collided and became one massive one with winds up to about two hundred miles per hour. Back in the storm we were constantly pelted with wreckage of every imaginable thing that was later determined to be roofing rocks and other pieces of the structure from the Walmart next door that was totally destroyed. Outside and inside the mighty storm raged on!

Debris piled up around us and on us. While lying there, we cried out to God to save us. But somewhere along the way, we became very much aware of something quite strange and eerie happening around us as well; another type of battle was going on at the same time. This one was perhaps more sinister. Sometime afterward, I wrote a story of our experiences and when my husband read it, he came to me to say that *he had experienced the exact same thing that I had during the storm.* Before that, for some reason, we had not mentioned this part of that awful night to each other. There seemed to be a very large, dark, evil mass pulling at us, trying desperately to overwhelm us. In retrospect, we realized that Satan, or most likely some of his demons, were in the room with us trying to consume us, attempting to take our very lives. We kept crying out to God to spare our lives, but this war inside the room, as well as outside, continued. It was like a game of tug-of-war, but this was no game; this was deadly serious! At times, it seemed the enemy was succeeding, and then somehow we were given inner strength to retaliate and get a temporary reprieve to hold on to life for the next round. There were moments when it seemed we were being engulfed in sheaths of something similar to black crepe that covered our heads like a hood, suffocating us. We would find ourselves giving in and momentarily slipping off into a sea of darkness. Then, somehow, we would regain our consciousness and inhale another big drag of oxygen into our lungs. But death was stealthily and steadily waiting for us to succumb. We kept praying and pleading for God to spare us, and though at times it seemed we were losing the war, at last the monumental and prodigious tornado lessened. And death, too, had slung his menacing robe around his ugly form and slunk off into his haven of darkness to plan his next move. The next sound came from my husband as he said, "I'm hurt! Are you hurt badly too?" Then quite strangely and very calmly, he said, "You will have to try to call and get help." Honestly, my first reaction was that he must be kidding! I thought he would be the one going for help. But he insisted and explained that he was hurt badly and that I should attempt to reach someone at the motel office on the phone. Much to my horror it was like a second tornado had hit, as we were being hit with another barrage of an intense force of winds and flying debris. I had to take cover back on the floor. My husband was in such intense pain, he couldn't move. While hovering over him to get down as far as possible, I felt something liquid, warm, and thick. Blood!

Again, a prayer for safety was sent up from my lips as I reached for the receiver to make a call that would probably mean the difference between life and death for both of us. My husband has AB negative blood type—the rarest in the world. We had to get help for him as well as for myself, and quickly! Surely we had not just fought and won a battle with dark forces to be reckoned with beyond anything anyone could imagine only to let my husband bleed to death. Therefore, far from bravery, but out of necessity, I dialed the zero for the motel operator. A young man answered, but so faintly I could barely understand him. But, thank God, he answered. I simply stated, "This is Room 114; we are badly hurt. Please get help for us!" He asked me to repeat the message, but the line went dead. Thanks be unto God He was definitely looking out for us.

The winds began to diminish quickly and this same young man, along with a friend, came to our room with flashlights to see what we needed. He said that our call was the only one that went through the switchboard before the lines went dead. Of course, the electricity was out. He used his flashlight to survey the situation and saw that we were both beaten up badly, and the puddle of blood around my husband's right leg alerted him to the seriousness of the situation. These two young men ran outside into the storm to attempt to get transportation to the hospital for us. There was a flash flood so with that, and an active thunderstorm, most cars were off the streets. In spite of that, just as they approached the front of the motel, which overlooked the street, the first vehicle they saw was a police car driving up into the raised parking lot area of the motel to get off the flooded street. The young men relayed the message to the officer, and he quickly called for help. Almost immediately, they saw an ambulance approaching. The emergency medical personnel were driving around attempting to find people just like us in need of emergency service. Only God could have orchestrated the timing of all of this for us.

It was determined right away that my husband's right leg was badly broken with bleeding lacerations and a hole straight through it. After a very painful failed attempt to set it, the paramedics loaded us, and we began a torturous ride to the hospital. The hospital wasn't that far away, but with so many limbs, whole trees, and power lines down, as well as transformers blowing up, it was an arduous task.

Finally, we arrived at the hospital only to discover that many others had preceded us. Although my husband was bleeding badly, they were triaging and were too busy to do anything for him. At long last, a couple of doctors stopped to see where all the blood was coming from. We explained and again emphasized that his blood type was AB negative. They quickly took him into surgery, stitched up all the lacerations, and set his right leg in a cast. His leg was broken just below the knee and badly lacerated from his knee to the calf. The force of the wind had been so strong that apparently one of the roofing rocks had penetrated his leg, and it had gone in the front and exited the back side of his leg. The surgeon said had he not known the truth, he would have assumed he had been shot. He was in the hospital for about a week with his leg elevated. Gratefully, all of these injuries healed within a few months, with the exception of some outbursts of bleeding around his right ankle where blood had accumulated in small pockets from the injuries.

Basically, my injuries included a badly swollen right shoulder with lacerations and a large lump on my forehead, with very little external bleeding. Since there was no actual pain initially, it was later thought that I was in shock due to a brain concussion and contusions with hematomas. Emotionally, it was tough for me each time a storm headed my way. Looking back, it seemed that I suffered from something similar to post-traumatic stress syndrome. When storms came, I relived that night in living color for many years. Although the Lord had allowed it to happen, He did an amazing thing. He divinely intervened at just the right moment. I know if He spoke the world into being, and He did, according to the Bible, then that was nothing in comparison. All we know is that He delivered us! We give Him praise and thanksgiving!

"'I love You, O Lord, my strength.' The Lord is my Rock and my Fortress and my Deliverer, my God, my Rock, in whom I take refuge; my Shield and the Horn of my salvation, my Stronghold. I will call upon the Lord, who is worthy to be praised, and I am saved from my enemies" (Psalm 18:1–3, NASB). "He delivered me from my strong enemy, from those who hated me, for they were too strong for me" (2 Samuel 22: 18, NASB).

Chapter 6

God Meant It for Good

You have probably heard someone say that good and evil move on parallel tracks. How could anything good possibly come from all that I have told you so far? You probably have also heard that sometimes we have to be knocked over the head before God can finally get our attention.

On the day my husband was finally to be discharged from the hospital, a friend of ours, who was a pilot and had flown with my husband, chartered a twin-engine airplane. He, along with a friend of his and my husband's dad, all flew out to transport my husband and me to his family home in Tennessee. We did most of our recuperating there. Because we had already sold our house in South Carolina and the people who purchased it needed to take possession, we were moved out of our house and our home furnishings were put into storage while we were still recuperating in Tennessee.

After considerable time, we were physically able for our friend to fly us on to South Carolina so we could conclude our personal business back there and move on to the mid-South. Yes, unbelievably, we did continue with our plans to move there! Because so many homes were destroyed, we had no choice but to return to that same motel and wait for the new place to become available. Strangely, our room had been the only one destroyed during the tornado. Several people had been killed across the city, hundreds were hospitalized, and numerous houses and businesses were demolished. Over three hundred people were treated at the hospital where we were. That motel was not a fun place to revisit, but our Sovereign God was not finished with this story yet. The rooms had radiators that made incredibly loud noises as they cycled repeatedly each night. Many nights my husband and I would awaken and jettison ourselves out of bed to take cover, convinced it was another tornado. Somewhere along the way we would come to our senses. We were sleep deprived the entire time we were there.

Somewhere along the way, the Holy Spirit of God began to speak to my spirit that all was not well with my soul. He enabled me to understand that had I died that night, I had no assurance that I would spend eternity with Jesus Christ in heaven. That was a very sobering thought and one of extreme concern to me—we now lived in Tornado Alley. You might remember that I was sure I was a Christian since I had joined the church and was baptized many years prior to that. Yet, who can argue with the power of the Holy Spirit and a message like that? Eventually, He showed me that I needed to confess my sin life, repent, turn away from it, acknowledge Jesus Christ as my Savior and Lord, and begin to follow Him according to the teachings of His Word before I could have any assurance of spending an eternity with Him. The Bible says that the demons believe He is God and they tremble (James 2:19). But Jesus is not their Savior. They chose to follow Lucifer when he rebelled against God, and all were thrown out of heaven. I knew about other religious leaders and their teachings, but I didn't follow their teachings either. That's sort of the way I was with God back then. I just believed about Him intellectually; I didn't believe on Him by faith from my heart and had not committed to follow His teachings.

~ Author's Note ~

You know, if you really believe something from your heart, you will follow that teaching, won't you? I had never really begun to do that. Up until that point in my life, I was just practicing religion. There is a little test that is very helpful in making a decision about whether Jesus Christ is truly God. If you visit the grave of the man that people call Buddha, who, by the way, never claimed to be a god, whose remains do you find there? Buddha's, of course. If you visit other religious leaders' graves, you will find their remains there as well. Who do you find when you visit Jesus Christ's grave? No one! You won't find Him there! No! He was crucified and buried, but He arose on the third day, and He lives today and forever. He is the only One Who can lay claim to that fact. Both secular and Christian historians attest to this fact. It is worth your time to purchase the booklet, Is Jesus God? from East-West Ministries in Dallas, Texas. It is filled with information to support all of this. Of course, there are great authors with books filled with this info. And, most importantly, there is the Bible!

Still though, without having all of that information clear in my mind yet, at the strong urging of the Holy Spirit of God, I slipped out of my bed, went into the little bathroom there, fell upon my knees, and prayed a little prayer that went something like this: "Lord, please forgive my sins; come into my heart and make me the person You want me to be. Thank You, Lord, in Jesus' name." Immediately, a feeling of peace and joy flooded over my soul, and it felt as though Someone had just reached over and lifted the weight of the world off my shoulders. It was indescribable! In the same motel where we had almost lost our lives, had I now found mine? Yes, my eternal life. This time it was by surrender, running up the white flag to the God Who said, "For I know the plans that I have for you, declares the Lord, plans for welfare and not for calamity to give you a future and a hope" (Jeremiah 29:11, NASB). It was my desire to let Him take over and make something beautiful out of my life. (The only time you will ever achieve victory by surrendering is when you totally surrender yourself to God.)

How I wish I could tell you that I left that room and continually walked in the path of obedience and righteousness. I did not. We did get into a church, and I made an attempt to get involved there. However, it was like Paul said in 2 Corinthians 7:5 (NASB), "For even when we came into Macedonia, our flesh had no rest, but we were afflicted on every side: conflicts without and fears within."

Having lived through that horrific tornado, and living in Tornado Alley, incredible fear consumed me. It seemed we were watching the skies for tornado development, headed for cover in our bathroom, or racing with our neighbors to another neighbor's storm cellar. Some people sympathized but others laughed that I was so fearful. Like Paul said in Romans 7:18–19 (NASB), "For I know that nothing good dwells in me, that is, in my flesh; for the willing is present in me, but the doing of the good is not. For the good that I want, I do not do; but I practice the very evil that I do not want." Either I was still not saved or I was such a baby Christian that I was still not living as I should. I figured it was probably the latter since the devil does not give up easily.

Soon after we settled in, my husband received a promotion. Even though we lived within fifteen or twenty minutes of his company, his employer said it would be necessary for us to live in that small town where the headquarters were located. Just as we were getting settled in and had begun to meet people and become involved in that city, suddenly we were uprooted again. So within a year we had made two moves, both just after we had experienced the huge trauma of the storm—yet again to another very small town of approximately six thousand people.

Not too long after our second move, just around Christmas, I began having some weird symptoms that made me feel like I was getting a strange flu bug. After going to a doctor for a time, thinking I was having a miscarriage and not getting better, it seemed the rational thing would be to get another opinion. It was about that time that I met a nurse who suggested the name of an OB/GYN in a much larger city. Surprisingly, we received the good news that I had not yet actually had a miscarriage but indeed was pregnant. We were so excited! He gave me injections to stabilize everything and sent me home. Everything went well for a few months.

We were excited and making plans. My mother-in-law flew in to visit us and planned to meet me at my normal doctor's appointment. We had fun times planned, but my mother-in-law got a shock when she entered the doctor's office—I had gone into labor quite unexpectedly! The doctor was very optimistic and initially was able to stop the labor. He was sure it was all over, so he sent me home. On the drive back to our home, my labor began again. When we got home, my husband and mother-in-law took me to meet the doctor at the hospital.

Several hours later, our precious baby boy was born. Unfortunately, he lived only a short while before he went to be with the Lord. Within ten days of being one year since the tornado, we had experienced yet another tragedy. *God, in His infinite wisdom*, took our child home to be with Him. It was very traumatic for me to lose that child!

Shortly afterward, I went into severe depression for several months. Later on, as I learned more, I believe I was then suffering from postpartum depression combined with what seems now to have been a bit of posttraumatic stress from the storm experience. When other people heard about it, they would tell me "how lucky" we were that our baby boy was not ten or eighteen, or some random age like that, as though we should not be hurting because, after all, he was just a premature baby. We hadn't even been able to bring him home from the hospital! People meant well, I know, but it would behoove us to think before we speak such things.

Thankfully, now there are support groups for everything. I also experienced the sensation of Empty Arms Syndrome, which is not truly a medical term but one that doctors are very familiar with. Although I was never able to hold my baby, it felt as though he had been in my arms and someone had simply reached over and had taken him away from me. As I stuffed my emotions, the dense fog of depression tightened around my head, and my mind simply could not find a way out.

As the months progressed, emotionally I sank even deeper. One day, home alone, as I stood in my shower, it suddenly dawned upon me that the only way out would be by suicide, so I made the decision to do so as soon as I finished getting dressed and putting my make up on. (Studies show that women usually make themselves lovely prior to harming themselves in this way. That is why they *normally* do not use violent means to commit suicide.) The most unbelievable thing happened at the precise moment that thought became a viable option in my mind. Still standing in my shower, it seemed as if something had pierced the base of my spine, and chills raced all the way up the back of my neck. It felt to me that the hairs on my neck stood straight out. Amazingly, for the first time in many months, a sudden clear and rational thought seemed to take over and envelope my mind, pushing the darkness away. That thought was to get out of that shower and call for help, which is exactly what I did.

Interestingly, a new acquaintance we had met stopped by for a few quick minutes the day before. Because we were aware that she had attempted suicide herself a couple of times, she mentioned that she had recently discovered a wonderful doctor at a nearby university who had done wonders for her. His name was quite different and difficult; however, at this unique and special time, it came to me clearly. He answered the phone quickly and after listening for a few minutes, he insisted that I come right in to see him, which I did. He very sympathetically asked questions and let me weep and weep and weep. He just kept handing me tissues while all the pent-up emotions came tumbling out.

After only a couple of follow-up visits, he was convinced they were no longer necessary. He was correct. My circumstances were still the same, but the depression had lifted so it was much easier for me to cope.

~ Author's Note ~

Some psychologists say that making a move, even within the same area, can equal that of a death in the family, psychologically. Upon reflection, it is easy to understand that with posttraumatic stress from the tornado, the two moves so close, and postpartum depression, is it any wonder that such serious depression occurred? That is why it is of such major significance that we have a support system around us when we go through these things. But God was standing right beside us all the time, yearning for us to turn to Him for the Holy Spirit, the Comforter, to come to our aid. We are reminded of that in the book of Genesis when Joseph was going through such incredibly difficult times after his brothers sold him into slavery, and when Potiphar's wife falsely accused him of rape. The scriptures tell us repeatedly that the Lord was with him.

In Joshua 1:9 (NASB), we're told, "Have I not commanded you? Be strong and courageous! Do not tremble or be dismayed, for the Lord your God will be with you wherever you go." God is there for us always. This particular verse has come to me many times for myself and others at just the most perfect timing. I am quite convinced that even though I still had not learned how to turn to Him for help and wasn't living my life sold out to Him, it was He Who pierced my heart and mind with the clear thought to get out of that shower and call for help. If I had only known how to seek the Lord in His Word and in prayer during that time, He would have been able to comfort me in a much more personal way. As it was, He had to allow me to endure much more. Yet even in my distance from Him at that time in my life, He continually poured out His love to me in many ways and again preserved my life. I shall forever, through all eternity, sing His praises and offer up to Him the sacrifice of thanksgiving and love. He is a God of faithfulness! That is why we can put our total faith and trust in Him. Our confidence in Him and His promises will never be misplaced. We can have absolute assurance of that. If you doubt that, just do a study of the prophecies in the Old Testament and the New Testament, and you will see that He has met every one of them that are to be fulfilled up to this date. "For the Lord is good; His mercy is everlasting and His truth endures to all generations" (Psalm 100:5, NKJV).

Chapter 7

An Upward Turn in the Road

Sometime later, we moved to Virginia, where we got into an Evangelical Protestant Church that reaffirmed that the Bible is God's Word, written by God through men inspired by the Holy Spirit. Or simply put, it is "God-breathed," and it tells us that Jesus is God. It became even clearer to us that Christianity is not just another religion; it is having a personal relationship with the living and Almighty God through Jesus Christ our Savior, Who gave His life and paid the supreme penalty for our sins so that we would not be held accountable for our own sins.

~ Author's Note ~

His death on the cross was a fulfillment of a prophecy made in the Old Testament Psalms whereby Jesus would be crucified. Crucifixion, when it was first prophesied, had not yet begun to take place and would not for many years to come.

When Jesus Christ gave His life on the cross, He took the sins of the whole world's population of all time upon Himself at that time, suffering agonizing pain in a way no other human being would ever understand. Thereby, this provided a way for anyone who places his faith in Him as the Messiah, Savior of the world, to be "born again" (John 3) and begin an immediate personal relationship with Him on this earth, which would then last for all eternity. The cross of Calvary is a reminder to us all of the purest form of unconditional love. Agape love is God's supernatural love for us. Only by Him and through Him can we learn to love with agape love. Though Jesus Christ paid a high price for us, His salvation is a free gift to us. All we have to do is receive it by faith. His Word tells us, "For by grace you have been saved through faith, and that not of ourselves; it is the gift of God, not of works, lest anyone should boast" (Ephesians 2:8–9, **NKJV**).

Many people believe we have to work to earn our salvation. If so, then why did Christ die? At the moment on the cross of Calvary when Christ voluntarily gave up His life, He said, "It is finished!" Then the temple veil was rent in two enabling us to freely approach the throne of grace and speak to our Lord without any mediator. If you are not quite sure and you still need help, get a good translation of the Bible and begin reading in the gospel of John. Tell the Lord that you are willing to give your heart to Him and accept Him as Lord and Savior, and ask Him to please reveal Himself to you. The New American Standard Bible is the closest thing to the original manuscripts, according to Dr. Adrian Rogers, who is recognized around the world as one of the leading theologians and brilliantly gifted in the languages of the day. Others believe the King James Version is the best. That's a tough one for me to read. At least try the New King James Version. It is important that you have a willing heart. After you receive this free gift, you must then desire to be in obedience to Him. Out of your love for Him, you will be available to Him for anything that He asks of you. Just make sure it is from Him. James 2:17 (NASB) says, ". . . faith, if it has no works, is dead, being of itself." That does not mean that you must earn your salvation; we have just seen that it is a free gift. But you can know whether you have truly received it by your heart's desires. If there is still no desire to follow His teaching, then you are not yet committed to Him. It is also one of the ways to be a testimony of Who He is to others so that they might come to know Him as well.

We need to understand that God loves us and has a much better plan for our lives than we could ever imagine. "'For I know the plans that I have for you,' declares the Lord, 'plans for welfare and not for calamity to give you a future and a hope'" (Jeremiah 29:11, NASB). When you are ready to totally commit your life to Him, follow His teaching, and allow Him to guide you, then bow before Him, express remorse for your sins with true repentance and godly sorrow, confess that you are a sinner, and ask Him to come into your heart and make you into that person that He wants you to be. If you are truly sincere, He will do it. In the book of Revelation, He said, "Behold, I stand at the door and knock; if anyone hears My voice and opens the door I will come in to him and will dine with him, and he with Me" (Revelation,

3:20, *NASB*). That simply means He will come to live in our hearts in the person of the Holy Spirit immediately upon our inviting Him. He will never leave us alone nor forsake us.

He supernaturally enables us to live the life that is pleasing to God the Father through Jesus Christ, if we will allow Him. "All have sinned and fall short of the glory of God" (Romans 3:23, *NASB*). "For the wages of sin is death, but the free gift of God is eternal life in Christ Jesus our Lord" (Romans 6:23, *NASB*). Sin is an archer's term, which means missing the mark. We are all guilty of that. Every single one of us. We cannot earn His forgiveness; He freely gives it, if we come to Him with the right heart and mind and ask for it and if we are willing to follow His teaching.

Some people think they are so good they don't need God. I recently heard somewhere that some people think they are so good that when they get to heaven, the Holy Trinity will become a quartet! That's a joke, but we act like that at times. But that is not what God says in Romans 3:23. We are all born sinners in need of a Savior. He also tells us there is only one way to the Father, and that is through Jesus Christ, His Son. "Jesus said to him, 'I am the way, and the truth, and the life; no one comes to the Father but through Me." (John 14:6, *NASB*). He did not say that He was a way; He said the way. That means He is the only way to God the Father and heaven. If you have a problem with that thinking, then you have a problem with Him, not with me. That is Jesus speaking His truth in love to us. We are told in Romans 5:8 (*NASB*), "But God demonstrates His own love toward us, in that while we were yet sinners, Christ died for us." So there are none so good they do not need the Savior, and there are none so bad that He will not save. Amazing grace! It's God's unmerited favor, His gift to us. A good little acrostic for **GRACE** is: God's Riches At Christ's Expense. I don't know to whom to give thanks for that little piece of information, but it is good. Paul states the beautiful good news of the gospel of Jesus Christ: "For I delivered to you as of first importance what I also received, that Christ died for our sins according to the Scriptures, and that He was buried, and that He was raised on the third day, according to the Scriptures, and that He appeared to Cephas, then to the twelve. After that He appeared to more than five hundred brethren at one time . . .; then He appeared to James, then to all the apostles, and last of all, as it were to one untimely born, He appeared to me also" (1 Corinthians 15:3–8).

Oh the beauty of One so majestic! He is filled with such great love but tempered with His unspeakable holiness so that He gives unbelievable gifts generously and graciously. He will not withhold any good gift from His children, even to the giving of His own life in order for us to have a personal relationship with Him in the here and now and throughout eternity. What a Savior! " For God so loved the world, that He gave His only begotten Son that whoever believes in Him shall not perish but have eternal life" (John 3:16, **NASB**).

There is a great chasm between us and God, and no matter how we attempt to reach God in our own way, whether it is through a religion of good works, following some religious guru with his or her philosophical false teaching, or whatever, it will fail. Unless our pursuit of God is rooted and grounded in God's Word—the Holy Bible—and the teaching therein, our attempts will fail. God is a loving God, but He is also a just God. He does not want any to die and miss His plans on this earth and in heaven, but He will not force Himself on us either. It is simply our choice to make. We must surrender, repent, confess our sins, trust, and obey, or we will be eternally separated from Him and all others who have put their trust in Him. Jesus Christ, born of a virgin, is the Savior of the world. He is the Messiah, the Most High God. He is our only way to heaven. According to the Word of God, heaven is real, but so is hell. Hell is a place of eternal torment where people who do not accept Him are separated from Him and all that is good and lovely. Choosing life with Jesus Christ and His kingdom warriors is the right choice.

According to Jesus Christ, He came that we might have life and have it more abundantly, which means we can live life to its fullest (John 10:10). Yet, living for Jesus on this earth does not mean it is trouble free with no mountains to climb or trials to overcome. However, it does mean that we will have Him enabling us, guiding us, giving us strength for the day and wisdom for the way, protection, provision, and deliverance. "But, in all these things we overwhelmingly conquer through Him who loved us. For I am convinced that neither death, nor life, nor angels, nor principalities, nor things present, nor things to come, nor powers, nor height, nor depth, nor any other created thing, will be able to separate us from the love of God, which is in Christ Jesus our Lord" (Romans 8:37–39, NASB).

Somehow after my decision to give my life to Jesus Christ a few years earlier, it seemed like everything had deteriorated. I was even more miserable. Had it just been a "spiritual experience" with no resolve on my part to follow through? For sure, I was failing miserably in following after Him, and I needed to make perfectly sure. So, one day, I sought a quiet spot in our Virginia home, fell on my knees with my face to the floor, and once again cried out to the Lord. I told Him that this time I was very sincere in surrendering my life to Him and ready to forsake everything; I was willing to follow Him. I knew that I was unable to cope with things, and He would have to do it for me. That day, I very genuinely yielded my heart to God and decided to follow Jesus, no matter what. Do you know what happened? I got off my knees, walked away, and this time there were no bells or whistles going off, no feelings that Someone had lifted the weight of the world off my shoulders. It was nothing like that at all. But inside there was peace.

The next day, doing mundane chores around the house felt different. There was a song in my heart, a smile on my face, and my spirit soared with the joy of the Lord. There was a newfound desire to go to church and be with other believers. I also learned that after we make a decision to follow Jesus, if we want to get to know Him better, and have a personal relationship with Him, we have to spend time with Him. To spend time with God, we have to spend time with Him reading His Word and devoting good quality time with Him in prayer. As I began to do that, suddenly the Bible came alive to me, and I just devoured it. Before when I read the Bible, it made no sense and was just plain dull and boring. The Bible tells us that when we decide to commit our lives to Jesus and follow His teaching, the Holy Spirit of God immediately comes to indwell us. The Holy Spirit—the third Person of the Trinity—enables us to live our lives pleasing to God the Father through Jesus Christ our Savior. It is the Holy Spirit Who opens our eyes to the truth of

God's Word after we receive Him as our Savior, so that we can then understand it and take its meaning.

Some people become frustrated at the beginning of their new life in Christ Jesus because they don't instantly understand all of the Bible. One of our favorite quotes is: "To understand the part of the Bible you don't understand is to obey the part you do understand, and before long you'll begin to understand what you didn't understand. Understand?"[2].

Similar to Paul in Acts 9, I had my own type of Damascus Road experience. My entire outlook on life had suddenly taken on a different hue. The closer I got to Jesus and the better I knew Him, the more I wanted others to know Him too. I loved telling everyone about Jesus. I was working in Virginia as a recruiter for corporate positions. Even though this was a business office, I had people come into my office who needed something more in their lives than just a corporate change. They really needed a heart change. I had opportunities to tell them what Jesus had done and was continuing to do for me personally. As a result, some of them came to know Jesus Christ personally as well. Truly, the Giver of good gifts had given me my perfect life. I wouldn't have changed much of anything. I understand more fully now what the French scientist and Christian writer, Blaise Pascal, meant when he stated something like this: Every man has a God-shaped vacuum in his heart and only Jesus Christ can fill it. What a difference a day makes. I was finally surrendering my life to Jesus, and He was beginning the work in me that only He can do. Dying daily to self is so important, according to the apostle Paul.

A dear pastor friend explained something that I had never heard before. We can be saved (born again spiritually speaking, as Jesus Himself explained to Nicodemus in John 3:3) but not yet be a Christian. He said that being a Christian is a term that came

---

[2] Adrian Rogers, *Adrianisms: The Wit and Wisdom of Adrian Rogers, Volume Two* (Bartlett, TN: Love Worth Finding Ministries, 2007).

later on in the Word. It means a Christ follower, and that to Him that term identifies those who have surrendered to the Lord and are growing/maturing spiritually. If we are saved, we need also to be surrendered to know Him and fellowship with Him. I really believe I was saved in that motel room after the storm, but I didn't have the teaching and the tools to begin to grow up in that new life. Please understand, though, when we are born again (saved), we still have our old selves inside us. So we begin to have spiritual warfare. Our new selves in Christ Jesus, with the Holy Spirit inside us, will have war with our old selves (nature). However, the more we read the Bible, pray, attend the right church, and associate with like-minded people, our desire for the old will begins to fade and the new creation will begin to dominate. Just remember, Satan is a real foe, and his goal is to bring you down. So be on the alert! (see Ephesians 6:10–13).

Chapter 8

How God Speaks

"The Lord has His way in the whirlwind and in the storm . . ." (Nahum 1:3, NKJV). When I read that verse, I am reminded of how God finally began to get my attention. He speaks to us and through us in various ways. A lady spoke of a time when she was on a mission trip to South America with a church group when the Lord told her she would give her presentation in Spanish, a language she had never spoken before. She told Him she was unable to do so, as if He did not know that. I can almost hear Him saying, "Behold, I am the Lord, the God of all flesh. Is anything too hard for Me?" (Jeremiah 32:27, NKJV). True to His Word to her, when she began speaking to that group in South America, He spoke through her in Spanish for the entire presentation. I would say that is an extraordinary way of reaching people for Him. Speaking in "different kinds of tongues"(languages) (1 Corinthians 12:10, NKJV) is not too difficult for Him. "But one and the same Spirit works all these things, distributing to each one individually as He wills" (1 Corinthians 12:11, NKJV). "Call to Me, and I will answer you, and show you great and mighty things, which you do not know" (Jeremiah 33:3, NKJV).

"Pistol" Pete Marovich, a once famous basketball player, told his story at a church we attended years ago of how he had messed up his life. Fame and fortune had not given him meaning and purpose in life. He was spiraling downward, rather than living a satisfied life with all that had been given to him—something we see and hear of with so many other celebrities before and after Pete. After many years of this life, one night as he lay sleeping in his bed, he heard a voice calling his name. It was so loud and clear that he assumed it was audible, and his wife had heard it as well. However, she had not. As his name was repeatedly called, he finally realized it was God calling him to Himself. He got out of his bed, fell on his face, received Jesus Christ as his Savior, and was never the same again. He fell in love with Jesus, and it became his delight to travel the world and tell others about his relationship with Jesus, so they too could come to know Him. Although he was a legend in his day because of his basketball accomplishments and the acclaim that went with it, nothing filled the void in his heart or gave meaning and purpose in his life until he met and committed his life to Jesus Christ personally. After studying secular religions and finding nothing to compel him to endorse them, only Jesus could fill that void. Pete Marovich died a few years later at the age of forty. He had made a statement years earlier that he did not want to play basketball for the NBA for ten years and die of a heart attack at the age of forty; he died in the arms of Dr. James Dobson during a pickup basketball game after having just told Dr. Dobson that he felt the best he had ever felt. Although it was a sad day for everyone who loved him here on earth, there was rejoicing in heaven that day because Psalm 116:15 tells us, "Precious in the sight of the Lord is the death of His saints" (NKJV). Fortunately, for Pete, and for all of us, he will be there when we arrive in heaven, and we will be able to spend all eternity with him along with all the others who have made a sincere commitment to follow Jesus Christ all the days of their lives here on earth.

The apostle Paul was initially a persecutor of the Christians of his day. He, known as Saul at that time, stood by and witnessed the stoning of Stephen, the martyr, who died because of his Christian witness against the religious Jews, who denied that Jesus was the Christ. In fact, the other witnesses laid their coats at Saul's feet while they stoned Stephen. "Saul was in hearty agreement with putting him to death." After that incident, "Saul began ravaging the church, entering house after house, and dragging off men and women, he would put them in prison" (Acts 8:1, 3, NASB). "Now Saul, still breathing threats and murder against the disciples of the Lord, went to the high priest, and asked for letters from him to the synagogues at Damascus, so that if he found any belonging to the Way, both men and women, he might bring them bound to Jerusalem. As he was traveling, it happened that he was approaching Damascus, and suddenly a light from heaven flashed around him; and he fell to the ground and heard a voice saying to him, 'Saul, Saul, why are you persecuting Me?' and he said, 'Who are You, Lord?' And He said, 'I am Jesus, Whom you are persecuting, but get up and enter the city, and it will be told you what you must do.' The men who traveled with him stood speechless, hearing but seeing no one. Saul got up from the ground, and though his eyes were open, he could see nothing; and leading him by the hand, they brought him into Damascus. And, he was three days without sight, and neither ate nor drank" (Acts 9:1–9 NASB).

Just about that time, the Lord also spoke to a man called Ananias in a vision and told him to go find Saul. He told him exactly which house to go in, and He told him that Saul would also know about him from a vision the Lord was giving him. He told Saul that this man would come and lay hands on him so that he could regain his sight. He also told Ananias that Saul, later renamed Paul by the Lord, was His chosen instrument to bear His name before the Gentiles, kings, and the sons of Israel, and He showed Saul how much he must suffer for His name's sake. Ananias did go and lay hands on Paul, and he later went on to become one of the greatest apostles of all time. Enduring much suffering, yet he continued to proclaim the name of Jesus everywhere the Lord sent him. Paul's conversion experience can be found in the book of Acts, chapters 8 and 9.

***

Jessie, a native Filipino, was residing in Hong Kong when she heard I was writing a book, and she wanted to contribute her story: "As a young lady in the Philippines, I was a rebellious and disobedient child before I came to know Christ in a personal way. Not only was I disobedient within the sight of my own family and others, but more importantly, I was disobedient in the sight of God. Christianity had been taught at home since my relatives are missionaries. Also, my elder sister had shared about God's love and saving grace with my family. Yes, I suppose I believed that there was a God who can save sinners like me, but as for me, all of those things were very vague and meaningless at that time. All I know is that I received some happiness in whatever it pleased me to do, even getting married at an early age.

"However, in my first year of high school, I was invited to attend a Campus Crusade for Christ Fellowship that was called 'College Life.' After the happy fellowship, someone shared with me about Jesus Christ from a booklet called the Four Spiritual Laws. He said that Jesus died for my sins because He loved me so much and that He wants to offer me eternal life. He said that Jesus is only waiting for me to open the door of my life so He could come in. In the book of the Revelation 3:20 (NASB) it says this, 'Behold, I stand at the door and knock; if anyone hears My voice, and opens the door, I will come in to Him, and will dine with Him, and He with Me.' That verse really struck me and spoke to my heart. It led me to a decision to repent and ask forgiveness for my sins. I then received Jesus Christ to be my personal Savior. It was then, too, that I gave Him my will and let Christ change my life to a new and meaningful life that God wanted to offer me. Unfortunately, because of unexpected circumstances that had come my way, and because of my lack of commitment, I began to fall away from what I knew to be right. I was not growing spiritually because I was not reading God's Word and praying as I should. I had become a stagnant Christian. In 1987, I moved to Hong Kong and it was there that I rededicated my life to Jesus. My Christian life was revived and deepened through the messages of my pastor in each worship service, by attending Sunday school, and various training that the church offered. God spoke to me through the words in John 10:27 saying, 'My sheep hear My voice, and I know them, and they follow Me . . .' (NASB). Gradually, God worked through me, and my changed life is proof that Christ loves me and cares for me.

"Now I can say that I serve the Lord with gladness and a committed heart. One of the areas I saw Him working to change me was with my chain smoking; He delivered me from that habit. Because of my heavy smoking, I had lost my sense of smell and my appetite. Because of this, I had lost a lot of weight. I was concerned that I would be a slave to this vice forever. But God is so good to me. It took time and I struggled, but 'with God nothing is impossible.' He made a way for me to get rid of that habit. Finally, I was able to stop smoking. You see, I believe that from the day I received Jesus Christ as my Savior, my body is no longer my own; it is a temple of the Holy Ghost. 'What? Know ye not that your body is the temple of the Holy Ghost which is in you, which ye have from God, and ye are not your own? For ye are bought with a price; therefore, glorify God in your body, and in your spirit, which are God's' (1 Corinthians 6:19, 20, KJV). Thanks to God, after I finally stopped smoking, I gained weight and regained my sense of smell. Through the years, I have continued to be in Bible studies and teaching Master Life Training."[3]

***

A friend of mine is Jewish by birth, but she has accepted that Jesus is the Messiah and that He is her only hope for salvation. She proclaims boldly that Christ is her Savior. As a result, the Lord opens doors for her to speak to others about Him. She met another Jewish lady somewhere along life's road that was also a follower of Jesus Christ.

One day she received an invitation from this lady to come visit her and her husband. She explained that he had Alzheimer's disease, and she was very concerned that he might die without accepting Jesus Christ as his Savior. She knew if he did die in that condition, he would be eternally separated from Jesus Christ and her. My friend quite happily accepted the invitation to go speak with them. Sometime after her arrival, and while she was speaking with the gentleman, suddenly he rallied and became quite cognizant and listened attentively to what she was telling him about Jesus Christ. After telling him about the gospel of Jesus Christ, this precious elderly gentleman very quickly acknowledged that he believed what she had told him was true, that Jesus is both God and man, and that as man He died on the cross for all of our sins. When given the opportunity to pray a little prayer whereby he would accept Jesus as his Savior, he happily did so.

Later on that day, she spoke with her friend again. The lady told my friend that she had become concerned that perhaps her husband had not actually understood after all. That evening, she approached him and asked him what his memory of the day entailed. The dear man excitedly told her that he had accepted

---

[3] Master Life is an advanced Bible study for more mature believers. Jessie is now teaching this advanced study. All praise and honor and glory to our God.

Jesus Christ as his Savior. She, of course, was elated. She went on to say that shortly afterward, he lapsed back into a state where he had normally been living, seemingly totally unaware of his surroundings. Not too long after that, the gentleman died. The best part of this story is that he was immediately in the presence of his Savior, and no doubt will probably be one of the first waiting to greet his precious wife just after the Lord welcomes her into her eternal home.

Some people may ask how we know this to be true. Have you ever heard the words, "Absent from the body, present with the Lord"? The actual scripture where this is written is in 2 Corinthians 5:6–8 where Paul said, "Therefore, being always of good courage, and knowing that while we are at home in the body we are absent from the Lord for we walk by faith, not by sight—we are of good courage, I say, and prefer rather to be absent from the body and to be at home with the Lord" (NASB). El Shaddhai, Almighty God, is a great and awesome God. He is faithful. If there is a heart that will turn to Him, He will readily receive, but He will not override our will. He is a very patient God; however, He will not wait forever. It is my understanding that if you have a rebellious heart and prefer to turn away from Him, He will allow the enemy to come and nudge you in that direction. However, if you have the least bit of interest in knowing Jesus, He will send the Holy Spirit to give you a nudge in the right direction. He will use whatever means He needs to reach us, but if we harden our hearts, He will eventually turn away and convict us no more.

From the stories above, you can see how gracious and loving our Lord is in His display of patience, kindness, goodness, faithfulness, grace, mercy, compassion, and so much more, with His provisions for us through the gift of eternal life through Christ Jesus. When we hear that people have come to know Jesus Christ in a personal way, or have been "born again" (Jesus' words, John 3:3, NASB), we need to come alongside these people and be a vessel our God can use to help them grow in the grace and knowledge of our Lord and Savior, Jesus Christ (Colossians 1:9–12).

Sometimes it appears that people may have just had a religious experience, rather than a true conversion, because we do not see any fruit. Maybe so, only God knows for sure. It could be that He is still working in them to bring them into the kingdom. Or it could be that they really have accepted Jesus as their Savior and haven't had proper teaching to enable them to grow up spiritually. Paul says that when we are first born again, we are compared to a baby eating baby food: "like newborn babes, long for the pure milk of the word, so that by it you may grow in respect to salvation, if you have tasted the kindness of the Lord" (1 Peter 2:2, NASB). But when we begin to grow, we can feast more on other lovely foods (meat) so we aren't just receiving the basics; we are beginning to give back. It is so important for all of us to daily read God's Word, pray, spend time in church, and fellowship with other believers. We need to be obedient to Him in service where He calls us and be careful to fill our minds with things that are lovely and wholesome. We need to mature and get to know Jesus Christ more intimately and be of service to Him in His kingdom work here on earth. It also behooves us to come alongside others to introduce them to Jesus the Christ and then to assist them in their growth. Jesus said that we are to, "Go therefore and make disciples . . ." (Matthew 28:19, NASB). We should begin by telling others (confessing) what He has done for us. "Therefore, whoever confesses Me before men, him I will also confess before My Father who is in heaven. But whoever shall deny Me before men, I will also deny him before My Father who is in heaven" (Matthew 10:32–33, NKJV). The quicker you do this, the better it will be. Then, just begin obeying what you already know and allow God to grow you up and use you. Even as a new follower of Jesus Christ, when you begin to experience the excitement of what God is doing in you, and what it means to be a "new creation," you will probably discover that it will begin to spill out to others. You don't have to be a trained evangelist; the Holy Spirit of God will just do it through you. Some say that salvation is as much caught as taught. When others see your excitement and what God is doing for you, they too will want to know Him. However, as we begin to mature spiritually, God allows trials for several reasons.

One is so that we learn to cling to Him and depend on Him more and more. Another is that He might be able to grow our character to be more like Him, so He will be able to see His reflection in us. Still another is that we will become more compassionate to those around us when they are going through tough times, and we will be able to comfort them. "Blessed be the God and Father of our Lord Jesus Christ, the Father of mercies and God of all comfort, who comforts us in all our tribulations, that we will may be able to comfort those who are in any trouble, with the comfort with which we ourselves are comforted by God. For as the sufferings of Christ abound in us, so our consolation also abounds through Christ. Now, if we are afflicted, it is for your consolation and salvation, which is effective for enduring the same sufferings which we also suffer. Or if we are comforted, it is for your consolation and salvation. And our hope for you is steadfast, because we know that as you are partakers of our sufferings, so also you will partake of our comfort" (2 Corinthians 1:3–7, NKJV).

Again, we must recall that our God's ways and thoughts are quite different and much higher than ours. "'For My thoughts are not your thoughts, nor are your ways My ways,' declares the LORD. 'For as the heavens are higher than the earth, so are My ways higher than your ways, and My thoughts than your thoughts'" (Isaiah 55:8, 9, NASB). Jesus is our Teacher, and He sends the Holy Spirit to enable us to grow spiritually. It's an inside job, precipitated by the Holy Spirit's work; however, we must surrender to Him and be willing to change. It seems to me that we are all little porcelain vessels broken into hundreds of pieces by the time most of us reach out to our Master Potter. When we do, He takes the mess that we have made of our lives, and puts all the pieces back together into something more practical and useful. This new creation shows His reflection more and more as we allow Him to work in us so that we can be used in His kingdom work.

Upon His final act of mercy toward us, He scoops us up and brings us up to the third heaven where He resides. There, we are suddenly changed into something more beautiful than we can imagine, for we will be perfected, and there we will live with Him for all eternity serving Him for His glory and honor, face to face! God not only uses extraordinary means for us to come to know Him, He also uses various means for us to grow up in Him. Therefore, we want to be vigilant to listen to God when He speaks, whatever the occasion. Please understand that *if* we are His children, He will always be working to bring us closer to Him. Another Adrianism goes something like this: God will never let us flunk a class; He just re-enrolls us.

Chapter 9

_____

An Exciting Walk with God

Although nothing in our physical lives had changed, I now had God's truth, love, and acceptance factored into everything, which was quickly changing the very fabric of my everyday life for the better. God the Holy Spirit was beginning to fill the hollow places in my life. Now that I had truly found my perfect life, I was ready to simply settle in and enjoy. However, Father God had something else in mind for me. The Holy Spirit had begun speaking to me in the middle of the night, saying, "Take a step in faith and quit your job." Initially, I thought He was ringing up the wrong number. No way could that message be for me! Back then, I liked to think of myself as very logical. Well, I couldn't think of one logical reason why I should quit my job. I loved the business world and had no desire to leave it; we didn't have any children for me to stay home with. So I didn't quit. But this thought began to consume me, waking me up at all hours night after night with the same message. But I still wouldn't quit. I had no experience with God speaking to me in that way, so I needed to be sure.

On Christmas Eve of that year, I thought I had another miscarriage. Once again, depression set in. It was all so disappointing and frustrating. A few days after that latest disappointment, I was in my bathroom putting on my makeup and getting ready for work. I began thinking about what I wanted to speak with God about in my time alone with Him before going to work. This was something that I had begun to do daily, and I had learned many believers call it their "quiet time." This is the time when we seek His presence through adoration, praise, and thanksgiving, and we seek His power through confessions, intercession for others, and petitions for ourselves and others. I was going to tell Him that I was hurting once again because of the miscarriage, and I wanted Him to help me through it. Suddenly, it was like I was no longer looking at myself in the mirror, and somehow the light in the bathroom was replaced by an incredibly bright—brighter than the noonday sun—light. I was filled with the most incredible and indescribable heightened sense of peace, love, and joy that I had ever known, before or since. Out of my peripheral vision, I could see someone standing right beside me. He was clothed in the most spectacularly, dazzlingly, bright and luminously shining white garments. It was beyond anything this world has to offer! I did not see His face and He did not speak to me audibly, but these words were etched right across my mind as He spoke to my spirit, "Don't worry! You will be fulfilled, not necessarily with children. I have a plan for you!" Then, just as quickly, I was back looking at myself in the mirror again just as before, yet still feeling an incomparably heightened sense of peace, joy, and love—and no more depression.

The Bible speaks of messages being delivered by angels, and there are times when it speaks of "the angel of the Lord," which means that it is Jesus manifesting Himself as an angel. Either way is just fine with me, but He spoke in the first person, which convinces me that it was Jesus Himself. Why He chose to do this for me, I will never know, at least not while I'm here on earth. I have always believed that He gave me a tiny glimpse of what it will be like in heaven. It was a few moments of total perfection and bliss, like I had been caught up in paradise and given a precious few moments in the presence of the King of kings. Frankly, it was difficult to just move on with the cares of the day! I wanted nothing more than to savor the ecstasy and delight in the pleasures of His company in that special way. Momentarily caught up in all of this, and pondering it all, suddenly I realized there was no more depression. Unexpectedly, these words were clearly spoken to my spirit as well, "Call Barbara------."

Barbara and her husband, Phil (not their real names), were simply two acquaintances at the church we attended. She was probably one of the last people I would think of to tell about some spiritual experience I just had. So I didn't call her. Having no answers for all of this, I did the only thing I knew to do—continue to go through my day as normal. But this thought about calling her joined the other one about taking a step in faith and quitting my job.

Night after night I was awakened with these thoughts permeating my mind. Unable to continue losing sleep, I asked my husband for his advice. He listened very attentively and then he said, "It's really very simple. If these two things are bothering you, then just do them. Quit your job and call Barbara." That was a huge leap for him because quitting would drastically change our lifestyles. Yet, even with his support, I still couldn't bring myself to do it. More time passed and with each day it seemed everything was turning up roses at work.

I had a management position, and the owner gave me accolades for the team's accomplishments one Friday. We had just finished the best week of sales we had ever had, and my last thoughts before beginning the weekend were, *This is wonderful. I will never quit this job!* We must remember to be careful how we make those declarative statements, especially as His children, because God has a purpose for our lives. When I returned to work the following Monday, I discovered that all the work we had just finished had gone away. What we thought were completed sales were not. We certainly can be very slow learners. I began to quickly see that God was using these circumstances to get my attention. In my office, I surrendered to the Holy Spirit.

Now on a new mission, I strolled into my employer's office to inform him of my new plans. After much debate, he accepted my resignation as I took that step of faith and quit my job. Next, I called Barbara. She listened to me very sweetly until I finished my story. She said, "I'm so glad you called. Phil and I just got off our knees this morning from praying and asking God to send someone like you to me." She told me about an international Christian outreach organization and that she and a national representative and other local ladies were starting a new group for business and professional ladies. They had planned on having a guest night dinner the next evening, and she invited us to go. She "just happened" to have two extra tickets. Barbara was the chairman of a luncheon group there, and they were also starting a brunch group. That night turned out to be one of the most wonderful nights of our lives.

Typically, once per year the women's clubs will have a guest night where they will invite their husbands or friends, which is what we attended. They meet in beautiful venues whenever possible. They will have special features that interest women, and men, like fashion shows, music, and a contemporary Christian speaker who usually shares his or her testimony. The guest speaker the night we attended was an incredibly talented NFL football player. He spoke of his life in football, but mostly, he spoke about his personal life. He said that he had made it to the top doing the things he loved more than anything else in the world—playing football and making lots of money doing it. However, he also spoke of how his life was filled with creating strife and discord everywhere he went. He further added that he felt for quite some time that the Holy Spirit had been convicting him to turn his life over to Jesus Christ, but he refused. His biggest concern was that if he did accept Jesus Christ as his Savior, God would take football away from him. At some point, he found a quiet place, fell onto his face before the Lord, and invited Jesus Christ to come into his life. He surrendered and asked the Lord to take control of his life and do with it whatever He wanted. He told of how he got up off of his knees a fully changed man, filled with the Holy Spirit. Soon afterward, he went to training camp with his team.

The coach called him into his office to talk to him, and he let the coach know he had something to tell him too. Graciously, the coach allowed him to go first. He told the coach about his new life in Christ Jesus and how it had totally changed his life for the good. He said the coach listened intently, and when he had finished, the coach said, "When I called you into my office, I called you in to cut you from the team, not because of your abilities, but because of your rotten attitude. After listening to what you have just told me, if you really have changed, I'm going to give you another chance." He assured the coach that he had changed, and the coach kept his word. He went on to have several more successful years in football. He realized that the very thing he had worried about, that is, postponing turning his life over to the Lord and losing football, was the very thing that God had given him—football. Essentially, if he had not accepted Christ as His Savior and faced the coach without being in the family of God, he would have been cut from the team. God is so amazing! God gave him the very thing he was afraid of losing. He does not withhold any good gifts from His children. What a generous and loving God we serve. He is Jehovah Jireh, our Provider.

At the end of that lovely evening, he gave any unbelievers there the opportunity to pray a sinner's prayer and thereby, by faith, invite Jesus Christ into their lives as their Savior. Upon hearing this incredible athlete's personal story, and upon learning how God had blessed him in return, my husband sincerely prayed that simple prayer by faith. He acknowledged his need for the Lord Jesus to be his Savior and surrendered to Him as much as he knew to do at that time. From there, he began his new walk with the Lord through serving Him in obedience by attending a Bible-based church, participating in Bible studies, having personal quiet times of prayer, reading the Word, and giving through tithes and offerings. Both he and I attended a class on learning how to share our faith with others, and we began generally allowing God to remake our lives for Jesus' sake.

My husband had been very religious most of his life, but he had never known until much later in his life that he needed to have a personal relationship with Jesus Christ. He had never been encouraged to read the Bible and learn what it was like to follow after Christ in obedience on a daily basis, not just ritually, but because of Christ's love for him and his love in return. He grew up attending and serving in the church from the time he was a very young boy and, generally speaking, he had grown up to be a good man. However, he came to realize there is much more to being right with God. He had finally understood that religion is simply man attempting to work his way to God and heaven. Christianity is God loving us so much that He sent His Son, Jesus, to earth as a man to ultimately suffer and die on the cross paying the penalty for our sins by His shed blood. Not only does this step in faith enable us to discern God's will and plan for our lives on this earth, but this free gift of salvation from God assures us of eternal life with Him in heaven after this life. Another wonderful benefit is that God created us to fellowship with Him. Through Jesus, we are able to have an intimate relationship with God. We can speak directly to Him with no mediator. He always answers our prayers with a yes, no, or wait—it may not be audibly or immediately. But He hears the prayers of His children if we keep ourselves cleansed by constant confession and repentance and live for Him day by day. Jesus said, "The thief comes only to steal and kill and destroy; I came that they may have life and have it abundantly" (John 10:10, NASB). Also, Jesus said, "I am the way, the truth, and the life; no one comes to the Father but through Me" (John 14:6, NASB). It is a truth; we have no other choice than to receive it, or else we will be separated from God for all eternity.

We thank God for sending us to hear that special NFL player that night. It was the single most important evening in my husband's life—he made the decision to choose light and life with Jesus Christ rather than darkness and death with the devil. Our decision to turn our lives over to Him is the single most important decision we have made as a couple. My husband's salvation was the greatest news from that first encounter with that international Christian outreach organization. However, God had other reasons for sending us to that guest night evening.

That Christian women's organization was planting a group for the business and professional ladies there. Shortly after that evening, Barbara and the national representative assisting with that endeavor invited me to be the chairman of that new group. Quickly thereafter, it became quite clear why God was insistent in His whispers to take a step in faith and quit my job and call Barbara. It was a bit of a change, but the Lord was eager to teach me. He is very gracious and patient with us and when He calls us to do something for Him, He also equips us and enables us. Before long, I slid into the swing of things. Until this day, I cannot thank Him enough for calling me into that type of ministry. "Then Job answered the LORD and said, "I know that You can do all things, and that no purpose of Yours can be thwarted" (Job 42:1, 2, NASB). That initial evening was just the beginning of a long career with that international outreach organization.

Sometime after being named chairman of the group in Virginia, I began to understand that the Lord was calling me to prepare my personal story for approval by their headquarters. I had trouble coming up with a beginning and an end, but one day when I sat down to write, He gave me the words to say. They just poured out of me—eighteen legal pad pages later, I was done. I would later use this testimony to speak to people wherever a door was opened.

A situation arose that required three of us ladies to have a meeting with the top leader of the organization. Our destination was The Homestead, one of our nation's elegant and premier hotels set in the Allegheny Mountains in Virginia, which was hosting a regional conference. The founder and chairman of that wonderful organization was our hostess. The three of us, along with a couple other ladies, had a meeting set in The Homestead. After a brief time of introductory conversation, we were invited to place our chairs in a circle. The founder and chairman had another chair added, which was left seemingly unoccupied, but designated by her for our Lord Jesus Christ. Then, the three of us were given an opportunity to present the situation that had precipitated the convening of the meeting. They listened respectfully, made comments, and then we had prayer time. Jesus Christ's presence was definitely there, as He is when He is invited.

Afterward, we were invited to join them downstairs in the Great Hall of the Homestead for tea. That lady, the founder and chairman, was a very engaging and delightful lady. I knew right away there was something special about her. I could feel the presence of the Lord in her presence in a way that I had never known before, or since, with anyone else. The Great Hall is just that. It is a long, extremely wide, and incredibly beautiful hall reminiscent of magnificent Southern plantation homes, but on a much larger and grander scale. There were conversation areas set all along the way on both sides of the hall with handsome sofas and club chairs, tables, lamps, a fireplace, and even strolling violinists. There were a considerable number of people enjoying themselves in the hall that afternoon. It appeared that many were business people associated with corporate conferences.

As we were enjoying our afternoon tea, an interesting gentleman suddenly approached us from a group across the hall.

It is worth mentioning here again that the space between the conversation areas across the hall from each other is quite wide. When he approached us, he said that it was particularly noticeable to him that we seemed to be having so much fun without imbibing in any alcohol. In fact, he went on to say that we seemed to be having so much more fun than the others in the hall that day, and he wondered why. With that encouragement, our founder stepped up and very quietly and passionately began to explain to him the gospel of Jesus Christ and what it means to those of us who have received Him as our Savior. I honestly do not recall exactly what she told him that day, but Jesus said, "I am *the* way, and *the* truth, and *the* life; no one comes to the Father but through Me" (John 14:6, NASB, emphasis added). He also says that it is through Him and Him alone that we can have life and have it more abundantly (John 10:10), which simply means it can be full and meaningful. Amazingly, in just a few short minutes, standing there with so many people from so many walks of life surrounding him, there in our little circle of ladies, this gentleman, a complete stranger to us all, prayed and invited Jesus Christ into his life. And if he was sincere, he suddenly had become our brother in the family of God and coheir with Jesus Christ Himself, according to the scriptures. Who would have guessed that our afternoon tea would go in that direction? But our Father God had known it before time began.

Not too long after this gentleman walked away, surprisingly a lady strolled over to join us from another group and expressed her own interest in what was so different about us and why we seemed to be having so much fun. Again, our founder and chairman stepped forward and began speaking to her. As it turned out, this lady thought she was a Christian, but she had not been living her life accordingly. How great is our God?

We certainly give all praise and honor to Him. He and He alone must draw people to Himself and when they yield to Him, it is He that does the life change in that surrendered life. Because the Word of God teaches that it is not God's will for any to perish but for all to have eternal life with Him, we must believe that we will be called to Him at some point in life. Please don't harden your hearts so that you miss it and never come to know Him. To those of us who are already believers, there is one thing of significance here from our side of the equation that you will hear from me repeatedly: we are always witnesses for Jesus Christ once we come into fellowship with Him. Are we good witnesses or bad witnesses? As you have probably heard before, if we are arrested because we are Christians, is there enough evidence to convict us? When people see us out in the market place, at play, or in our homes, what do they see? Do they see us reflecting Jesus Christ, a transformed person from death to life spiritually, as was obvious that day from our founder and the other ladies? Do they see us reflecting Jesus in a way that the Holy Spirit could use to draw people to Jesus Christ? Or do they see someone who reflects worldliness? I know most of us fail Him miserably at times. If we do not show the fruit of our Christianity for all to see, we certainly need to quickly repent and surrender our lives to Him.

I heard our former pastor once say something like: The moment we decide to give our lives to Jesus Christ and do it, that is the last independent decision we should ever make. We belong to Him from that point on, and we should seek Him and His wisdom in everything and then follow it. We should also thank Him *for* and *in* everything. Yes. He is Sovereign. He knows much better than we do about what is best for us. He is a God of love, but He is also a holy God, so that His plans and His gifts are always good. We should make it a point to be so surrendered to Him that we seek Him for every decision, large or small. When He makes His will known to us, we should be obedient and do it as soon as it is clear that it is from Him, something I am always striving to do. Some people say they don't want anyone controlling them and making their plans for them. However, just in case you aren't aware, according to the Word of God, there are only two choices: Satan and the world or Jesus Christ. Jesus Christ wins hands down, and the ultimate payoff is out of this world! Remember, Satan is a created being. Our great God is the Creator. He desires for you to accept Him as Savior, then He will become your Father. The scripture says that we are to pray for all the believers. Let's do it! Satan is a liar and wants nothing more than to prevent true believers from trusting and obeying our Lord. He definitely wants us to be bad representatives of Him. "And pray in the Spirit on all occasions with all kinds of prayers and requests. With this in mind be alert and always keep on praying for all the saints" (Ephesians 6:18, NIV).

Chapter 10

Continuing the Walk

Another important factor that came out of my husband's decision to accept Jesus Christ as his Savior and follow only His teaching was a beautiful story of obedience by him and what God did with it. It didn't come easily.

Just a few short months after he was born again, God tested him. Our pastor in Virginia announced one Sunday that the members of the church were to submit their pledge cards that evening to inform the church leadership of everyone's intentions regarding tithes for the coming year so plans could be made accordingly. It was a decision that I had made earlier with my husband's blessings regarding my income, but it was not one that he had made regarding his salary. We had some conversations about it, but he had not yet felt it necessary to tithe at least 10 percent of our gross income plus additional offerings or giving, as was my belief.

On the way to church that night, the subject came up again. I said, "You will never be able to out give God!" Immediately, he took the pledge card out of his jacket and tossed it over to my lap and said rather gruffly, "Fine, fill it in. I'll do it!" Laughing, my response was that God loves a cheerful giver so perhaps he should wait until his attitude was correct. (Back then, he occasionally would have to remind me that I was not his Holy Spirit!) "Now this I say, he who sows sparingly will also reap sparingly, and he who sows bountifully will also reap bountifully. Each one must purpose in his heart, not grudgingly or under compulsion, for God loves a cheerful giver (2 Corinthians 9:6–8, NASB). Shortly after I mentioned the quick phrase from verse 7, he said, "No, I know it is the right thing. Let's do it!" And he did. In fact, he has been a very faithful tither from that day on. The Holy Spirit of God had reminded him that the tithe is to be out of the firstfruits. It is all God's anyway. If we are faithful to tithe accordingly, He will be faithful to pour out blessings until there is no more need, not greed. However, if we aren't faithful, that breaks God's covenant with us. Once my husband became faithful to write that check and contribute his tithes to God what was due Him first, out of his gross pay, it was an amazing thing to see the blessings the Lord poured out on him financially and in other ways. I might add, too, that he quickly began to love giving above the tithe, which has blessed me and others through the years. Remember, I had quit my job and was now working without bringing in an income.

Before long, my husband was given an unexpected raise and promotion. At the end of the year, it was incredible that we had made almost the same thing as if I had never quit my job, and we were tithing 10 percent of our gross income! God is so faithful! If God says it, it will be done! However, we must be careful to remember that many promises of God in His Word indicate that we have a part that must be done before we can count on Him fulfilling the promise. "'Bring the whole tithe into the storehouse, so that there may be food in My house, and test Me now in this,' says the LORD of hosts, 'if I will not open for you the windows of heaven and pour out for you a blessing until it overflows'" (Malachi 3:10, NASB).

Continuing to speak of His faithfulness and His provisions, while still living in Virginia, we received good news from a home pregnancy test. Soon afterward, it was confirmed by the doctor that I was pregnant once again. We couldn't help but get excited! Everything went well for a time, but the news changed rather dramatically when I went in for a checkup with my gynecologist. I still remember his words that day: "I am so sorry to have to tell you this, but this baby is no longer living. And since you didn't miscarry this time, I'm going to send you home and let you wait for nature to take its course." In an instant, we had to deal with yet another huge tragedy. Imagine getting up and walking around every day knowing that the child you are carrying, and love, is no longer living. My husband and I had gone through quite a lot of painful ordeals in our lives already, and this was just way too much for me to bear without supernatural help. Most of the times in the past, I had dealt with the trials in all the wrong ways. Things were different now. I had an Advocate to help me through this. I remember going home from the doctor's office and very slowly trudging up that winding staircase in our lovely home with only one thing on my mind—getting to the place where I had recently surrendered everything to God.

I fell on my face before Him and cried out, "Father God, I cannot handle this. You have to take care of this for me." And He did! Unbelievably so! During the entire time that I was in that waiting period, it was like I was being carried along on a pillow or a cloud. I was never depressed. Disappointed? Oh, you better believe it. We both were. But never depressed, which had been the usual way I had responded. At the time it was like our Lord carried me in such a way that it literally felt like my feet could not touch the ground, nor could I have been depressed even if I wanted to. In fact, it was like I was on a spiritual high as I experienced God's power and presence in a way I had never known before. Even now

I am filled with praise and thanksgiving to Him. What a mighty God we serve!

That experience seemed to depict our lives running on parallel lines like a train track. While we saw God working out great blessings for us in ways we *could* understand, we were also players in His big plan for our lives in painful ways we could never understand. We should learn from the suffering of those in the Bible. Like with Joseph in Genesis, "he was laid in iron" (Psalm 105:18, KJV). After so many painful trials, he reached a point where he was no longer a young boy. Somewhere along the way, he became a man. But the scripture continued to say, "The Lord was with him." And He is with us. God has a plan to grow us up in Him where we can be used for His kingdom work, for His glory, and for His own name's sake so that our joy will be made full. One day we will spend all eternity with Him, and it will be worth it all. In 2 Chronicles 20:3, we see where Jehoshaphat and all of Judah were surrounded by enemies. "Jehoshaphat was afraid and turned his attention to seek the LORD, and proclaimed a fast throughout all Judah. So Judah gathered together to seek help from the LORD . . ." (NASB). He began to pray to the Lord, recognizing His power and His might. He noted that they were powerless before such a great multitude, and they did not know what to do, but their eyes were on Him. God responded with, "Do not fear or be dismayed because of this great multitude, for the battle is not yours but God's." Then they organized themselves and went out in obedience to what God had laid out for them to do, which in itself was rather bazaar. The enemy literally became confused, and they ended up killing each other (see 2 Chronicles 20:22). If you haven't read 2 Chronicles 20, I encourage you to do so.

So what do we need to do when we are presented with something too big for us to bear? We need to fast, pray, seek God's help, follow in obedience, offer up songs of praise and thanksgiving in faith, and trust in the Lord. Stand by and see the goodness of the Lord. Our God will perform His wonderful works to get us through the difficult times. In due time, we will see His rewards. As someone once said, "First the suffering, then the glory."

Our pastor in Virginia had said that we should use our time, our talents, and our money to serve the Lord. By this time, I had become pretty much involved in full-time Christian ministry, and loving it. Unbeknownst to me, the statements by the pastor had hit a nerve with my husband. Years before, as he struggled with the decision to leave the flying world, he expressed that he wanted to be in a flying club so that he could continue his love of flying, to which I heartily agreed. Therefore, since he had access to great aircraft in the club where we were members, he felt the Lord leading him to dedicate his time, his talents, and his money to fly our pastor to events when needed, which was much quicker than scheduling a commercial flight. Living in Virginia always meant going through Atlanta or Washington, D.C., and it required too much time for people on extremely tight schedules. His last flight for this ministry took place shortly before we moved away from Virginia.

Our pastor, the chairman of the deacon board, my husband, and I all departed one Sunday afternoon in a twin-engine Duchess bound for Murray, Kentucky, for a deacon ordination service. As we climbed out and began our trip across the West Virginia mountains, we met a weather front that was an unfriendly companion that kept us company all the way to our destination. Later, after the services and upon checking the weather at the airport, my husband insisted it was safe for us to return home that night. So at approximately midnight, we set out and caught up that same horrible front as we crossed back over the mountains of West Virginia heading east. The updrafts and downdrafts were causing us to seemingly fall out of the sky and then shoot right back up, tossing that airplane around like it was a toy, just as it had heading west earlier. My husband the pilot was loving the challenge! I'm sure the two in the back were praying fervently, as was I. Hours later, upon approaching the airport in

Virginia, there was a very strong crosswind. My husband called the tower and asked which runway most pilots had been choosing earlier that evening. Because of the winds, the tower's response was, "No one has attempted to land here in several hours." He went on to remind us that the alternate airport was Raleigh, North Carolina. My husband explained to us that he was going to make one attempt to land, that we were to make sure our seat belts were snug and hang on. If it didn't look just right, he would abort the landing and head for Raleigh.

As we came in on the final approach, the cross wind was so strong the airplane was totally crabbing (flying sideways). Rather than the nose of the airplane facing the runway, that night the right side of the aircraft was approaching the runway until just before the wheels touched down for the roll out. Then, at the last moment, my husband hit the right rudder hard bringing the aircraft around, and he literally greased it in on the runway as though it was a lovely sunny and still afternoon. The tower said, "Captain, if you can land it in this type of weather, you can land it anywhere." We knew that he was a wonderful pilot, and we took nothing away from his God-given skill, but we also recognize there was no doubt that the Lord gave an extra measure of grace to all of us that night, much in part to the cries of His children on board that airplane.

Soon afterward, we heard that the people from the church had been very concerned about us because of the bad weather they were experiencing and had a prayer vigil going for us all that evening. Certainly the prayers of the people at the church in Kentucky were among those I'm sure the Lord heard. God is in the business of providing and protecting His children, and He definitely did it for us on that mission trip. Bless the name of the Lord! God is our shield, according to Psalm 18:2. In Ephesians 6, the shield of faith is to be used to extinguish all the flaming missiles of the evil one. I encourage you to read all of Psalm 91 for emphasis about God's protective care. "I will say to the Lord, 'My refuge (defender) and my fortress (protector), My God, in whom I trust!" (Psalm 91:2, NASB). "For He will give His angels charge concerning you, to guard you in all your ways" (Psalm 91:11, NASB).

> O God, You are my God; I shall seek You earnestly;
> My soul thirsts for You, my flesh yearns for You;
> In a dry and weary land where there is no water.
> Thus I have seen You in the sanctuary, to see Your
> power and your glory.
> Because Your loving kindness is better than life,
> My lips will praise You.
> So I will bless You as long as I live;
> I will lift up my hands in Your name
> (Psalm 63:1–4, NASB).

"The Lord will rescue me from every evil deed, and will bring me safely to His heavenly kingdom; to Him be the glory forever and ever. Amen" (2 Timothy 4:18, NASB).

Chapter 11

God Executing His Plan

God is mighty to save and faithful to accomplish what concerns us (Psalm 138:8) no matter what the need might be. That entire trip to Kentucky and the return to Virginia with the incredible landing turned out to be God's special blessing that night for yet another reason.

After arriving back home and getting in bed at approximately three o'clock in the morning, my husband, after only about three hours of sleep, had to be back at the airport to depart commercially for his initial interview at nine o'clock with a major transportation corporation in Tennessee.

***

Let me back up to give you a little background information leading up to his decision to make that trip. My husband's position with the company he was with for quite a few years gave him human resource management experience. He had tried unsuccessfully to get the other members of management to agree with him to make critical changes for these people, but he could not get them to agree. One particular week my husband had spent time at that location once again. As before, he was unsuccessful in getting the other members of management to agree with him to make changes. On his last day there, he got up and had his quiet time with the Lord, reading the Bible and spending time in prayer. Afterward, he finished preparing for his day, picked up his briefcase, and as he started out the door, he felt a distinct impression that the Holy Spirit was encouraging Him to go back into the room and pray about the situation at the plant. He had already done that; however, since the impression was so strong, he decided to do so. He returned to the room and knelt by the bed. He cried out to the Lord: "Lord, I would really like for You to change these things for these people, but if You won't change them, please help me to accept them just the way they are. If not, if there is a company out there somewhere that I would be better suited in, please show me that too." He left the room and headed home in the middle of the afternoon prior to going to his office just to bring me up to date. Seeing him home at that time certainly surprised me, but as he walked in the door, the telephone rang. A lady asked to speak to my husband. That lady turned out to be a headhunter he had used for staffing executives at another location. She was calling to invite him to go on an interview with the transportation corporation because of his experience as a pilot and with human resources.

***

He was approved for the position! I must tell you, it looked just like someone had written a job description specifically for my husband, and we know, of course, that Someone did! He spent twenty-five years with them, and with it came wonderful experiences that only God could have orchestrated. Now, I'm quite sure that my husband didn't pray that prayer that morning in the motel room and immediately say, "Oh thank You, Lord, for putting those words into my mouth." However, I'm also quite sure that he didn't just think them up on his own either. How could he have imagined that God already had the answer ready and had prepared for a headhunter to contact him on that very day at that precise moment that he would walk into his house in the middle of the afternoon? Is our God amazing or what? Coincidence? No way. His timing is perfect. Amazingly, too, somewhere in the recesses of my mind, an idea had formed some time before all of this happened.

As a baby Christian there in Virginia, I asked the Lord to give my husband a position with an airline. He had been like a fish out of water in the industry he was with after giving up a flying career for us to have more time together. Considering what you have just read, neither did it cross my mind that it was perhaps God's idea that He simply placed into my mind and sent back up to Himself through me. But it is my understanding from the wonderful prayer warriors that teach on prayer and are much deeper in theology than I, that those are the prayers that are heard and answered by Him. Jeremiah 29:11–12 states, "'For I know the plans I have for you,' declares the Lord, 'plans for welfare and not for calamity to give you a future and a hope. Then you will call upon Me, and come and pray to Me, and I will listen to you'" (NASB). Ultimately, we are to pray for His will to be done on earth as it is in heaven, in whatever our circumstances, and for Him to enable us to be faithful to the end. We certainly may pray for many things, according to His will. But we are to pray fervently when He lays things on our hearts. Psalm 66:1, 2 says, "Shout joyfully to God, all the earth; sing the glory of His name; make His praise glorious. Say to God 'How awesome are Thy works'" (NASB).

As exciting as the opportunity was for my husband and me, there were down sides. First, our baby son was born and died in the hospital in the city of our new location. And the new location was only a short hop from where we were in that awful tornado. I was not sure that I was emotionally equipped to go back to that area. The other thing was that I had just found my "perfect life." I was so totally happy with where the Lord had brought me, and I could not imagine giving that up. I had been asked to serve at least a two-year term as the chairman of that new group for business and professional women. My first term was not over. I remember telling the Lord, "I know that You put me into this position." To which He quickly responded, "I didn't say you were to die there." Oh well. I guess you have to "know when to hold them and know when to fold them," as Kenny Rogers sings. So, I agreed to the move.

Yes, He is Jehovah, Almighty God. He displays His faithfulness everywhere if we will only look on His works and behold His majesty. It is all around for us to see. He doesn't hide it from us. Even when it looks like the situation is a trial not a blessing, do not be deceived because God is busy orchestrating things in our lives. While it may seem like God has looked away, or doesn't even care if He is aware, behind the scenes, He is making it into something good. "And we know that all things work together for good to those who love God and are called according to His purpose" (Romans 8:28, NKJV). In Genesis, regarding Joseph, one of my favorite biblical characters, the scripture says that what men intend for evil, God takes it and turns it into good. Oh yes, our great God is always looking out for us. We could not begin to imagine at that time just how He would bless our obedience in moving. But He knew. There was to be a lot of growth for both of us, but there were other magnificent gifts as well.

Chapter 12

God Orchestrating Things for Good

In the early days of collecting stories for this book, my oldest brother contributed this story, and it is one of my favorites. World War II had been over only a few months when a small group of Christians were involved in a ministry that took them by train through the Rio Grande Valley. As they passed through a Texas border town, they discussed how devoid the area was of any genuine Christian ministry. The older man, who was the leader of the group, said to those sitting near him, "This would be a good place for someone to come and give his life to serving God without expecting any notice or recognition." Those words did not leave the mind of one young man, and a few years later he returned with his wife and young family to begin a lifetime of serving God in that Texas town, where Spanish was the language of the streets.

The events of the next few years were difficult ones for the young missionary and his family, but they were years in which they often saw the Lord provide their needs, whether it was daily sustenance for the family, property and materials for their growing ministry, or conviction and conversion of many souls. One of the more spectacular events involved a piece of property, which had been purchased for use by the Christian school and for a warehouse for their clothing ministry. The large parcel of land had been purchased with a small down payment with scheduled installments and a specific deadline for the final payment set four years in advance. One condition of the loan was that the property would be repossessed by the lender at the due date of the last payment unless all of the money had been paid.

As the date for the final payment of five thousand dollars drew near, the missionary went to the post office each day with hope and expectancy that money would arrive. To the surprise and bewilderment of himself and his staff, who had prayed diligently for the Lord's provision, no money came for that need. On the day the payment was due, after the mail had been posted in the post office and no money had come, the missionary took his helpers to the warehouse and began unpacking some boxes of old clothes, which had been given by a kindly YMCA director in Chicago. The missionary's heart was really not in his work as he pulled shirts, trousers, and coats from the boxes and shook them to remove some of the dust and trash, as well as any varmint stowaways. He shook a coat and something "jumped" from a pocket and rolled across the floor. The missionary gasped, and his heart raced as he saw the color of the round thing resting on the floor. It was the color of money! Everyone gathered around as he picked up the roll of money. He unrolled the money and noticed that the top bills were of large denominations. As he began to count the bills, laying them on the nearby table, everyone's excitement rose when they realized that the roll contained a sizeable sum of money. He counted one thousand, two thousand, three thousand . . . and then everyone counted in unison as he finished counting the bundle. They had exactly five thousand dollars, the exact amount of the final payment on the property. There was just one problem; they did not know if the money was really theirs.

The missionary called the YMCA director in Chicago and made inquiry concerning the possibility of finding the owner of the coat in which the money had been found. He told the missionary that the clothes had been stacked in the storage room at the "Y" for about four years, and he was just glad to be rid of them. The phenomenal part of this story is that not only did the Lord supply the money needed for the final installment on a piece of property, but He also provided the final payment at the same time the property was purchased. "It will also come to pass that before they call, I will answer; and while they are still speaking, I will hear" (Isaiah 65:24, NASB). ". . . For it is God who is at work in you, both to will and to work for His good pleasure" (Philippians 2:13, NASB). "Be anxious for nothing, but in everything by prayer and supplication with thanksgiving let your requests be made known to God. And the peace of God, which surpasses all comprehension, will guard your hearts and your minds in Christ Jesus. . . . And my God will supply all your needs according to His riches in glory in Christ Jesus" (Philippians 4:6–7, 19, NASB). Praise the Lord!

No Coincidence

Most of us respect firemen and, as a whole, they are incredibly wonderful human beings, like most policemen, military personnel, etc. because they lay down their lives for us all of the time. They are our true day-to-day unsung heroes. To all of you, and you know who you are, we thank you from the bottom of our hearts. We take this opportunity to salute you. A retired fireman, who had become a deliveryman, became the image of an angel to a wonderful old man on life support in the hospital.

One day he was delivering a basket of flowers to a patient in a local hospital. He was there so often that it was rote for him to park the van, pick out the designated flowers for the designated patient, and head to the room. He got off the elevator at the appropriate floor and headed to the patient's room. When he got there, he knocked on the door, quietly at first, but, getting no response, he knocked a little louder. Still receiving no response, he pushed the door open slightly, ever so gently. There was no one with the patient, so he pushed the door open further and walked into the room. It was quite dark inside, but as his eyes began to take in the picture in the room, suddenly he went into fireman mode. He had found a little elderly gentleman crunched way down on the bed and draped around and entangled in the side railings. He had disconnected his life support system during the melee and appeared to be either comatose or dead. The fireman pulled him up on the bed immediately, reconnected the tube to his life support system, and then called the nurses on duty. They arrived and found the little old man beginning to breathe again. The immediate danger was foiled, thanks to another faithful on-the-job, 24/7 fireman. Even though he no longer receives an income as a fireman, he is still a fireman in his heart. Looking out for others' welfare is what they do.

Later, as he stood there speaking with one of the nurses for a moment after everything had calmed down, they glanced down at the name and number on the card of the bouquet of flowers. He realized he was on the wrong floor of the hospital. He had gone to the fifth floor rather than the third floor. As this story filled my heart, realization dawned once again at how incredibly gracious our holy God is. Who knows how long before they would have found that little man, and in what condition. We do know that God knew and was so wonderful to allow this man, this trained-for-emergencies retired fireman, the privilege to be just the perfect one to enter that room at just the precise moment to save that little elderly man's life. How great is our God! For some reason, the Lord wasn't finished with that little old man on this earth. "Great is the Lord and greatly to be praised, and His greatness is unsearchable!" (Psalm 145:3, NASB). "Surely the righteous will give thanks to Your name; the upright will dwell in Your presence" (Psalm 140:13, NASB).

Miracle Escape in Monzi

This particular story is regarding a missionary couple in Swaziland, in southeast Africa, that a church in Sydney, Australia, supported at the time. This couple considered that support the lifeline that kept them going. This missionary couple and their two small children were home minding their own business when armed men with AK47s and other weapons broke into their place and began attacking them. Fortunately, the two small children were in bed. They reported that it was an unbelievable experience, but God gave them amazing—obviously divine—power to send them off in all directions. They stated that the most amazing miracles took place. The husband dived at the gunman firing at him with the AK47. His wife dived alongside him, and they fought for their lives and for the lives of their children. They heard one of the gunmen shouting for his accomplice in the next room, so the husband ran to the next room to take care of that assailant. His wife restrained the first gunman on her own, a man larger than her husband.

At one point, the husband saw one of the gunmen deliver a blow to his wife's forehead, which even the surgeons said should have fractured her skull. The husband charged him and broke the AK47 with his hands. (God is amazing!) The butt of the gun cracked, and the firing pin was dislodged together with other pieces of metal. Their daughter told them later that she woke up and above all their shouting she heard: THE MIGHTY NAME OF JESUS—YES, LORD, YOU ARE HERE! THANK YOU, JESUS. She also saw angels all around the property. Their son slept through it all and was unharmed. Most amazing was this couple's attitude. They said they think they now know what David must have felt when he slew a bear, a lion, and Goliath—victorious, excited, and happy. Obviously, they no longer trusted the local security forces for their safety, but they did take other security measures. The Bible states, "Some trust in chariots, some in horses, but we trust in the name of the Lord our God" (Psalm 20:7, NIV).

This should serve as a reminder of what a mighty God we serve. But it should also remind us to pray for the people He has called to serve as missionaries in dangerous parts of the world, who are willing to give their lives for the cause of Christ that others may hear of His gospel and turn to Him and be saved.

Chapter 13

𝓜𝓸𝓿𝓲𝓷𝓰 𝓞𝓷

The day of our move to our new location had come. Looking back up at our beautiful house in Virginia, while the movers were taking care of their last-minute errands, we took pictures and spoke of how beautiful it was there. I recall my husband saying, "We can live a lot of places, but we will never live in a place more beautiful," to which I agreed. Our home was positioned approximately five minutes off of the Blue Ridge Parkway, and from our vantage point in the valley, we had a scenic view of God's handiwork on the mountains surrounding us. We had watched with great excitement each year as our heavenly Landscaper turned the pages from season to season, making magnificent bold strokes with His brush to capture everyone's attention. Spring brought all things new and green with beautiful flowers that lasted all summer long. Then fall came blazing in with the most unbelievable brilliance of colors, just daring winter to top that. However, not to be outdone, the snow-capped mountains made their own magnificent and bold statement. To be sure, it is a place with its own splendid magnificence. Something about being in that valley gave us a sense of protection and coziness lacking on the plains where the tornadoes sweep through with a mind of their own. Even two feet of snow on the ground for six weeks at a time could never diminish that. It was never as cold as it gets in other places where the humidity is so high. But it seemed to be God's timing for us to be moving on as He set the hands of time to begin the sweep of new and exciting plans and places.

Once we arrived in Tennessee, my husband very quickly became immersed in his new duties with the new company. In fact, he loved it, and it almost immediately consumed his life. As for me, I floundered a bit at the beginning—I was in a new city and knew no one. It seemed I continuously took two steps forward and three steps back. However, we did join a church whose pastor was very gifted and anointed in the Holy Spirit. He was known in many parts of the world.

Little did I know what a packed schedule our pastor kept. Since our previous pastors were usually very accessible, I called his administrative assistant and asked for a counseling appointment with him. She explained that he would see me, but that it might take a little while. After about three weeks, I was invited to come in to speak with him. I explained what was going on in my life and that I was not doing well, even though I was praying and reading the Bible. He listened attentively and said, "You are going to think this is strange coming from your pastor, but you have *spiritual indigestion*!" He went on to explain that I needed balance in my life and suggested that whatever hobby was enjoyable to me, I should do it. Bible study and prayer are essential for Christians, but we *do* need a balance. It was great advice!

The headhunters that had sought my husband and lured him to the new company had hired me on the phone prior to our moving there. Other opportunities came up, but the business world was no longer a place for me. Apparently, the Lord had other plans. Fortunately, the international Christian women's organization had a local Christian women's club with which I became involved. Initially, there was only a large luncheon group there. After only a year or two, the Lord gave me a vision to plant a dinner group. Although anyone was welcome, of course, it was primarily for business and professional women who needed a place to hear Christian speakers and attend Bible studies. It is difficult to imagine that need in the South where nowadays many churches provide all of that for their members, and others, who want to attend, but it was not so much back then. After much prayer and some hard work getting the groundwork done, a national representative was sent from the headquarters to assist us in continuing the project. With her leadership, and the assistance of a team of local ladies the Lord had led us to, God brought it to fruition. This group was active for many years, and He used that platform to spread the gospel of Jesus. Only in heaven will we know the legacy of all He accomplished through the ladies' hard work through that one outreach group.

My testimony had previously been approved, for speaking, by the headquarters, and while the national representative was working with us locally, she invited me to be the Christian speaker for the grand opening night at that new dinner group. From there, He launched me onto a speaking career that spanned many years across the United States and even to Asia. Having been quite shy as a young girl, and not living for the Lord until later on, it is no surprise to me when I come upon the verse in the Bible that says, ". . . God has chosen the foolish things of the world to shame (confound) the wise, and God has chosen the weak things of the world to shame the things which are strong, and the base things of the world and the despised God has chosen, the things that are not, so that He may nullify the things that are, so that no man may boast before God. But by His doing you are in Christ Jesus, who became to us wisdom from God, and righteousness and sanctification and redemption, so that, just as it is written, 'LET

HIM WHO BOASTS, BOAST IN THE LORD"' (1 Corinthians 1:27–31, NASB, emphasis added). I give Him all praise and glory for all He has done in and through my life. When I go to heaven, His work will be done in me. His finished work on the cross made that possible.

~ Author's Note ~

He now sees us in beautiful white robes of righteousness if we have come into His family, but He is still working it out in us while we are here on earth so others can see and want to come to know Him. What a joy to know, and how I long for that day when I see Him face to face. I am nothing special, except for the grace of God. I, along with all true followers of Jesus Christ, am on a journey with Him here on earth as He uses me (us) for His glory in His kingdom work, until He knows it's time to bring us home to be with Him.

There was a time during those years of speaking that I knew I was not walking with Him in a manner befitting Him and His call on my life. I remember telling Him that I needed a break until I could get my life back where it needed to be. I took some time off. No one called. One day, I told Him I was ready to begin again. That very day I received a call to speak somewhere, and it all began anew. What a wonderful Father God we serve, and how exciting it is to walk the walk with Him. I didn't keep a diary of those days, but sometimes now I wish that I had. I believe He impressed it upon my mind that I should not for reasons only He knows for sure. But I thank Him for all the opportunities I had to tell the good news of Jesus Christ both at home and abroad. And He has a plan for you too. Maybe not necessarily the same plan I had but, whatever it is, it will be perfect for you—if you are willing.

During those years my husband was promoted to an officer's position at the company in the International Personnel Department and had begun traveling extensively internationally. On rare occasions he would be home when my speaking engagements had me away and vice versa. In all of those many years, we only missed speaking to each other a couple of days. That was no easy feat considering the time zones where either of us might be on a particular day, and the fact that we didn't necessarily stay in the same city each night. But God in His goodness worked it all out for us.

There was one thing that was such a blessing to me and a special gift from God. My husband had my traveling agenda for each week and told me that wherever he was, the Lord would remind him to pray for me about the time that he knew that I would be speaking. If he was at work, if he could, he would shut his office door, get down on his knees, and pray for me. However, if he was in some other part of the world, and it was time for me to speak when he was sleeping, the Lord would wake him up so he could pray. That brings tears to my eyes even all of these many years later. What a blessing!

While my husband traveled international first class and stayed in five-star hotels, my situation wasn't quite the same. Usually the honorarium I received was just enough to cover the cost of the airline tickets if I traveled standby. Most often, lovely people's homes were made available to me during my stay in their area. As much as I enjoyed the majority of those stays, it did add a certain amount of stress to each trip. If there were speaking engagements in several surrounding cities, then I might stay in two to three different homes in a week's time. The families were extremely considerate, but on occasion there were incidental things that were bothersome, such as the thermostat being set too low for me in the Northern states or too high in the lower Southern states, so that getting enough sleep was difficult. Occasionally, when fatigue was a huge concern, my husband would treat me with reservations in a lovely hotel or motel. At times, grand old homes were made available where every comfort and care was given to me.

On one occasion, there was a breakdown in communication about the home that was to be available, and the host already had guests. Someone else offered their lake home, which was so far out in the boonies that someone had to lead me out there. The next morning, I was to be able to find my way back out and to the military base, without a GPS, and find the Officers' Club where I was to present my talk with nary a ruffled feather. I decided to follow them back into the little town and find a room. There were no motels readily available in the vicinity, so I ended up staying in what could be called a "flophouse" down on the city square where vagrants normally hung out. I do not recall having dinner that evening except for snacks that I brought in with me. The door was flimsy and not secure. The entire situation was so unnerving that when I spoke to my husband much later on, he told me to drag a big overstuffed chair over to block the entrance. The nearby trains were so loud I got very little sleep. The next morning, when my adrenaline wasn't soaring, it was almost impossible for me to move that chair! So without much sleep, and quite hungry, I began my day. When I arrived at the place I was to speak this day, the leaders were aghast when they heard where I had stayed and were very apologetic. The Holy Spirit met us there and people's hearts were turned to Jesus.

Thinking back, it could have been a test the Lord allowed for me to check my dedication to His call. Obviously, He knew how I would handle it. While it didn't seem so entertaining at the time, it has always been one of the funniest memories of those days.

Sometimes the venues where I spoke were small restaurants in small rural towns with an area sectioned off with curtains. It was often in beautiful country clubs, hotel ballrooms, a beautiful country estate, someone's grand private home, a bar closed for the day, or a retirement community club house. At one of those retirement communities, several women seemed to be snoozing during my presentation. I thought I could just slide down behind the podium, and they would never miss me. It was always amazing how the Holy Spirit of God would show up in places at just the right time. He is the One Who points people to Jesus. He did, He does, and He will continue until Christ comes again. If He can use a donkey to speak, imagine what He can do with a heart turned toward Him (see Numbers 22:28). In the years of my speaking in large cities to rural towns, driving or flying standby, the Lord made sure I reached the destination on time—there was only one exception. That is still remarkable to me I do give Him the praise.

On one trip to Ohio, I had missed my connecting flight through Atlanta due to bad weather. I had several speaking engagements lined up over several days. After desperate attempts to get onto another flight that day, it was to no avail. Accepting defeat for the day, and planning to try again the following morning, I placed a call to my oldest brother, who lived in the vicinity, and he came and drove me to his house. Once there, my sister-in-law gave me a message to call my hostess in Ohio. When I did, this dear lady explained that their area had been hit with a terrible ice storm quite unexpectedly, and all the clubs where I was scheduled to speak had been canceled. Of course, the first question was, why didn't they call me earlier in order for me to stay home? The answer was simple. God had other plans for me. My sister-in-law had been ill and housebound for quite some time and had wanted me to come spend some time with her, but she knew I couldn't because of my previous engagements. But God countermanded my plans and showed me His plans, which included visiting with my sister-in-law. Because my previous flight schedule routed my return back through Atlanta, all I did was stay those designated days with them and boarded my return flight home at the originally scheduled time later in the week.

~ Author's Note ~

He is indeed an awesome God, our sovereign Lord, our Supreme Leader; He has His ways to bring about His providential will in our lives. Another verse states, "Whatever the LORD pleases, He does. In Heaven and earth, in seas and in all deeps" (Psalm 135:6, NASB). Sometimes that is a tough verse to accept when big trials are causing us sorrow and affliction, but He is a trustworthy God who will do what is right for us in every situation. We must remember this verse: "For I consider that the sufferings of this present time are not worthy to be compared with the glory that is to be revealed to us" (Romans 8:18, NASB). "But as for me, the nearness of God is my good; I have made the LORD God my Refuge, that I may tell of all Your works" (Psalm 73:28, NASB).

When our flight was canceled that day, and before I called my brother, others were attempting to make connections as well. Somehow, a very interesting man became my shadow all that afternoon. He, too, was trying to get to Ohio. No matter what I tried, I could not shake this man. He had a deep, gravelly voice that was very annoying. Even when I spoke to my husband back at home, he stood by a short distance away until I completed my conversation. He invited me to join him in one of the private airline clubs nearby in the terminal where he tried to obtain seats for us on another flight. Upon hearing that it was necessary for me to get to my speaking engagements beginning the next day, he even offered to rent a car and drive me to Ohio, which, of course, I would never consider. If the Lord wanted me to get to Ohio, it would definitely have to be in a different mode of travel. Finally, he invited me to sit and have a sandwich with him. Feeling tired and hungry, I joined him in one of the little sandwich shops there in the terminal. Entering into conversation, I learned he was Jewish and that he was a booking agent for sporting events in coliseums. He offered to be my booking agent, but I informed him that God was my Booking Agent and that He was very good at it. He was quite perplexed at my response. Then he asked me about the topic of my talk. He was quite interested in coming to hear me speak that week, but since that didn't seem likely to happen, I offered to send him an audio copy of my talk, which he was happy to receive. On the audio, he heard the entire plan of salvation and how he, too, could receive Jesus Christ as his Savior. After listening to it, he returned it with a note a few weeks later, and I have never heard from him since. Only in eternity will we know the results of that day. But our Father God gave him an opportunity to come to know Jesus Christ as his Savior. It is, quite simply, his choice to make—Jesus and light, life, and eternity in heaven with Him in unbelievable beauty and bliss, or darkness and eternal life separated from God in hell. The One and only all-knowing, all-wise God is always on the job. One must wonder what else He did that day in changing the agenda in the lives of all of those people who missed their flights that day.

I have had so many interesting experiences while speaking for that organization. Having just completed several speaking engagements back in Virginia, our flight had departed with no problems, and we were settled in for a short flight to Charlotte, North Carolina, where I would be changing for my final leg. Only shortly after we started crossing the mountains, we found ourselves in the worst thunderstorm that I had ever experienced. The airplane was pitching and swaying and seemingly falling out of the sky as it plowed its way through the updrafts and downdrafts over the Blue Ridge Mountains. At one point it felt like some giant hand had grabbed the aircraft and was shaking it violently. Later on, my husband told me that you never want to be in an aircraft when it is shaking like that because the aircraft could literally come apart.

People were screaming and crying. I was pleading with God to get us through to Charlotte and on the ground to safety. I sneaked a glance at my seatmate to my left, who had been strangely quiet during all of this. What I saw totally shocked me! That businessman looked like someone had poured a tub of water over his head; there did not seem to be a dry hair on his head, and all of his hair was literally plastered to his head like it was oiled down. His white shirt was also soaking wet and plastered to his skin. He stared straight ahead and seemed to be catatonic. My husband had always labeled me a white-knuckle flyer, which I was at times, but this guy seemed to be the very definition of the term. I felt great compassion for him, but it certainly did not increase my comfort level for a man to be reacting in that way. He was totally freaked out. In the midst of all of this, the captain came on the microphone and apologized for the inconvenience this was causing us; he had to deviate so much to attempt to get us into better air. Imagine what the center of the storm must have been like! He also apologized for getting us into that horrible storm in the first place and that he had read the conditions wrong before takeoff. Our confidence in him was *not* boosted by that announcement. One gentleman said that he had flown around the world for thirty years and had never been in anything like that before. The Lord got us on the ground safely in Charlotte, where I had to make a decision whether to get on my connecting flight to Tennessee or rent a car and drive for two days. The weather in Charlotte looked good, so I decided to fly. Even though the weather was better, we still had a pretty bumpy ride home. I recall telling the Lord, "Lord, if You don't make things easier for me to travel, I'm not sure I can continue doing this *for You.*" Obviously, He was waiting for me because His response came quickly and sliced me to the core: "Paul was shipwrecked for My sake." Let me hasten to add, He let me off lightly that day because He could have very easily added that Paul was shipwrecked three times, for His sake, beaten with a cat-of-nine tails, robbed, imprisoned, snake bitten, and persecuted probably more than anyone other than Jesus, and yet sang God's praises while imprisoned in a filthy prison. Assuredly, I was very ashamed of my shallow walk with Him that day, and even until this day.

~ Author's Note ~

There is no comparison with my life and the lives of any of those dear saints of God who walked the earth during biblical days, and many since then who have gotten the gospel message out about Jesus Christ and His great love for us. He showed that in so many ways, before and since, but certainly very impressively on the cross of Calvary. What an awesome role model He is. Our wonderful God knows our names, and He knows our frames; He knows just how much we can bear, and He will not put more on us than we can bear without providing a way of escape. He is always there for us to dump our loads on Him because He promises that, "A bruised reed He will not break, and a dimly burning wick He will not extinguish" (Isaiah 42:3, NASB). He is kind, compassionate, and just. He demands obedience, yet He is patient—up to a point. His Word contains commandments, principles, and promises, and they are not merely suggestions.

Gratefully, He looks on our hearts, and He doesn't give up on us easily as long as we have the desire to follow after Him, stay surrendered to Him, and attempt to follow Him. He will provide a way.

After living in a lovely colonial Williamsburg house in Virginia, my husband decided we should try something different—condominium living. Actually, there was some logic behind his thoughts and the promise of new furniture in the deal, and that we would move if it was not enjoyable, so it really wasn't a very difficult choice. The entire complex was very attractive, and we purchased an end unit overlooking the lovely courtyard. Together with an interior designer who had decorated the models there, we created a very stunning interior. We had only lived in the condominium a few short months when we decided it was all a mistake. We did not like the neighborhood or that section of the city. Unfortunately, the housing market was depressed at the time and nothing was selling. Some of the other homeowners in that complex had their homes on the market for approximately three years. So we settled in to wait it out. During the wait, we attempted to make the best of it, but it was too much at times to endure the local area. We began to pray and ask the Lord what to do. On a spring day one year, my husband told me that he believed the Lord was telling us to put the condo on the market in May. We decided we would attempt to sell it ourselves rather than use a realtor. On May 2, a well-known local couple came to our door and asked to see the property. They loved the decor and everything about it, and within a short time, we signed the papers and closed on it. Free at last! During that time, we had found a new house in a lovely neighborhood in close proximity to the interstate, which would be helpful in my husband's commute. We were able to close on it and make one move directly from the condominium to the house. Who knew that our great and wonderful Lord would also be our personal heavenly Realtor? We were so incredibly blown away. It was a great faith-growing opportunity to see Him work in our lives like that in answering our prayers.

After many years, we have learned that we don't always get to hear from the Lord so clearly about things in which we are seeking His will. We still need to pray through until we either hear from Him or have the peace deep down in our hearts that whatever we are about to do is His plan for us. If we are abiding in Him (according to John 15:4), seeking His will, and trusting in Him with all of our hearts and not leaning on our own understanding, I do believe that He will make our paths straight (Proverbs 3:5–6). Let me hasten to warn you that sometimes Satan gives a false peace. He is a counterfeiter, remember. Whatever your decision, it cannot be in God's will if it is something He has spoken against in the Word of God. There are some things we just don't need to pray about.

Years ago, a lady told me it was God's will for her to divorce her husband, yet she had no scriptural basis for a divorce whatsoever. She told her story to a group of ladies in our Bible study class. They, like I, explained that it could not be from God. She refused to listen. Sadly, the very day the divorce was final, suddenly she was aware she had been hoodwinked by the devil. She went to her husband, who had never wanted the divorce, and explained that she had made a mistake. He refused to accept her back. The last time we spoke she was still a very sad lady. Satan will attempt to deceive you, and once you agree with him and act on his leading, he will turn it around and use it against you, heaping guilt on you. So be careful. But it is a wonderful thing to abide in Christ and to know and do the will of God.

Whether it is selling a house or other needs, we always need to seek Him for His wisdom, guidance, strength, and ability. The good news is, He is waiting to assist us in any way we need Him. Still, He uses even the bad things to eventually work out His good blessings for us in all situations. "And we know that God causes all things to work together for good to those who love God, to those who are called according to His purpose" (Romans 8:28, NASB). "Remember His wonders which He has done, His marvels, and the judgments uttered by His mouth" (Psalm 105:5, NASB). "Your Word is a lamp unto my feet and a light to my path" (Psalm 119:105, NASB).

Chapter 14

―――――――――

God's Plans Not Ours

Sometime after moving to our new location, we made the decision to adopt a baby. What we were told upon our inquiry was shocking to say the least. Just imagine our surprise when we were informed right up front that it would be impossible for me to adopt a baby because I was too old. At the time, I was thirty-nine. Anyone who knew me guessed my age at least ten years younger.

At that time my life had been an extremely active one, not only in the business world, and in community service and Christian work, but I had a dedicated exercise life as well—jumping rope, jogging, walking, etc. But that meant nothing to the adoption representative who explained that we might be able to adopt a three-year-old, but then quickly said that that, too, would be impossible because of the shortage of really little children as well as babies. She suggested that we adopt a seven-year-old child. Right or wrong, we made the decision that was not for us.

On a couple of different occasions we had tried to get to know very young teenage girls from an orphanage. We brought them to our homes, took them shopping, etc. with the hopes of being a blessing in their lives. However, probably because of their backgrounds, things just didn't work out between us. Perhaps that was factored in our decision making regarding an older child at the time.

We did pursue going through Christian sources. Not too terribly long after our initial pursuit in that direction, a call came from our contact while my husband was still at his office. Our source informed me that another pastor had contacted him to see if he knew of anyone interested in adopting a baby that was to be born in just a few short weeks. Interested? I was more than interested! Ecstatic was the word! I was so excited that I had to be reminded to speak with my husband about it and that we would need to seek God's will first. Pray about it? This was an *answer* to prayer. What was there to pray about? Pray indeed. Still, I at least controlled myself and waited for my husband to come home that evening to inform him that we had a baby coming soon. I told him everything, with no mention of a need for prayer. Imagine my surprise when he then said that he would pray about it and get back to me when he had his answer from the Lord. I was undone! How could these two men come to the same conclusion when the answer was so clear to me? Why could they not see that this was God's gift to us after all of these years? Still, I had no choice but to wait. Our contact had said that we needed to get back to him as quickly as possible so other plans could be made if we were not to be the parents. That was not my concern. My concern was in a totally different direction—that if we didn't get back to them soon, someone else would step up to the plate and take the baby right away from us. So, very impatiently, I waited. Later, I thought that perhaps I, too, should be praying. So, I prayed. Incredibly, when I attempted to ask the Lord if we were to adopt this child, the answer came so immediately and so overwhelmingly that I could not believe it. It was like someone raking his fingernails across a blackboard! With it came the answer—a resounding, "No!" To say that I was stunned is an understatement. In fact, it still seemed to be such a no-brainer that I was convinced it was just my approach. So I tried another prayer with the same response, then another and another. Unequivocally, our great God was denying my request. Disappointment again. What a roller-coaster ride it had been for us in our quest for a child. Interestingly though, at that moment, my concern was more about what my husband was going to think when he received my answer. Oh me of little faith, like our Father God was going to give him a different answer. When my husband returned home that evening with his answer, he was very sorry to tell me it was a very definitive no. He was surprised that I was on the same page with him. We called our source and explained our answer. Bottom line: never assume you know God's plans for your life without consulting Him, unless it is specifically addressed in His Word.

After that occasion, my husband and I made the decision that we would not put ourselves through that type of psychological trauma again. We accepted the fact that we would not have children and went about making our life plans with the knowledge that we would be without children here on earth. Of course, we know that we have children in heaven.

Many years went by before it was possible for me to ask our contact if he knew what had become of the baby. He had said that he also felt it best, under the circumstances, not to pursue it. We only know that our great God is an awesome God Who knows what is best for us all. We do know that if we will only stay close to Him, He will allow us to get to know Him more intimately, guide us with His righteous right hand, and make His will known to us as we need it. We may not delight in His answers all of the time, but we must accept them graciously. To do otherwise is to hurt our Lord God and to bring harm to ourselves. "In quietness and trust is your strength" (Isaiah 30:15, NASB). In time, He did take the sting out of His response to us, and He gave us peace in such a wonderful way. Yet even with that peace, the desire for a child never left us. That has stayed with us all these many years. There are still those moments when it is refreshed in many different ways. One day we will understand it; until then, we simply accept His ways, His will, and trust in Him. The Lord said, "'For My thoughts are not your thoughts, nor are your ways My ways,' declares the LORD. 'As the heavens are higher than the earth, so are My ways higher than your ways, and My thoughts than your thoughts'" (Isaiah 55:8–9, NIV).

Though we have never known the answer as to precisely why God chose to take our children home to be with Him so early, we do know that He has used those painful times in our lives to make us more compassionate and to enable us to comfort others in their painful times. These are times when we must also look past the pain for the greater good—of others and ourselves. These times have been a part of my personal story when He has opened doors for me to tell of His excellent greatness. Some young women have been really blessed by our summation that God, *in His infinite wisdom,* chose to take those babies home to be with Him. Additionally, after speaking in North Carolina, I was approached and permission was given to place a recording of my story into baskets in a North Carolina hospital to be given out to young ladies who had also lost their babies. It is another way to see how the Lord creatively uses these things for His glory and to bless others. It is His choice to make, because He is a sovereign God, and quite simply, that is all we have, but it is enough. He is sufficient! We must depend upon His infinite wisdom, not ours. Remember, He tells us in Jeremiah 29:11 (NIV), "For I know the plans that I have for you, declares the Lord, plans to prosper you not to harm you, to give you a future and a hope." Another translation words it like this: ". . . plans for welfare not for calamity" (NASB). If you read the surrounding passages, you will see that times were not good when He said that. Though it doesn't feel good at the time, we must push past the lies of the evil one and *know that God is good—all of the time.* "Oh come, let us sing to the LORD! Let us shout joyfully to the Rock of our salvation. Let us come before His Presence with thanksgiving; let us shout joyfully to Him with psalms. For the LORD is the great God, and the great King above all gods" (Psalm 95:1–3, NKJV).

Chapter 15

Canceled Florida Trip

We made plans to meet some of our Virginia friends in Florida for a week of fun and catching up. On the day we were to leave, we were all so excited that at the end of the day we would be winging our way to sunny weather and a fun time with our friends. When my husband got off work, he left his office and headed over to preflight the airplane before heading home to pick up me and our luggage. When he walked in the house he said, "We won't be going on vacation." He had discovered that the owner of the aircraft, who leased the aircraft to the flying club, had erased our names from the roster and was using it himself. Unbelievable! Without so much as an explanation, he had arbitrarily ruined our long-planned vacation. He could have given us notice at the very least or an explanation. Perhaps there would have been another aircraft available at the time. But now, nothing was available. We were both so very disappointed. I still remember not being able to wrap my mind around it. We called our friends and informed them. They, too, were very disappointed. However, they were already there and, as far as we knew at the time, stayed and had a lovely time without us. Although we were definitely disappointed, certainly it wasn't a life or death moment. Again, we just could not understand why God would even allow something like that to happen.

Sometime later on, He did give us a peek into His thinking. When we next spoke to our friends, they told us was an amazing story. The wife had become very seriously ill with a very rare virus during the time we were to join them. It was extremely serious and caused her to lose sight in one of her eyes. Interestingly, this virus was highly contagious, and we would have been exposed to it and, quite possibly, could have contracted the virus ourselves. When we learned this, we found ourselves thanking our Lord that He had provided a way of safety for us. Some might say this was happenstance. We knew differently. El Shaddhai, Almighty God, was working on our behalf, protecting us from that ordeal. It was definitely another way to remind us to trust His plans for us and to show His great protection for us. Why He allowed it to happen to our friends, we will never know until we see Jesus face to face. One thing for sure, we will forever be grateful.

Accepting God's nos isn't something we enjoy initially, but when we are reminded of how He can take it and use it for His glory, our good, and the good of others makes the adjustment much easier. Looking around us, we can usually find plenty of people who are going through much tougher times. Most of us in the United States don't understand *real* suffering. Immediately, I think about the story of Peter being delivered from jail even as the church was praying fervently for him. If you are unfamiliar with the story, read the entire account in the Acts chapter 12. Essentially what happened is that King Herod had begun mistreating some of the Jesus' followers. In fact, he had just had James, the brother of John, put to death with a sword. When he saw that it pleased the Jews, King Herod then had Peter arrested as well and planned some sordid persecution against him, perhaps death (some Bible scholars believe this to be true). Some of Peter's friends in the church were meeting together, fervently praying for his release.

Although he was bound and chained to two soldiers with four squads of soldiers surrounding him, God blessed him in answer to prayer and sent an angel to set him free. The angel ushered him right out of the jail. As they approached the gate, it swung open for them with no earthly being in complicity with them. Imagine that. What an incredible prison break for Peter! The question is, why didn't James get the same break? We don't know. We do know that the early Christians suffered terrible persecutions even unto death in horrible ways because they were followers of Jesus. Even Peter was crucified later. Look at John the Baptist. It's widely reported that all of the disciples were martyred with the exception of the apostle John, who died of old age in Ephesus, and Judas Iscariot died a horrible death of his own causing. Through the ages other followers of Jesus, like the apostle Paul, suffered greatly. People still die today for Christ.

If you doubt that, please read the book, *The Insanity of God* by Nik Ripken, which will totally amaze you. The incredible accounts of the modern-day persecutions of true followers of Jesus Christ will keep you turning the pages. There are many around the world! If you are like me, you will come to realize that many of us are shallow Christian who have been blessed immeasurably with the freedoms in this country, yet with which we have done so little for the kingdom of God in recent decades. We need to count our blessings and give Him our thanksgiving when we receive a pass from suffering times, and indeed we need to offer up the sacrifice of thanksgiving and praise when He allows the trials to come. Again, we don't understand His thoughts nor His ways, but we must trust Him. His view of the tapestry of our lives and our views are quite different, since He looks down from above and sees His perfectly managed pieces of work, while we simply see the back side with all the knots and snarls. We are to praise Him in all things, rejoice always according to the Word, and remember that sometimes He says yes and sometimes He says no. And sometimes, He simply says wait. "For it is God who is at work in you, both to will and to work for His good pleasure" (Philippians 2:13, NASB). "God is our Refuge and strength, a very present help in trouble. Therefore, we will not fear, though the earth should change and though the mountains slip into the heart of the sea; though its waters roar and foam, though the mountains quake at its swelling pride. Selah" (Psalm 46:1–3, NASB). "Rejoice in the Lord always; again I will say rejoice!" (Philippians 4:4 NASB).

Chapter 16

A God of Comfort

At the height of my husband's professional career, he experienced a real gut blow like never before. To those who don't know him, he is a very loyal, dedicated company man. So much so that in the early years of our marriage, he could be found working such long hours that books were written about him. Okay maybe not literally, but they could have been. Books like *The Work Trap* by Martin C. Helldorfer are "spot on" about people like him, and it took God having someone give that particular book to him—in addition to the wisdom from a few Christian seminar leaders, pastors, and teachers—to open his mind to the fact that he was a workaholic. Frankly, he loved his work and gave it his best. God exalted him and kept him in favor for twenty-five years with this company. With that in mind, imagine his surprise when he was passed over for a well-earned promotion in a division that was made for him but was given to someone else with zero experience in that particular side of the industry. Actually, that person was a friend who we admired and respected.

In the ensuing months, my husband was very frequently on the phone in the evenings with the people in that division seeking his advice on how to maintain the integrity and efficiency of the day-to-day workload. When my husband first heard the news, He was across the city from his office. Instead of returning to his office, he left and took a walk down the sidewalks of a very busy street and poured his hurts out to God. And He comforted him. That was his first move and the best decision! Scripture tells us to, "Humble yourselves, therefore, under the mighty hand of God, that He may exalt you at the proper time, casting all your anxiety (cares) upon Him, because He cares for you. Be of sober spirit, be on the alert. Your adversary, the devil, prowls about like a roaring lion, seeking someone to devour. But resist him, firm in your faith, knowing that the same experiences of suffering are being accomplished by your brethren who are in the world. And, after you have suffered for a little while, the God of all grace, who called you to His eternal glory in Christ, will Himself perfect, confirm, strengthen, and establish you. To Him be dominion forever and ever! Amen" (1 Peter 5:6–11, NASB). Then he simply went on about his business of doing his job "as unto God."

My husband had accumulated a wide range of business experience in his field, as well as in aviation. Suddenly, he was promoted to an entirely different area. God had saved a very special blessing for him in that he found that he loved this new area even more than what he had been doing originally. He found it challenging, fascinating, and exciting! He was quite happy that God had allowed him to suffer in the original position in order for him to be in the right place for this new opportunity. Then one day on an extended business trip around the world, he was contacted by a special company executive and was told that he desperately needed him to take the position where he was originally passed over. The executive told him that he was doing such a wonderful job for the company where he was, he wondered if he would manage both positions. This was quite a high compliment. My husband took on the challenge of managing both positions. Later on, he was promoted again. With God's wisdom, grace, and strength, he served in varying positions with great success and earned the highest awards along the way. We give God all the glory!

As the years progressed, it became known to me that when he held meetings with many people in the audience, he would encourage people to put God first, their family second, and their company a distant third. He had come a long way in his walk with the Lord by that time, although his workload sometimes made it seem to those observing that wasn't the case. I knew where his heart was, and he had my support.

I am reminded that in life, painful things occur. During those times we are to seek our Lord's wisdom and the comfort of the sweet Holy Spirit. Once, as I prayed for the Lord's comfort, I was writing a prayer request in my prayer journal with one hand while holding my Bible in the other. I had been reading in Isaiah chapter 55 and meditating on how our God's thoughts and ways differ from ours. As I completed writing the request, my eyes were drawn back to the open page. The following words seemed to sink into my waiting heart as the Holy Spirit of God comforted me, and will comfort you as well:

> "O afflicted one, storm-tossed, and not comforted, behold, I will set your stones in antimony, and your foundations I will lay in sapphires. Moreover, I will make your battlements of rubies, and your gates of crystal, and your entire wall of precious stones, and all your sons will be taught of the Lord; and the well-being of your sons will be great. In righteousness you will be established; you will be far from oppression, for you will not fear; and from terror, for it will not come near you. If anyone fiercely assails you, it will not be from Me. Whoever assails you will fall because of you. Behold, I Myself have created the smith who blows the fire of coals, and brings out a weapon for

its work; and I have created the destroyer to ruin. No weapon that is formed against you shall prosper; and every tongue that accuses you in judgment you will condemn. This is the heritage of the servants of the Lord, and their vindication is from Me," declares the LORD (Isaiah 54:11–17, NASB).

As the days passed, Philippians 4:4–9, 19; Psalm 37; Isaiah 41:10, 13 and 20; and others all became very meaningful to me. Our precious God, Who is the only true God, is a God Who provides "all of your needs according to His riches in glory in Christ Jesus" (Philippians 4:19, NASB). We need only go to the foot of the throne, humble ourselves and pray, and ask for our needs to be met, and they will be. It may not be in the way we think or expect because He may have something better in mind for us! And as a song goes: "He may not come when you want Him to, but He is always right on time."[4] This is a message to all of us living in these troubled spiritually, economically, and politically unbalanced times. So remember, when He says no to our prayers, He just has something better in mind. "'For My thoughts are not your thoughts, nor your ways My ways,' declares the LORD. 'For as the heavens are higher than the earth, so are My ways higher than your ways, and My thoughts than your thoughts'" (Isaiah 55:8–9, NASB).

He is in control. He is sovereign, and He is waiting to bring us the comfort and care that is His best if we will only bring our cares to Him and wait on Him. Frankly, He knows that we are but dust; He knows the circumstances of troubled times before we become aware. Let's all take everything to God in prayer and trust in Him. "Bless the LORD, O my soul, and all that is within me, bless His holy name" (Psalm 103:1, NKJV).

---

[4] "He's an On Time God," words and music by Dottie Peoples, © 1994 Peer Music Corporation, International Atlanta Music, Dottie Peoples Publishing. International Copyright Secured. All Rights Reserved.

Chapter 17

Facing Giants

There came a time in my life when it seemed obvious the Lord was pointing me to prayer. After selling the condominium, we purchased a beautifully appointed model home in a new neighborhood that was just far enough out of the city that you could see deer—one of my favorites of God's creations—meandering around the wooded areas near the lakes that the homes surrounded. We were getting settled in and really loving it there, yet we were both so busy we had no time to get to know any of our neighbors very well. But God was teaching me lots of things. We had begun to know the importance of prayer, even fasting and praying. God had begun teaching me and using me to teach that subject.

After we had lived there for a time, I returned from a trip to find a flyer from a couple of my neighbors laying on the island butcher block in our kitchen. It was an invitation to attend a Bible study at one of the lady's homes. It was very interesting to learn that we had lovely neighbors, some even Christians. It would have been delightful to commit to attend that Bible study. In fact, it was something I loved doing. Unfortunately, this was just not the time for me. Being away so much, plus running the house, made it impossible for me to consider it as much as I would have wanted to . . . or so I thought. When my husband came into the kitchen, he brought the subject up and told me that he had placed that flyer there for me to see because he wanted me to attend that Bible study. I loved him being the spiritual leader of our home, just not this at this particular time in my life. I told him it wasn't a good time. He calmly insisted and was very resolute in his answer that I attend. I remember thinking, *How unreasonable and inconsiderate!* However, I also knew that as a believer and follower of Jesus Christ, I am under the authority of my husband, just as he is under authority of Jesus Christ. When there is a difference of opinion between the two of us that can't be reconciled, then I am to submit to his decision, unless it is immoral or illegal, at which point I submit to the higher law of Jesus Christ. Peter said,

> ". . . you wives, be submissive to your own husbands so that even if any of them are disobedient to the word, they may be won without a word by the behavior of their wives, as they observe your chaste and respectful behavior. Your adornment must not be *merely* external—braiding the hair, and wearing gold jewelry, or putting on dresses; but let it be the hidden person of the heart, with the imperishable quality of a gentle and quiet spirit, *which is precious in the sight of God.* For in this way in former times the holy women also, who hoped in God, used to adorn themselves, being submissive to their own husbands; just as Sarah obeyed Abraham, calling him lord, and you have become her children if you do what is right without being frightened by any fear" (1 Peter 3:1–7, NASB, emphasis added).

I know what many of you ladies are thinking right now. It definitely isn't popular to observe these principles, nay commandments, today in our independent, feminist, liberated society. But God's ways haven't changed nor have His commandments. It is not always easy for us to "die to self" (1 Corinthians 15:31, KJV) as He also commands all of us to do if we are to follow Him. As I honored God and attended the Bible study, it was such a blessing. Not only did we enjoy getting to know our neighbors in this way, but we became a support group for each other in prayer. After completing the Bible study, we continued on as a prayer group. They prayed for me when I traveled to speak, and on occasion some of them would go with me. Some would fast and pray that God would specially anoint me and use me, and that the women would have open hearts to His message for them. We saw God answer our prayers in remarkable ways in each of our lives and the lives of those around us.

Many years later, circumstances caused us to go in separate ways, but some of us are still in contact with each other, and we still pray for each other when we have special needs. God continued to point me to prayer. It seemed everything around me was teaching me about the importance of prayer. In addition to that prayer group, I was invited to lead a Bible study on prayer at the headquarters of my husband's employer. by some of the female managers. Prayer became important enough that I began to make a special request each time a chairman of the Christian women's organization invited me to speak. I requested that they have several ladies commit to pray for twelve hours just prior to my speaking at their location, not only that God would provide for all of my needs but also for all of the coming events. We especially prayed for the hearts and minds of the ladies attending to have their hearts opened to receive the gospel of Jesus Christ. Each lady would be responsible to take a half-hour or a one-hour shift—not through the night. We could see that God blessed the prayers of

His people immeasurably. Whatever we expect of others, we need to ask of ourselves. At some point during those years, I was not only committed to prayer regarding these events, but it became my practice to fast (liquids only) for a day prior to a speaking trip.

One day, I received a message in my heart and mind that I was to call my church and tell them they needed to put more emphasis on prayer. That was *way* out of my comfort zone! Even though we were members there, neither one of us were serving in the church in any way. Like other times when the Lord had a plan for me, He relentlessly pursued me until it was on my heart and in my mind daily. Frankly, I didn't even know who to call. After speaking to my husband about this and praying about it, I did follow up and not too long after that day, I received a call from the Women's Ministry director of the church. She invited me to lunch. She and another lady met me and we enjoyed a delightful lunch together over which all that the Lord had laid on my mind was brought out. During the conversation, I explained to her that I was simply dumping the information to be obedient and what they did with it was up to them. She asked me what particular studies on prayer were meaningful to me, and I was happy to recommend a very introductory one to her. She explained to me that this other lady who had come to lunch with her that day had also been sent to her recently with a similar plea, and that was to restart a church prayer chain. She then further stated that our pastor had also been tapped by the Lord with a similar message—put more emphasis on prayer in our church. It was the most incredible thing for me to learn how God was working. As we talked, the director said she wanted to make it clear to me that they weren't just interested in the study; they were interested in my leading the class. It was such an honor for me to have that opportunity. After all was accomplished with the vetting and our praying through everything, God gave me the gift of being the leader of that group. How humbling! I think I must have felt like David when he slew the giant! At the end of that class, they extended an invitation for me to continue in the next session and teach the Bible study on *Prayer Life: Walking in Fellowship with God* by T. W. Hunt and Catherine Walker. What an incredible gift and opportunity that was. When the words "prayer warrior" come up, I think about T. W. Hunt.

At the end of those weeks of study, we had a churchwide seminar on prayer led by T. W. Hunt himself. My husband and I, members from our class's committee, our pastor and his wife, and other church leaders enjoyed having dinner together with Mr. and Mrs. Hunt. What a pleasure. God blessed us immensely with the ladies on that committee. There would have been no way for me to take on that job had He not surrounded me with incredible praying helpers. They were just as important in His mission for that class as any other person. We are only foot soldiers serving in the King's Army, but each of us is assigned tasks from Him. We are only as good as the people we surround ourselves with. God really blessed the obedience of those He touched with the message for more emphasis on prayer.

Our pastor appointed others in the church to set up a churchwide prayer chain. Hundreds of people showed up and participated in it. People were assigned times to pray with another person assigned to them. It was an awesome thing. And God blessed. I am reminded of a scripture reference that I use frequently: "but God has chosen the foolish things of the world to shame the wise . . ." (1 Corinthians 1:27, NASB). God is working. Join Him where He is working.

At that time in my life, facing a giant in that way was one of the most difficult things God could have given me to do. Going with a message like that to one of the world's most well-known and respected, even loved, pastors was indeed like David going out to meet Goliath to me. However, I felt like the bad guy—and the big church and their pastor the good guys—who just happened to be the giant. God knew my fears, but He also knew my heart for prayer, and He used it for His glory. There is no better foundation for a church, an individual's life, or for a country than one that is rooted and grounded in the Word of God and grown up in prayer.

Prayer is an integral part of each of our lives. It should be a message to all of us to concentrate more on this incredible arrangement that our heavenly Father has set up in order for us to be in communication and fellowship with Him. He desires it and He delights in it. Prayer is a beautiful gift, yet I believe it's a resource that we overlook more than any one thing in our Christian lives. "The effectual fervent prayer of a righteous man avails much" (James 5:16b, NKJV). A great word picture of this is with a woman—Hannah.

She prayed persistently and in faith for the Lord to give her a son. Her husband had chosen a different path when the wife he loved could not bear sons for him. He just married another woman. But Hannah was so grieved that she went to the temple and prayed and prayed—very unselfishly too. She promised to give him back to the Lord to serve in His temple all the days of his life. The Lord heard and blessed her persistent prayer and filled her barren womb. She gave birth to Samuel, which means "answered prayer," and then she fulfilled her promise by giving him back to the Lord for service in the temple. For the complete story, read the book of 1 Samuel. Of course, accounts of God's faithfulness to hearing the prayers of His righteous children continue all the way through the Bible, and there are many more in this book. God is still faithful—the same yesterday, today, and forever.

> "Is anyone of you in trouble? Let him pray" (James 5:13, NIV).

> "The eyes of the LORD are toward the righteous and His ears are open to their cry. The face of the LORD is against evildoers, to cut off the memory

of them from the earth. The righteous cry, and the Lord hears and delivers them out of all their troubles. The LORD is near to the brokenhearted and saves those who are crushed in spirit" (Psalm 34:15–18, NASB).

"Praise the LORD! Praise the name of the LORD; praise Him, O servants of the LORD! Praise the LORD, for the LORD is good. Sing praises to His name, for it is lovely" (Psalm 135:1, 3, NASB).

Chapter 18

An International Move

After many years of living in Tennessee, we would have told anyone who asked us that we would be there until retirement, and then move on. That's what we thought. However, our great Father God had another thought that He was about to pass along to us.

International travel had begun occupying a large part of my husband's life many years before. Early on, many countries around the world were interested in the company's brand and services coming into their countries, all of which kept my husband very busy. Their desires were that the company would open offices in their respective countries, bringing the privileges of the phenomenal services that only this company could provide. On occasion, my husband would be met at the airport by a minister of transportation in his limousine with the little flags of each specific country flying on the sides of the limousine; this is similar to what the president of the United States travels in.

One day my husband told me that it was thought among top company officials that since they were now an international company, perhaps they should open international headquarters in certain parts of the world. With this came the idea they would reassign select officers of the company to move there with their families to enable them to better understand the various cultures and enhance their business acumen. Since the company was losing a lot of money in the international realm, this certainly seemed to be a sound business plan. Brussels, Belgium, was the preferred location for the European headquarters. My husband further stated that an Asian location was undecided at that time, but that it might possibly affect us. He stressed firmly the importance of total confidentiality regarding this. After telling me about the plans for international headquarters, we didn't really discuss it anymore. That was pretty much the end of it. But it was tucked somewhere in the recesses of my mind as a possibility for us.

Months later, I was preparing to leave for a week of several speaking engagements. It seemed easier to drive so I could have my own independence and not have to be concerned with others driving me from one location to another all week. Just prior to my departure, a friend and neighbor passed along an audio tape of a friend of hers that she really wanted me to listen to. I was glad to have it to pass the time while driving. I had heard about this lady from another friend and was quite interested in hearing her speak, so I tossed the cassette in the front passenger seat thinking I would listen to it on the way. Somehow, my mind was on other things, and I didn't get around to it, which as it turned out, was a really good thing—planned by the Lord. The week's assignment had gone well, but I was tired and eager to get home. Heading home, it suddenly occurred to me that it was a good time to listen to the tape. I popped it into the player and began to relax and enjoy my trip home . . . but not for long. The speaker was great, but almost from the beginning, she began telling of what the Lord had to do to convince her to give up her home and move with her husband and their two youngest daughters to Brussels, Belgium, leaving their two oldest daughters behind in the United States. Much earlier, even prior to the two youngest daughters' births, she had agreed with her husband that God had placed a call on their lives to become missionaries somewhere, possibly internationally. Circumstances never produced anything to confirm that belief regarding the international move, so they went on with their lives. Her husband had felt the call to leave the professional world and was on staff at a local church, and they had even had two additional daughters, with the thought of moving overseas as missionaries long forgotten . . . or so she thought. She certainly learned that God's timing is perfect, not ours. He had not forgotten. In her lovely and humorous presentation of all these events, she related how He tapped them on their shoulders one day and reminded them of His call and their commitment to Him. She was devastated! After all those years, and the thought of having to leave her two oldest daughters behind, this reminder from the Lord was almost too much for her. Over a period of time, she, her husband, and their two youngest daughters did indeed move to Brussels, Belgium, where they remained for many years. God rewarded their obedience and used them in His work there and later in another country, prior to repatriation. As I listened to her testimony that day, the Holy Spirit of God began speaking to me that this was a message to me from Him with specific consequences. This was not just a speaker with a lovely message to listen to on my "relaxing" ride home. Oh no. It was a life-changing moment, a defining moment to prepare me for news that awaited me at home. I somehow just *knew* that deep inside my heart. I really believed that the Lord was saying that my husband and I would be making a big move; most likely we would be one of the families to move to Brussels, Belgium, with him being tapped as one of the officers set to establish the European international headquarters office there. I certainly knew the Lord would not ask me to move to Asia. Tears were flowing down my face, and it was difficult to concentrate on driving. So many concerns and fears raced through my mind. I'd have to give up the life that I knew, give up my home, give up my friends, move far from our families, give up my church, give up my ministry of speaking and teaching . . . Yes, indeed, it was all about me! However, as many of you can relate, our Father God can be pretty persistent when He wants to be. So, somewhere on the return home, I surrendered to Him and I told Him I would go wherever He called us.

Shortly after I arrived, my husband called me. He told me that the CEO and chairman of the company had just called and asked him to come to his office. My husband said he thought he might be talking about his career, so he encouraged me to be praying, which I did. Deep down in my heart though, I already knew what that was all about. Around six o'clock that evening, my husband arrived home with the most peculiar and tentative look on his face. He blurted out, "What do you think about moving to Hong Kong?" I said, "No! We're moving to Belgium!" That response certainly took him aback, so to this he quickly asked, "Where in the world did you get that idea?" "From God I thought," was my response. Well, at least I had the message right; I just missed it on the location. The next few hours were amazingly dramatic with even a few tears shed on both sides. Definitely, if the Lord was collecting our tears that night, He stored up quite a bit more of mine. My husband and I talked well into the evening about this. By early the next morning, we had made our decision to go, if that was God's plan for us. The final decision was made by the CEO a few weeks later that we would indeed be moving to Hong Kong just as quickly as we could accomplish all that we had to do to make an international move. If you have ever moved, you know what an ordeal that can be. Well, you could triple that intensity for an international move.

We made a whirlwind house-hunting trip to find a place to live in Hong Kong. All along the way, it seemed the Lord just made a way for us where there seemed to be no way. He helped us sell our house, settle all other business and personal issues, and He even gave us a beautiful apartment in a brand-new building on the fifteenth floor with a magnificent panoramic view overlooking

Hong Kong Island, the busy international harbor, and Kowloon. The sad part of this new setup was that our precious little chocolate toy poodle would have to go to "prison" for six months. It was the required amount of time for incoming pets to be quarantined. We were heartbroken. We knew that she wouldn't survive this six-month stint. Then one day, Almighty God gave us a rich blessing—Hong Kong had dropped their required six-month quarantine. The updated quarantine requirement had just changed to thirty days. I remember standing in the shower and saying, "Lord, I will minister to the up and outers, and I will minister to the down and outers." Reflecting years later, I could see that He had taken me up on that commitment to Him quite literally.

All of this was kept very confidential until almost the end of my teaching year in Bible study. Unbeknownst to me, until almost the last day of Bible study, our pastor's wife, who happened to be in our class, came up with the idea to have a special prayer time for me (and for my husband in absentia), while she and the members of the class' committee laid hands on me. Additionally, she invited the other ladies from our Prayer Life Bible Study class, as well as any others who were there from other Bible study classes, who would join them in committing to pray for my husband and me *every day for three years*. As I was bowing my head, I glanced around the room and saw hands stretching out to show symbolically the laying on of hands. Ladies, who didn't even know us or didn't know us well, were committing to pray for us every day for three years. Then as our pastor's wife prayed, she asked our great God to provide for us and use us in His service during our three-year appointment in Hong Kong.

People told us that at the Wednesday night prayer service after our departure, our pastor announced to the congregation that we had moved to Hong Kong. He further stated, "God is sending them, but the company is paying for it!" And so He did. We were so blessed by Him and all that we saw Him do in that first three years we were there (we ended up staying an additional year). It seemed that nothing could slow or stop anything that we felt He called on us to do, proving once again what Job said in Chapter 42 (NASB), "I know that you can do all things, and no purpose of Yours can be thwarted."

We were called on to attend to spiritual needs or minister across the board to people of every socioeconomic standing. Some of the time it was one-on-one or two-on-one occasions, but much of the time it was in groups. Other expatriates, local residents, and we were to join up with God where He assigned us to work as teams to accomplish His work there. Sometimes it would be for my husband in a professional situation, or for us personally as we traveled throughout Asia. Most often it was through the wonderful church we were blessed to be affiliated with during that four-year period. In addition, we were ministered to in unbelievable ways.

Hospitality is key to the Asian culture, and we had certainly received that! Since that time, I have often stated, "I went over there kicking and screaming and came home the same way." I felt loved and accepted like I have never been before or since. Our church there at the time had approximately one thousand members. We attended the international Sunday morning worship service, which had approximately 250 attending. In that small contingent of worshipers, we had approximately thirty-five nationalities. People from varying cultures from around the world gathered there to pay homage to our wonderful Lord Jesus Christ or come to know Him. I believe it was during our second visit to church there that I leaned over to my husband and said, "This must be what heaven is like." No one seemed to mind the vast cultural or socioeconomic differences as we met to worship the one true God, Jesus our Savior. And the exciting thing is, He met us there! Time and time again. He had a work to do, and He was busy bringing it about. He used everyone in unique ways. If you had come from good basic training, you were enlisted! No bench warming there!

People moved in and out of that city with regularity. Change was the one thing that was constant. Just as we see in the Word of God, you didn't have to work your way up from the bottom just because you hadn't served there for many years. God used people who knew a work was being done and were excited to be a part of His kingdom work, even in a small way. We were so blessed to be called to a beautiful mission field such as Hong Kong (approximately 7 or 8 million people and only 2 percent Christians).

For three years, it seemed that each time we were called to do some special task through the church, God just swept us up like a rushing tide and carried us through, accomplishing whatever it was He had called us to do. Although we had been a part of incredible work of the Lord prior to our moving there, we knew the power and the presence of the sweet Holy Spirit in ways we never had before.

During the fourth year, however, spiritually speaking, we experienced something quite different and quite difficult. Even though we were still being called on for service, it seemed that for no reason it was like pushing a boulder up a steep grade. There seemed to be no explanation and no way around it. It just was. And then I remembered something: with the fluidity of people moving from one Bible study class to another back home, and with many of those ladies in that original group who committed to pray for us coming in from other churches just for the weekly Bible studies, there was just no way to announce that we were staying in Hong Kong for an additional year. Understandably, there was no assurance they would have agreed to continue to pray so faithfully every day anyway. Who would blame them when they received no updates for all those years? We do know that many friends, including our pastor and his wife, were continuing to pray, but we did not have the daily throng approaching the throne of grace on our behalf as before. What a difference!

~ Author's Note ~

People, prayer is a powerful thing. Who can really understand it? Acts 12:5 says, "So Peter was kept in prison, but prayer for him was being made fervently by the church of God" (NASB). James 5:16 says, "The effectual fervent prayer of a righteous man availeth much" (KJV). But we do know that our great and wonderful God has this plan where we can fellowship with Him, petition for our needs to be met, and it happens. "Pray without ceasing" (1 Thessalonians 5:17, NASB). Even when one person comes to our Savior with cleansed hearts, God is always anxious to meet with us, and He will answer those prayers, giving us His best in His perfect timing. It may be yes, no, or wait, but He will answer. We should always pray for God's will to be done on earth for His glory in each and every situation. Until this day, Hong Kong has turned out to be the highlight of our lives spiritually, personally, and professionally.

Most of the people there were involved in worshiping foreign gods or practicing certain philosophies—Hinduism, Buddhism, Taoism, Confucianism. However, it wasn't at all unusual to visit a Buddhist or Hindu temple and also see a crucifix there. Most of them were open to people telling them about Jesus Christ. People practicing those secular religions certainly don't mind taking in additional gods in conjunction with their own form of worship, just to make sure they are covered in all areas. But our great and awesome God, the One true and living God, doesn't share His glory with another. In order to know Him and the power of His excellent greatness, we must turn away from all other gods, surrender our lives to Him, and live in obedience to Him as outlined by His Word, the Bible. Then we can have access to Him and enjoy His favor upon us. We don't have to work for it; we don't have to earn it. Just prior to voluntarily giving up His life on the cross, Jesus said, "It is finished" (John 19:30, NASB). Nothing has to be added, not even good works. Otherwise, for what purpose did Jesus die? However, He does require works after we have come to Him by faith. The shedding of His perfect unblemished blood on the cross of Calvary paid the cost—ONCE AND FOR ALL (Hebrews 10). Hallelujah! What a Savior! "For just as the body without the spirit is dead, so also faith without works is dead" (James 2:26, NASB).

Our first Asian vacation was to Phuket, Thailand, the largest island of Thailand, to the exclusive Amanpuri Resort, one of the lovely Aman Resorts that are sprinkled around the world. It was located on the Andaman Sea alongside the lovely white sands of Pansea Beach. However lovely, it was a very small beach that curved around to where large boulders lay and extended to high bluffs. One day my husband came up with the idea that we walk around on the boulders and explore what lay around on the other side of the bluffs. I decided it was not a good idea for me, but he thought it a good idea so he set out. I found a perch on one of the boulders there in the shallow water and settled down to wait for him. He was gone for quite a long time. I became anxious and began to wonder what in the world I would do to find him if he didn't return soon, as the day was fading fast. I don't remember exactly, but I'm quite sure I was beseeching the Lord to bring him back to me safely. With an extremely grateful heart, I finally spotted him gingerly making his way back around to where I was waiting. He quickly began relating an experience he had just encountered. While walking along the other side of the bluffs enjoying the view, he came upon quite a few little shrines to man-made gods where incense was burned. That was a very common thing for us to see since they were all around Hong Kong too. Thinking nothing much about it, he simply continued on his way. He strolled back down toward the edge of the bluffs and began heading back around to where he would meet me. Suddenly, he felt an overpowering presence of evil spirits, and he said he knew in his heart that their desire was for him to go over the cliff. Without hesitation, he firmly spoke aloud, "Be gone in the name of JESUS!" Immediately, he felt their departure and continued peacefully on his walk back to the beach to meet me, but not without knowing with assurance firsthand the power of the awesome name of Jesus, his Lord and Savior.

On that same trip to Phuket, my husband hired a car and driver to guide us around the island so we could enjoy the local culture. He also hired a boat captain and a guide to take us for a tour around the back side of the island. It was pretty amazing to think that we were in Thailand and just across the way from that side of the island was Vietnam. As we were taking in the incredible views, we realized there were other much larger boats, gun boats actually, with the crew watching everything we did. When we turned in a certain direction, they too changed their position and followed our every move. They looked quite sinister, and although they had legitimate concerns regarding possible drug and human trafficking and were simply doing their jobs, they certainly made us appreciate our freedoms in the United States. Truthfully, we are always being watched. The sinister minister of evil, the devil, has minions watching over us to do us harm at any time they can. However, our wonderful Lord is looking over us always; He promises never to leave us nor forsake us.

Driving back to the resort late that afternoon, the sun had dropped just below the horizon and the twilight of the evening was upon us. Suddenly, our driver excitedly remarked that something fantastic was taking place just up the road that we should stop and see. We were out in a rural place with no one around, that I could see, and it made me nervous. As we drove just a little farther, we could see there were cars parked along the road on either side and people were standing along one side of the road. Our driver was adamant that we stop and see this wonderful thing. This particular week was the week of the festival of the gods so, as it turned out, this was another celebration of some god (read 1 Kings 18). There was a huge god erected alongside a low, colorful building just off to our right and someone on drums was pouring out a repetitive beat. As our eyesight became adjusted to the evening light, we noticed that several young, handsome Thai men were coming out in our direction from the colorful building doing a little shuffle/dance in time with the beat of the drums. As they did, they advanced toward a cleared area closer to the side of the road where we, along with many others, were watching. These young men were dressed in beautifully colored red tight pants, and they were as handsome as any young men could ever be. As they danced a little nearer, it looked to me that they held roses in their mouths like flamenco dancers. My husband said, "No, that's a spike driven through their mouths and that's blood you see on their faces!" They had reached a position to where there was no doubt in what I saw, and then they each began self-flagellating their backs with a steel ball with spikes at the end of a chain. Each time they struck themselves, the blood would flow down their backs. Initially, it was difficult to understand how they could endure such torture and just keep dancing around. As they turned toward us, we could see that their eyes were rolled back in their heads; they were all in a trance! The "celebration" continued with the raising of a huge prayer pole where possibly hundreds of prayers on small pieces of paper had been attached. We learned that once this was accomplished fireworks, also attached to the pole, were set off, which was supposed to frighten off any demons that might be a hindrance to their prayers being heard. After a time, we returned to our car and were finally deposited safely at our resort. As we began walking to our cottage, the manager of the resort, who happened to be from the United States, approached us and engaged us in conversation. He was most interested to know if we were enjoying our stay and all that was available on this picturesque island. Once he learned that we had been touring by land and by sea, he couldn't wait to tell us of the most exciting "celebration" that was taking place somewhere right near the resort. As he began describing it, we told him we had just seen it. He was totally shocked and more than a little jealous. He explained, "I have lived here three years, and I have never had an opportunity to see it!" Why it meant so much to him we never knew. Why the Lord allowed us to "happen up" on it that day we probably will never know for sure. We do know that experience made us realize what an awesome privilege we have to know the One true God, Jesus the risen Savior. He certainly doesn't require us to do as those dancers did since He did the finished work of paying the penalty for our sins on the cross of Calvary. We will definitely have trials and tribulations in this world, as He speaks of in His Word, but we do not have to shed our blood to pay any price for our salvation.

~ Author's Note ~

Some in the family of God have given their lives because of their belief in Jesus as Lord. Once we have come into His family, we do not have to do anything to have our prayers heard, as long as we are seeking to live for Him and keeping our sins confessed and repented. How sad for people who do not know our Jesus Christ. "If you have died with Christ to the elementary principles of the world, why, as if you were living in the world, do you submit yourself to decrees, such as 'Do not handle, do not taste, do not touch!' (which all refer to things destined to perish with use)—in accordance with *the commandments and teachings of men? These are matters which have, to be sure, the appearance of wisdom in self-made religion and self-abasement and severe treatment of the body, but are of no value against fleshly indulgence" (Colossians 2:20–23, NASB). How blessed we are to know the One true God, Jesus Christ, and to have the hope within us that we will soon be with Him in heaven for ALL eternity. It is not only an awesome privilege to know Him, but with that comes the knowledge there is much responsibility on our part to make sure others have that same information so they, too, can come to the saving knowledge of Jesus Christ. "To whom much is given, from him much will be required" (Luke 12:48, NKJV). Jesus is a powerful friend!*

Back from our vacation in Thailand, while sleeping one night, I awoke with the knowledge that I was being choked. I somehow knew in my spirit that I was under attack from evil spirits, but I could not move nor could I speak a word aloud! I had complete knowledge that unless something was done quickly I would succumb. It suddenly came to my mind to simply cry out in my spirit to the One Who could assist me—JESUS! Although I couldn't cry out loud to Him, as soon as I turned to Him in my mind and said His majestic name in the spirit, I was released! Indeed, what a great and mighty God is our God!

***

Although this next story didn't take place in the Orient, it is, however, in keeping with the subject matter. I was on a speaking trip, the older lady who was to be my hostess during the week greeted me so very warmly upon my arrival, but soon afterward she began to tell a story that seemed as though she was simply "spinning a yarn." However, this was a much-respected lady and her story was credible to the people who knew her. Just a few days prior, she had hosted a Bible study in her home. Those in attendance had left quite late, and she, being rather tired, had gone to bed soon afterward. Sometime during the evening she woke up and walked into the short hallway toward the bathroom. Something caught her attention; a little red light was glowing back down the hallway to the area where the Bible study group had met. She went to take care of that and was on her way back to her bedroom where something hit her on the back of her head, knocking her to the floor. After regaining consciousness, and living alone, she knew she had to get help for herself. Having no cordless or cell phone, she had to somehow get to the hall phone, which she finally managed to do by crawling. She called the police and they responded. When they arrived, they entered the house and were totally surprised to find no apparent point of entry for a perpetrator. Initially, their thinking was that she must have been confused and had simply fallen down and struck her head on something. The doctors at the hospital confirmed what she had said; she had been struck from behind and had sustained a very serious injury requiring a few days of hospitalization. Perplexed, the policemen decided to make a more complete investigation. They still could not see how anyone could have come from the outside into her house; all the windows and doors were locked up tight. Somehow this dear lady had been accosted by something or someone sinister within the confines of her home in the middle of the night.

After a few days, this brave woman was able to return home to continue her convalescence. Soon she began to encounter strange happenings, like furniture being moved around from its normal places. This was about the time I arrived. Usually, if I stayed in someone's home, it was a sweet retreat where, when possible, I could have all the time I needed between engagements. My initial impression of this lady and her lovely home was that this would be just the retreat that I needed.

My first evening seemed to begin well, except for the full disclosure of what had just transpired in the house. As the evening progressed, I became a bit nervous as my eyes darted around during our visit. At bedtime, now in our respective rooms, I snuggled down into my bed for hopefully a good night's sleep prior to a big day ahead. Very quickly I felt an evil presence in that room; actually, it felt like they were all around me. I quickly sat up, turned on the lights, and said, "Be gone in the name of JESUS! I have been bought and paid for by the precious blood of Jesus Christ, and I am His child. You have no rights over me and you must leave!" Suddenly, the room seemed different. Peaceful. Once again our gracious God, our Protector and our Deliverer, had come to the rescue. Jesus said, "Truly I say to you, whatever you bind on earth shall have been bound in heaven; and whatever you loose on earth shall have been loosed in heaven" (Matthew 18:18, NASB).

When Jesus walked on this earth, He used the Word of God to ward off temptation by Satan. Our loving God is always just a call away! We should begin our day by laying everything in His hands to provide and protect, and we should put on the full armor of God: " Finally, be strong in the Lord and in the strength of His might. Put on the full armor of God, so that you will be able to stand firm against the schemes of the devil. For our struggle is not against flesh and blood, but against the rulers, against the powers, against the world forces of this darkness, against the spiritual forces of wickedness in the heavenly places. Therefore, take up the full armor of God, so that you will be able to resist in the evil day, and having done everything, to stand firm" (Ephesians 6:10–13, NASB). I encourage you to open your Bible if you have one—and if not, get one—and read the rest of the scriptures in Ephesians 6, instructing you on each piece of the armor to put on. My husband

and I pray that together daily. You may want to pray it at other times during the day also.

Afterward that initial evening, all went well for the few days I was with this lady, with the exception of one little thing. I had asked her about the moving chairs and wondered myself if it was attributed to her age and the trauma she had just gone through. It was just like our Lord to actually *show* me. We were in the kitchen for breakfast one morning before leaving for several hours. Later on, when we returned, we walked into the kitchen to find a stool that she had moved over to one side of the room back in the center of the kitchen. It only required that one time for me to believe her! Who knows what really goes on around us in the supernatural world and what the Lord is protecting us from. One lesson we can remember, where God is working, Satan is always working, as well, attempting to destroy any good our Lord is accomplishing or prevent it from happening. "It's a fact of earthly life that when God opens the windows of heaven to bless us, the devil opens the doors of hell to blast us. When God begins moving, the devil fires up all his artillery."[5]

O Lord, enable us to always have the name of Jesus on the tip of our tongues. If we are pure, continuously praising You, thanking You, exalting You, witnessing for You in a positive manner, serving You, reading and meditating on Your Word, we will always be prepared. Please may it be so! We pray in Your mighty name, JESUS, because we are Your children if we have truly invited You to come into our hearts and have allowed You to take over our lives. Thank You, precious Lord, for what You have done, for what You are doing, and for what You will do for us from this day and all through eternity. May our lives continuously reflect who we are in Christ Jesus. We pray in Jesus' name. Amen.

---

[5] Adrian Rogers, "When You're Up to Your Eyeballs in Trouble, Part 1," Love Worth Finding articles, http://www.oneplace.com/ministries/love-worth-find-ing/read/articles/when-youre-up-to-your-eyeballs-in-trouble-part-1-11784.html

Chapter 19

_____

More Stories from the Orient

One particular vacation to Bali, Indonesia, proved to be successful in the way that really matters in the eternal scheme. We had spent several days in one of the fantastic Aman Resorts. Unlike most areas, there were three resorts within a few miles around Bali near the mountains and the coast. The one we spent our vacation in was on the coast, and it was fabulous. One was quite near the airport we were departing from, so the day prior to our departure, we decided to move there to cut down the travel time the next day. For some reason, just a short time before our departure, I suddenly had an overwhelming urge to have a manicure before leaving the resort. Why? I don't know. That was out of the ordinary for me. My husband was perplexed as well since we only had a very short time before we were to depart, but he graciously sat in the lovely private garden outside our cottage while the young Balinese lady did the manicure for me. When she began working, we began talking. Soon the Lord emboldened me and gave me the words to share the gospel of Jesus Christ with her. She spoke broken English, which was much better than my ability to speak her language. Gratefully, she understood my Southern-style English very well, and in short order, she readily accepted Jesus Christ as her Savior. Hallelujah! That day a precious young Balinese lady that I will simply call N. L. came into the kingdom of God and became my sister in Christ. It was very good news for a lovely friend of hers who worked there as well; her friend was already a Christian and had been telling her about Jesus. Now this young woman would be able to share her new life in Jesus Christ with her friend. Because of circumstances, we were unable to keep in touch; however, our pastor followed up for me and contacted an Indonesian pastor there. They were able to provide a Bible and other literature and follow up with her. From time to time, the Lord still reminds me to pray for her. What an incredible opportunity that was. As our former pastor used to say, "It was like picking ripe fruit!" It was obvious that the Holy Spirit had already prepared her—through her friend and perhaps others—and had already laid the groundwork so that she was ready that day to receive Jesus Christ as her Savior. We had just the right amount of time to get my manicure, but more importantly, spend the time we needed to let the Lord win her to His kingdom and still depart right on time. There is a little song that says, "Our God is an on-time God." The question that comes to my mind is, if the Holy Spirit is always speaking to us, what if we are simply too busy, have our own agendas, and don't want to do what He is asking and end up missing an important assignment? I will always be grateful that neither my husband nor I said no to His prompting that day!

***

I read somewhere about why God blesses certain people with certain gifts. It is the work of the Holy Spirit, so we cannot take credit for these gifts. Each of us is given at least one special spiritual gift the moment we are born again. If you have an extremely fine, intelligent mind, you should not be arrogant, and it is definitely not for you to make fun of others who are not blessed in that way. It is to be used to help those very people and for God to get the glory. So, if you ever wonder why you are so blessed, remember, it is not about you specifically. It is about our wonderful God choosing us to be used in His kingdom work in specific ways. It is all biblically based in the New Testament. As I write this, I wonder just how frequently I have missed that calling on my own life, and perhaps this applies to you too. It's my heart's desire that wherever I am and whatever I am blessed with, I will remember it is not for my own good pleasure. There's much more involved. I pray that all the saints will come together according to the Word of the Lord in these end-times. As our former pastor used to say, "Those gifts are not for enjoyment, but for employment." If you are using them for His glory, you will enjoy the fruit of it either here or in heaven. Acts 4:32–35 says, "All the believers were in one heart and mind. No one claimed that any of his possessions was his own, but they shared everything they had. With great power the apostles continued to testify to the resurrection of the Lord Jesus, and much grace was upon them all. There were no needy persons among them. For from time to time those who owned lands or houses sold them, brought the money from the sales and put it at the apostles' feet, and it was distributed to anyone as he had need" (NASB). I am not suggesting that we must do that specifically, although the way the world is going, it may come to that for Christians. However, I do believe that those of us who understand the verse "For by grace you have been saved through faith; and that not of yourselves, it is the gift of God; not as a result of works, so that no one may boast" (Ephesians 2:8–9, NASB) that sometimes we are not as committed to works as much as we should be. Unfortunately, that is true among some who are more financially blessed. We forget that the God of all creation can give, and He can certainly take away. I recall a message by Dr. Charles Stanley many years ago that covered this same topic. The gist of it was that when we are less fortunate financially, we are in church serving and loving the Lord, very dependent upon Him. Yet, when He begins to bless us more financially, we buy boats, airplanes, other homes, or we are traveling so much that we just can't seem to take an assigned position of service because it is just too inconvenient. It interferes with our lifestyles. Later on, the Lord begins to allow certain trials to come into our lives to hamper that chosen lifestyle. The next thing you know, we are back in church more regularly, but we are whining and whimpering about how the Lord has allowed this awful thing in our lives that we just can't understand. Why would a good God let bad things happen to good people? More importantly, we should ask, why does He bless any of us in such fashion? We become so self-centered that we truly think it is all about us. He gives to bless us in order that we might be used in His kingdom work in all the places He ordains to glorify Him and so that our joy will be made full. I believe that He also entrusts these things to us.

> For this reason I kneel before the Father, from whom His whole family in heaven and on earth derives its name. I pray that out of His glorious riches, He may strengthen you with power through His Spirit in your inner being, so that Christ may dwell in your hearts through faith. And I pray that you, being rooted and established in love, may have power, together with all the saints (all believers or followers of Jesus Christ), to grasp how wide and long and high and deep is the love of Christ, and to know this love that surpasses knowledge—that you may be filled to the measure of all the fullness of God. Now to Him who is able to do immeasurably more than all we ask or imagine, according to His power that is at work within us, to Him be glory in the church and in Christ Jesus throughout all generations, forever and ever! Amen (Ephesians 3:14–21, NIV).

I also pray that we ". . . will no longer be infants, tossed back and forth by the waves, and blown here and there by every wind of teaching and by the cunning and craftiness of men in their deceitful scheming. Instead, speaking the truth in love, we will in all things grow up in Him who is the Head, that is, Christ. From Him the whole body, joined and held together by every supporting ligament, grows and builds itself up in love, as each part does its work" (Ephesians 4:14–16, NIV). "For I know the plans I have for you, declares the Lord, plans for welfare and not for calamity, to give you a future and a hope" (Jeremiah 29:11, NASB).

***

There was another time where our wonderful Father made plans for me. He put His special touch on those plans to assure me that it was indeed of Him. And if we have that assurance, we might as well sit back and watch as He "accomplishes what concerns us" (Psalm 138:8, NASB). A couple from Tennessee had moved to Tokyo, Japan, about the same time we had moved to Hong Kong. She and I had become friends through the international Christian women's organization; her husband was with another company, but she and I had stayed in touch. One day I had the pleasant surprise of receiving a phone call from the chairman of the group in Tokyo, inviting me to come and speak to their group. I knew of that group already because they had been known in the United States as having the largest attendance in the world, so it was exciting to have the opportunity to speak there. Although my husband had been to Japan from time to time on business trips, I had yet to have an occasion to travel there. I had been battling a health issue, which made it difficult for me to travel alone. Therefore, I had to explain to this chairman that I would have to ask my Lord and my husband and see where that led me. It had always been my policy to go wherever the Lord opened doors, so I was really interested to see how He worked that out. I was thinking perhaps my husband could take a little respite from work for a few days to travel with me there. Our limitless God could do a number of things. Amazingly, very quickly after getting off the telephone, it rang again and it was my husband. Excitedly, I explained about their invitation for me to come speak to that group. He was so pleased to tell me that he had just discovered that he needed to make a business trip to Tokyo at the precise time I needed to be there. He was calling to see if I would like to go with him. Our great God is simply so awesome and majestic in all of His splendor, yet He is involved in every detail of our lives. Should we even begin to hesitate to trust Him? Never! Praises to Him, we did go and I did get to speak to their lovely group, which consisted primarily of Japanese ladies. It was an opportunity for the Lord to get His message of hope out to them. Our trip went wonderfully and we had a great time exploring.

As stated before, while living in Hong Kong, it was our good pleasure to be used of the Lord in many different ways as were many other expatriates from around the world. One day after a lady rededicated her life to Jesus Christ at the end of Bible study, several more of her family members made the decision to acknowledge Him as their Savior and Lord and follow His teachings. One precious young lady seemed to be so very excited and wanted to know more about Jesus. Soon afterward, I started a one-on-one Bible study with her in our home. Like a sponge she was soaking it all up. One day she came in, excitedly held up the Bible, and asked, "Who wrote this book?" When she was told that God did, she looked all around on the outside cover and, not finding what she was looking for, then asked, "Why didn't He put His name on it?" We had quite a chuckle over that.

Another day when she arrived, we had a friend from San Antonio, Texas, visiting with us. We had decided she would assist me in leading the study that morning. Everything was going well until we reached a particular topic and neither my friend nor I could think of the answer we needed. We just drew a blank. Suddenly, this precious young lady, who knew practically nothing of Christianity, piped up with the very information we were searching our minds for. Stunned, we asked how she knew that. She replied, "I saw the movie on television." When we inquired as to which movie, her response was priceless: "The Ten Amendments." It was all my friend and I could do to keep a straight face. How precious was that! Of course, you know the movie she was speaking of was *The Ten Commandments*. But who cares? It was a moment to cherish! From time to time, we still think of our dear sister in Christ and that particular moment of insight from her and her source, and we always smile. I am sure the Lord smiled too.

Chapter 20

God Raises Up Leaders . . . Including Deacons

W hile in Hong Kong, we were blessed to know many young Filipino ladies who had left their country and families— many with husbands and children left behind—to work in Hong Kong. Because of contractual arrangements by the Hong Kong government, most of them worked tirelessly for twelve hours each day, six days a week, with Sunday being their typical day off. Many of the ladies, who did not attend church, could be seen gathering in the Central Business District with their friends with whom they had much in common. Most of the ones we knew spent almost all of their Sundays at churches with primarily Filipino congregations. Some had pastors who spoke both English and Tagalog, their primary language. There was a two-fold payoff because they enjoyed the worship services, and got to socialize with their friends or make new friends. Unfortunately, the majority of employers forbade them from having their friends over, even though each residence was built with private quarters in a separate part of the home. It is an industry made up primarily of females with very few positions geared toward males. We discovered that they selflessly sent most of the monies earned back to their families in the Philippines because of the economic difficulties there. It is that country's number one means of revenue. Since there were so many more women than men, the traditional teachings of the Bible for male leaders were sometimes set aside and women were placed in predominantly male roles. Some of these decisions caused spirited spiritual discussions among them from time to time. Even though some people suggested otherwise, my husband and I were delighted to have them meet in our home for Bible studies and socializing after they completed their regular work schedules. We were always amazed that they were eager to do so even when their employers were strict about their twelve-hour shifts. Some worked much later but still came when they were able, around 9:00 p.m. It was during one such heated discussion in our home that they sought me out for counsel.

One of their leaders had been asked by their pastor to be a deaconess in their church. The role of deacon is defined in many churches as simply a servant of the church congregation. However, in many churches it is much more than that, having to do with making church policy, finances, and other administrative decisions. Most of them believed that the Bible clearly states that a deacon is primarily a male role, according to 1 Timothy 3. Their pastor, an American, disagreed. My counsel was for them to study the Word of God regarding this subject in pertinent scriptures and pray it through until the Lord gave them their answer. In the meantime, I told them if they truly believed that the position of a deacon in their church was reserved for a godly male member of their chapel, they should begin to pray for the Lord to provide more godly men in their chapel who were qualified to fill the role. If it is of God, He will provide. If He did not provide and they still felt the same, then perhaps they should consider closing their assembly and joining other assemblies already staffed appropriately.

A few months passed. One day one of the young Filipino men, who himself was a deacon at their chapel, was visiting with us along with some of the young ladies. He reminded me of the counsel given them regarding prayer for God to send godly young men to assume the responsibility of deacons that was so badly needed in their chapel. He smiled and told me that shortly after they began praying, quite amazingly, God had sent eleven godly young men who qualified to take those positions. As always, God does provide in every circumstance that He is a part. "And my God will supply all your needs according to His riches in glory in Christ Jesus. Now to our God and Father be the glory forever and ever. Amen" (Philippians 4:19–20, NASB). If it is from Him, He will either provide immediately or cause you to wait on Him. Sometimes it may be to test you to see if you will abide by your beliefs or cave in and follow another's teaching. He will sometimes provide in a way not thought of previously, so don't box Him in. Occasionally, He will simply say no to us and we may never know why. He knows, and His way is always best. Oftentimes the enemy will tempt us to settle for less than God's best by sending a counterfeit. That is why we must stay in the Word of God, and in prayer with Him, and have a firm grasp on what He is telling us.

Not everyone is intended to be in leadership roles, but everyone needs to be serving God in some way. Some think we shouldn't accept any position that isn't covered by our spiritual gifts (grace gifts). If that were so, then only people who have the "gift of giving" would be expected by the Lord to give of their time, talents, or money. I heard somewhere once that not all people give because they love, but all people who love will be givers. And even though we see in His Word that we don't have to work for our salvation, it is a gift and obtained by faith in Him. But He also tells us that once we are saved, we are to work. "For just as the body without the spirit is dead, so also faith without works is dead" (James 2:26, NASB).

We need to abide in Christ and allow Him to do what He needs to do through us. There is a verse in Philippians about "working out your salvation," (2:12, NASB) but that isn't to gain our salvation; that is already taken care of if you are born again. Jesus paid it all on the old rugged cross of Calvary for the penalty for our sins. There is much power in the blood of Jesus! That means we are to allow Him to live in us and enable us to be like Him by doing good works so that others can see Jesus in us and want to come to know Him too. We become His mouth, hands, and feet. When we seek to know Jesus and enter into His family, we enter into a covenant relationship with Holy God. We need to read His Word, be in prayer, associate with godly people, attend a good Bible-based church, be apprised of what His will is for us, and then do it. So, let's be in prayer, listening for the Holy Spirit's leading, and available to go and do whatever He has in mind for us. But be careful to do it within the confines of His will.

Chapter 21

_____

My Spiritual Pilgrimage

By a Dear Chinese Brother in Christ Jesus

"We are the clay, and Thou art our Potter." Little did I know what God was going to mold me into when I became a Christian. Before I became a Christian, I was an executive at a big multinational computer company. My "god" was spelled g-o-l-f. My entire Saturday and Sunday each week was spent playing golf. My wife used to tell the children, "Learn to play golf or you will never see your father." When I was a kid, I went to Sunday school, but like many others, I drifted away. I came to believe that Christianity, like all kinds of secular religions, was only for the uninformed, not something that an intelligent, well-educated person can believe in. Everything in my life was going well and I had no need for God. My wife was a Christian by then, and was praying for me, but there was still no interest on my part. A few years ago, God jolted my attention.

My son was studying in the United States at the time, and I was in Hong Kong. He got into some trouble, which would prevent him from graduating from high school. I felt very hopeless and cried out, "God, if You are real, help me. If You do, I will go to church for the next seven weeks." Miraculously, the situation with my son turned around. And even though I still did not believe in God, I kept my end of the bargain. I went to church for the next seven Sundays before I went back to my golf games. (I might mention here that I had just had an operation on my shoulder and could not play golf for seven weeks anyway.)

One day I received an invitation to attend a four-week investigative Bible study at the church. It just happened that at the time I had another operation and had to be sidelined for five weeks. With some nudging from my wife, I went. That study answered many of my questions, and I reached a point that I did not reject the notion of God and Jesus Christ. Yet I still had no need for it and went back to my golf games. However, from that point on, I was less reluctant to attend Christian functions my wife and friends invited me to.

While at my office, I took out a tract, what I used to call "the do-it-yourself Christianity." I had read many similar tracts before. When I would come to the prayer part, I would toss them aside, believing that it was ridiculous that one can just say a prayer and become a Christian. This time though, I thought to myself, *Why not? At least I will find out if it doesn't work.* So, I prayed the prayer at the end of the booklet. Right away, I realized that I had accepted Jesus into my life. I immediately called my wife and told her the good news. Amazingly, it is just that simple, if you are sincerely looking for the truth. Almost immediately God began to change me for the good. Old things were no longer holding me captive. I had been set free to "walk in newness of life." He began enabling me to reprioritize my life to the things that were important and that would ultimately bring great joy in my home and in my daily life.

Sometime later, at a crossroad in my life, I decided to refocus my life from chasing after the world's riches to following Christ more closely. Since then, He has led me to work with Christians in the southwest part of China. These Christians are very poor and barely surviving. Their annual per capita income is less than $60. I devote my expertise to teaching them to break free from the bondage of poverty, and then they, too, can reach out to other nonbelievers in their neighborhood. I am now raising goats with the villagers and helping them generate more income. In addition, a work is in progress of building health-care clinics so that people will have access to affordable medical care. God has indeed molded me through these years from a computer executive to an investment banker and to a goat herder for His sake. His blessings overflow as he continues to involve me in His work. I need daily to arm myself to face the challenges He has set before me. And to remember always, "for it is God who is at work in you, both to will and to work for His good pleasure" (Philippians 2:13, NASB). Blessed be the name of the Lord!

~ Author's Note ~

If only you knew all of how the Lord brought this lovely man to Himself! It is truly a beautiful story and the transformation that has taken place is totally awesome. God has truly been using them through the years in a wonderful way. His story shows the magnificence of God's grace and the simplicity of taking that step of faith in Christ Jesus. We are blessed to be friends with this lovely couple and to witness God's excellent greatness in their lives.

This is a prayer that you, too, can pray to invite Jesus into your life so that you may know Him.

Dear Father, thank You for loving me and making a way for me to come to know You personally by sending the Lord Jesus Christ to die for all my sins. I accept Your forgiveness for my sins and also Your free gift of everlasting life. I invite Jesus Christ to take up His residence in my heart as my Lord and Master. Please lead me into a new life and fill me with Your life and strength and power. Thank You for now making me a new creation in Christ. In the name of Jesus the Lord, Amen.

The prayer is found in the back of one of Stonecroft Life Publications called "My Search!"[6] If you pray this prayer sincerely, and commit to live for the Lord all the days of your life, He will see that you have the abundant life with Him from that very day forward through all eternity. Life on this earth will not be a gravy train, but with Jesus at the helm, it will be worth it when we see Him. And He will be in it with us forever. Please keep in mind that once we invite Jesus into our lives, our hearts are changed immediately, but we are always to obey the command to ". . . work out your salvation in fear and trembling" (Philippians 2:12, NASB). There is no better way! The alternative is not a choice anyone should even contemplate. We must seek Him daily for His enabling to see us through this life, so that we ". . . endure to the end . . ." (Matthew 24:13, NASB). God is willing. Are you?

---

[6] Lambert Dolphin, Jr., physicist, "My Search!" a prayer, (Kansas City, MO: Stonecroft Life Publications, 1991).

Chapter 22

𝒟addy's 𝒟eath

After a full life with no illness other than a cold or flu, and a bout with a back issue many years earlier, in his eighties my daddy was in declining health due to congestive heart failure. Prior to that, he had actually continued riding horses on his farm, certainly something a lot of people much younger would love to have done. He had been as strong as an ox all of his life, with literally no one we knew coming close to being able to match his strength. He was a marksman, and he knew cattle and horses better than most people. In fact, he was so good in his younger days with breaking horses that he perhaps could have been known as a type of "horse whisperer." People had brought their horses to my daddy to break because he was good at it, and through the years I had heard the stories. However, things were changing with him.

He was experiencing symptoms that caused him to require constant care. One of my brothers had built a house next door to him on land that Daddy deeded to him. My brother was the one most responsible for Daddy's care. However, on occasion when my brother needed a few days away, he would enlist one of us to be there.

Once when my brother needed time away, he enlisted the help of one of my other brothers to be Daddy's caregiver. He was to bring Daddy to his house. Simultaneously, my husband had returned from Hong Kong to the United States for a meeting at the company's headquarters. While he was away, I had been invited to attend a Chinese opera with some of our lovely friends there. On that special evening, I had just finished dressing and was waiting for my friends to pick me up. The telephone rang and as I went to answer it, I was certain it was my friends. No. It was my eldest brother who said, "I'm sorry to have to tell you, but the time we have all been dreading has finally arrived. Dad died earlier this morning!" Apparently, as was usual during the night, Daddy needed assistance to go to the bathroom. My oldest brother explained that while he assisted him out of bed and into the bathroom, my daddy, who had a sense of humor, was joking about a Little Debbie cake calling his name. That, too, was a nightly occurrence. Just after entering the bathroom, my daddy sank down into my brother's arms and died suddenly, yet peacefully. My heart was broken. Here I was, so far away, half way around the world from my siblings and my husband. Although I was able to be up and around Hong Kong, it wasn't immediately clear to me that I would be able to travel alone because of health issues. However, almost immediately the Lord, our Most High God, began revealing that He was going before me and making the rough places smooth. My husband was able to purchase a first-class flight for me departing the next day. Friends assisted me in packing, getting me to the airport, and getting me checked in without the normal international issues in Hong Kong and the United States. He sent what seemed to be angels to care for me all the way through the rest of the trip. What a beautiful gift!

The trip from Hong Kong to San Francisco took fifteen and a half hours. Somewhere over the Pacific, when her workload had calmed down, one of the flight attendants sat beside me and offered her condolences regarding the death of my daddy and continued to engage me in conversation. She visited with me for quite some time and in speaking with her, I felt the freedom to let the tears spill over. I had a layover for a few hours, and then several hours to Tennessee. The next day, my husband and I drove ten hours to meet up with my family for the receiving of friends, the funeral, and visitation with friends and family for the next few days.

After a week, we headed back to Hong Kong. My deepest gratitude goes to my heavenly Father Who worked all of that out for my benefit! He goes before us to make the rough places smooth and the crooked places straight. "I will go before you and make the rough places smooth; I will shatter the doors of bronze and cut through their iron bars" (Isaiah 45:2–3, NASB). It was all a blur and unbelievably painful. Something profound still stands out to me. We really must be ready to leave this world. It was very obvious to me that my daddy didn't expect his departure from this world at that time. He was joking about eating a Little Debbie cake. Be prepared! If you have not before, then accept Jesus Christ as your Savior. Those of us who have accepted Him know where we're going. "Therefore, we do not lose heart. Even though our outward man is perishing, yet the inward man is being renewed day by day. For our light affliction, which is but for a moment, is working in us a far more exceeding and eternal weight of glory, while we do not look at the things that are seen, but at the things that are not seen. For the things which are seen are temporary, but the things which are unseen are eternal" (2 Corinthians 4:16–18, NKJV).

Jesus Christ is our Savior and Lord, our Friend, and Father God is our eternal Father. May He be forever exalted! The Holy Spirit of God lives within us if we are true believers and followers of the Lord Jesus Christ. He has pointed the way to Jesus since shortly after Jesus Christ's ascension into heaven. Our God is three Persons, but He is the One true God. Satan is our worst enemy, who has already been cast out of heaven but is being given a little time to kick up some dust before he will be tossed into hell. Even that will come to an end before too long.

Even though I never knew my earthly daddy as the dad who loved and accepted me in the way God instructs in His Word, and really don't know if I will ever see him again, I certainly desired to know him and to know his love. Oh, how I wish that would have been so. More importantly, I know Who my heavenly Father is. I will be able to spend all eternity with Him in heaven.

Chapter 23

Return from the Far East

When we arrived at the airport for our final departure and return to the United States, we found a group of friends waiting to see us off. What a delight that was! They gave us wonderful gifts to remember them by. As the time of boarding drew near, they hugged us and held on to us with tears flowing, knowing that we would most likely never see each other again this side of heaven. I've heard it said that the people who are left behind should know that even though we never see them again, they shall always be with us, for they are forever in our hearts. It's certainly true for me with these dear friends. It was an interesting ride on the approximately fifteen-and-a-half-hour flight from Hong Kong to San Francisco. We were on the periphery of a typhoon and it was bumpy, to say the least. It was scary at times. My husband, who always thinks the more adventuresome things are the best, actually awakened at one point (yes, he was sleeping) and said, "This could get really interesting!" Thankfully, after a long and uncomfortable ride, we arrived safely and in one piece, as did our luggage. One thing I do not miss—long international flights. We call it the bag drag.

Readjusting to the United States, believe it or not, was much more difficult in some ways than our initial adjustment to Asia. We had to return to strong racial tensions, crime-ridden cities, filthy television shows and movies, very loud music in restaurants, and little to no service in stores. In Hong Kong, while there are racial issues between differing groups, they are mostly civil to each other in society. In Hong Kong, Singapore, Japan, and probably other cities in Asia, everyone, women included, could walk the streets perfectly safe at any hour without fear of being raped, mugged, or assaulted. Asians have a lot of respect for family and wouldn't want to embarrass their families in any way. Our time there was while Hong Kong was still under British rule. As sad as it was to leave the land and the people we had come to know and love, it was still good to be back in our own native country. I still believe the United States to be the best country in the world to live in, despite the negatives.

We returned to the same city in Tennessee, the same church, and the same pastor whom we so loved and respected. The next year I was back leading Bible studies there in the Women's Ministry Department. What a blessing! Soon, the Lord also led me to lead Bible studies in our neighborhood, as well. Again, what a blessing it was to have the privilege of that call from the Lord. My husband had returned to another position, which was his ministry position after years in the international arena.

Before long, we had purchased a motor yacht. We named her *Morning Star*. We had come to believe the Lord was leading us to start a Bible study at a yacht club on a lake not far from our home. On our first weekend on the *Morning Star* we met a couple on a houseboat behind us. The wife was someone I had known for years. We had dinner with them that evening. As we discussed our thoughts about a Bible study to be held at the yacht club there, someone mentioned to us that a lady that worked at the fuel dock was interested in the same thing. After dinner, we walked over to meet her. In a matter of days, other friends joined us in our discussions. Finally, it was all arranged. One problem was that we didn't have a leader. We began to pray for that leader to present himself to us. One day as I prayed at home alone, I asked the Lord who the leader should be. Immediately, it seemed the Lord gave me the name. It was my husband. I thought, *Good choice!* He had co-led a men's Bible study in our church in Hong Kong and they had loved him. Why not lead a men and women's class? Unfortunately, my husband didn't think it was such a good idea . . . initially. The more everyone agreed it was to be him, the more he was determined it was not.

One morning at our church Bible study class, a gentleman gave his testimony. Part of it was about what the Lord had to do to reach him to go on a mission's trip to South America. During that gentleman's testimony, the Lord reached into my husband's heart with the clear understanding that it was from Him that he lead that class, so he surrendered to do so. He led that class for a couple of years. How great is our God! The group in the men's class in Hong Kong were called "The Drifters" because they all traveled out of Hong Kong on business so much of their time. My husband named the Bible study class at the yacht club "The Drifters" because people didn't go to their boats every weekend. So some weekends we would have a very low turnout, and at other times we would have a high turnout; either way, God met us there. In Matthew He commissioned His disciples to go make disciples, and that principle is there for us to do also.

Chapter 24

Incurable IBD

Years ago I had begun to have serious health issues that chiefly manifested in the intestinal area. It began in Virginia, continued during our time in Tennessee, Hong Kong, and back to Tennessee. I became so emaciated that some friends approached my husband and expressed their concern for me after seeing me in a swimsuit. Doctors in the city we lived in at the time were clueless. All the while I was losing more and more weight and existing on a very bland diet. Many patients find aloe vera juice to be beneficial. However, as the years came and went, other symptoms worsened and produced a very broad range of health problems. During our month's home leave the first summer, I found an internist who diligently attempted to diagnose the problem. I had symptoms similar to lupus, chronic fatigue syndrome, and other diseases. I was systematically tested for each of those, all of which were ruled out. Finally I was hospitalized and more tests were done.

Almost every morning and evening, I spent time with the Lord and left it all with Him in thanksgiving and praise, fully resting in Him to accomplish whatever needed to be done. In spite of everything the doctors and nurses were putting me through in the hospital, amazingly, He kept me in His peace through it all.

In addition to all the symptoms commonly associated with these other diseases that were ruled out, it was discovered that I had a significant problem with anemia, which brought the doctors to the decision to do a bone marrow biopsy. They were concerned it might be leukemia. I spent time with the Lord and, once again, I was in peace prior to the test. During the test, I silently sang praise songs and offered up the sacrifice of praise and thanksgiving to God. After some time, my doctor asked me if I was all right. She was perplexed when I told her I was just singing praise songs to God. She explained that all of her other patients going through this procedure would be very uncomfortable during this time. She went on to say that they would not only be in pain but would be writhing in pain at this juncture! But praises to my wonderful Lord; the only thing I experienced was a feeling of dull pressure on my lower spine. God, in His compassion and mercy, chose to remove that horrible pain for me that day, for which I will be eternally grateful. Later on, after the doctor left the room, her assistant told me that the doctor was not a Christian but that she was, so she understood that God sometimes still chooses to work miracles for people. Indeed He had given me a very special gift that day.

The test results came back negative for leukemia, but there was an intestinal disease that produced symptoms like mine. The biopsy they took showed positive for Inflammatory Bowel Disease (IBD), which is considered incurable. My gastroenterologist said there were only two major diseases under the heading of IBD—ulcerative colitis and Crohn's disease. It was not ulcerative colitis, so it was finally decided that it was Crohn's disease. My gastroenterologist in Hong Kong concurred. In spite of frequent attacks of IBD, any time that our Father God called on me to teach a Bible study, travel with my husband, counsel people, or anything else requiring strength and stamina, I would simply call out to Him and He would supply. There were many times, however, when I would lie in my bed and claim scripture verses of His promises to supply whatever my need was for the day. If He wanted me to do something, He would have to do the rest. Over and over again, He was faithful to do supernaturally what I was totally unable to do on my own. Of course, "Nothing is too difficult for God!" (Jeremiah 32:17c, NASB).

As the years progressed, so did the Crohn's disease until it seemed at times it would totally consume me. BUT GOD, my Deliverer, would eventually lift me back up again. In 2 Timothy 4:17–18 (NASB) he stated, ". . . the Lord stood with me and strengthened me . . . ! The Lord will rescue me from every evil deed and will bring me safely to His heavenly kingdom; to Him be the glory forever and ever. Amen."

Sometime after our repatriation to the United States, God blessed me by allowing me to lead the Bible study in our neighborhood entitled, "Experiencing God: Knowing and Doing the Will of God" by Blackaby and King.[7] He had previously allowed me to lead it in our women's ministry in our church, and I had participated in it in Hong Kong. During my preparation time one day, somehow something came alive to me that had not been so apparent in preparing my homework before. Henry Blackaby mentioned that one reason we do not see more people coming to the Lord today than in biblical times is that unbelievers do not see God doing the miracles through believers that He did in those times. Back then, they saw God doing things they knew could only be God doing it, and they could not explain it in any other way. I remember weeping and crying out to the Lord that I wanted to be one of those people that He could do something in and through, so people would know that God did it and there could be no other explanation.

---

[7] Henry Blackaby, Richard Blackaby, and Claude King, *Experiencing God: Knowing and Doing the Will of God* (Nashville, TN: B&H Publishing Group, 2008).

Time passed and my health worsened. There didn't seem to be any hope left that I could get well. I woke up one day and said, "Father, I KNOW intellectually that You love me, but I don't FEEL loved. Would You just show me somehow today that You love me, maybe even as I read Your Word?" Quickly the Holy Spirit of God impressed upon me in my spirit to read Psalm 118, so I opened my Bible and began reading verse 1: "Give thanks to the LORD for He is good; for His lovingkindness is everlasting" (NASB). As I continued to read the next few verses, I knew He had heard my cry and had answered me. But He encouraged me to continue reading, which I did. When I read verse 17, I knew the Lord was giving me a rhema word—a special word from the Word. It says, "I shall not die, but live, and tell of the works of the Lord." It was a promise especially for me! I knew it, claimed it, and thanked Him for it.

The Crohn's disease grew steadily worse over the following months. My husband was leading a Bible study class on Sunday mornings for boaters at the yacht club where our boat was docked, and we were there each weekend from Easter until Labor Day for two years. The yacht club was approximately one and a half hours from our home. My neighborhood class was still in progress during the week and my husband was still working there. Even though I was able to get to the lake one particular weekend, that Sunday morning it was impossible for me to get up and go with my husband to his class until, once again, I cried out to the Lord for His enabling. I dressed and went with my husband while he led the class, and afterward attended a brunch with several of the class members at one of our favorite restaurants on the lake. Amazingly, again, I felt totally well all during that time! Wonderful Lord! However, shortly after we returned to the boat, I became so ill, and I was in so much pain that it was necessary for me to interrupt my husband so he could take me home. I expected that I would end up in the hospital since the pain was almost unbearable.

My doctor decided to do a colonoscopy, and it was scheduled for Thursday of that week. Monday and Tuesday were ghastly days with little rest and the pain abating somewhat, only to have other symptoms becoming supercharged. On Tuesday evening, I finally fell asleep. By Wednesday morning, I awakened totally well! It was so bazaar. There was such a peace and tranquility about me, it seemed I was walking around in another world. Honestly, I truly did not know what had happened. I told my husband how I was feeling, but he just thought it was a calm between the storms. I suppose I did too. I decided to say nothing to my doctor and go in as planned for the procedure. When the doctor came in, he had his usual compassionate heart and whispered, "How are you doing this morning?" I replied, "I feel fine!" He inquired, "Then what are we doing here?" I just told him that we should just go ahead with the procedure, and so he did.

Later on I received a call from his nurse informing me that the doctor wanted me to return to his office so he could give me the results of the pathology. I just figured he could give me the results over the phone since I was feeling so well. She insisted and I relented. As quickly as I got off the phone, my mind went into worry mode. *What had he found? Had it turned into cancer? Am I in the eye of the storm as we had thought, and the worst is about to happen?* On and on the thoughts persisted. For some reason, not once did I remember to think positive thoughts. When the doctor came into the room, he had was holding my rather large medical file. He sat down in front of me and began flipping through the file . . . page after page. As he did so, he ran his other hand through his hair and kept saying, "I can't explain this! I just can't explain this!" After listening to this for a while, finally I said, "Explain what? Just tell me what it is. I can deal with facts, but I can't handle not knowing!" He said he thought the tests had been switched, so he returned them for retesting. The second time produced the same results. He said, "You do not have Crohn's disease any more. You have the most perfect intestinal tract I have ever seen. It is the right color, the right density . . . everything is perfect. Where there is usually disease and scarring, there is nothing. In fact, you're beautiful inside!" I just sat there staring at him. It was surreal. Finally, I said, "Well, people around the world have been praying for me. Recently I was put on our church's prayer chain." With that, he closed my file, jumped up, and laughingly said, "That's it! It's that 'tree thing' they do out there!" He was referring to the incredible Singing Christmas Tree program they do annually that celebrates the birth of Jesus Christ. Of course, he probably meant to be humorous. Some doctors need scientific answers and evidence for things to make sense. Other doctors know that God still does miracles! I left his office in kind of a daze myself, not able to put things in the proper perspective.

As I began to leave the parking area, the Holy Spirit began scrolling back to me all the previous conversations He had with me through His Word and the Bible study earlier that year, words that I had totally put aside until He reminded me. My Father God had answered prayers and He had healed me of the "incurable" Crohn's disease, fulfilling His promise to me when He led me to Psalm 118:17 many months previously: "I will not die, but live, to tell of the works of the Lord." Of course, there was much celebration time and times of praise and thanksgiving in our house and with friends who had been praying so diligently for me for years. Indeed our God had used me to show that He is the One Who still performs miracles. He did it just as I asked—in a way that no one could explain it other than God had done it! God healed what the medical field *still* says is an "incurable disease." Only God can get the glory!

A couple of days later, as I told my story with one of my faithful prayer partners, she said, "It is that 'tree thing.' It's because of the cross of Calvary!" Amen. All that was made possible for me because of what He has done for us already. He alone is the

Healer, Jehovah Rophe, whether it is spiritual, physical, emotional, relational, or any other way.

A few years later, another colonoscopy was done and it was still fine. Knowing that some doctors have a difficult time attributing healings to our wonderful God, that day while discussing the issue with my doctor, I asked him if he agreed that it had to have been the Lord Who healed me. He smiled and said, "May be, may be, I know that you had it; I just don't know where you put it." Sometime after that, while I was praying, I asked the Lord, "Whose prayers did you hear?" I quickly explained that I really didn't need to know that, but I asked that He give me some perspective regarding this issue. He quickly responded, "Many prayers were sent up on your behalf, but there is only one Healer!" Oh WOW! How very true! He would not only heal me, but He cared enough to speak to me in such a personal way. It's impossible to wrap my mind around it all. It still brings tears to my eyes. He does these special things for His children, and He will do it for you. Healing may not always come in this way, but He will give you His special gifts if you will give your all to Him and let Him rule and reign in your life.

One day while worshiping God, with tears in my eyes I said, "I worship You according to Your excellent greatness." As quickly as the words came from my mouth, He spoke to my spirit and said, "That's a book I want you to write about Me!" At the time He said it, it resonated in my heart that it was indeed my Father God speaking. Just to be sure, for several months I sought Him for confirmation before speaking to anyone regarding this. It seemed He was leading me to do it. This was all in order to "tell of the works of the Lord" (Psalm 118:17, NASB). I then mentioned it to my husband, who is usually good at protecting me from some huge task that is too much for me to take on. This time, however, he quickly agreed that he believed it was an assignment from the Lord. After that confirmation, several other prayer warriors were contacted, who all agreed with him. When I told the Lord, "I worship You according to Your excellent greatness," I did not remember that it was a verse in a Psalm. I'm certain that I had read it before, but I believe it was placed in my heart by the Holy Spirit. Finally, I sought my dear pastor's counsel. He was in hearty agreement and said, "You are just the one to do it." That was so encouraging! Would I have loved to have been a very strong and healthy person during that time? Yes. Many people, including my husband and me, prayed fervently for my healing. But then I would not have known Him in such a personal way. I really missed my years of good health when I was somewhat of an exerciseaholic, being able to haul my own luggage, or the numerous other activities that healthy people do. BUT GOD in His infinite wisdom had chosen another path for me. He has been building my character and enabling me to learn perseverance, patience, faith, endurance, and other eternal things (see James 1:2–4).

Those who love Jesus and follow Him will have to go through times of trials and tribulations, for He says in His Word, "In the world you have tribulation . . ." (John 16:33b, NASB). That's why it is so important that the true believers, followers of Jesus Christ, stand by those who are in such trials. We see in God's Word: "Beloved, do not think it strange concerning the fiery trial which is to try you, as though some strange thing happened to you: But rejoice to the extent that you partake of Christ's sufferings, that when His glory is revealed, you may also be glad with exceeding joy" (1 Peter 4:12–13, NKJV). Another important verse to remember is: "Although He was a Son, He (Jesus) learned obedience from the things which He suffered" (Hebrews 5:8, NASB). What a powerful verse! "Grain for bread is crushed, Indeed, he does not continue to thresh it forever" (Isaiah 28:18a, NASB). Yes, He allows these things, and He can take them and use them for the greater good to reach others for His purposes. We don't always know what to do, but our eyes should always be on Him. God our Deliverer will always show up right on time!

Chapter 25

𝒟aughter in 𝒟istress

On my way home from a speaking engagement, approximately one hour east of our home, my car suddenly became difficult to steer. I immediately decreased my speed and successfully pulled over onto the shoulder of the interstate. Carefully, I got out with the busy traffic zooming past, went around my car, and checked my tires. Just what I thought, my right front tire was quickly going flat. Now what? There was no way I was able to change that tire by myself. It was about six o'clock in the late afternoon, almost dusk. With fear and trembling, knowing how dangerous it was in that situation, I returned to my car and began to pray for God to send someone who would do the job, but where I would be safe. For quite some time, a young college-age man in a compact car with University of Kentucky stickers on his back window had been traveling along with me, passing me at times when I was held up in traffic, and then my passing him later on when he was held up in traffic. He would always eventually end up behind me. It was like he was my angel sent to provide protection for me. So naturally, my first inclination was to begin looking for him to come to my rescue.

Then, out of the blue, he appeared, but he hadn't seen me until it was too late, so he slowed a wee bit, waved, and kept on going. Oh no! I was so disappointed. It wasn't long before a much different scenario began taking shape. A big tractor-trailer rig passed me and began braking to stop. It took him some time but he finally stopped, then pulled off on the shoulder of the road far past me. Then he began backing up toward me. I was talking to the Lord fervently about the situation. It was not what I had envisioned. Oh, Lord, what had happened to the college-age young man? The driver of the big rig finally got out of his truck and began walking toward me. When he approached me, he began asking me questions about how to find the jack, etc. He then brought everything around to the right front tire, knelt down, and began working to change the tire. All seemed to be well until he began asking me personal questions. "Does your husband know you are out here all alone?" "Do you know how dangerous it is for you to be out here alone in this situation?" Considering the fact that there was a patch of woods in a field right beside us, all I could think of was that I could be dragged up there and become the next statistic for rape and murder. Little did he know that I was armed, and my hand was inside my purse with my finger ready to pull the trigger. Then he said, "Considering all of this, you need to be ready to go at any time." I blurted out, "Are you witnessing to me? You are about to scare me to death!" Yes, he had been witnessing to me. I told him that I was returning from a week of speaking engagements for a Christian women's organization and that I was already a born-again Christian. God had heard and answered my prayers and sent a godly man to change my tire. About the young college-age man . . . he actually returned! He apparently had gone to the next exit headed back east until he could make the loop and come back to me. However, when he returned, the truck driver was already there, so he simply slowed down, waved again, and drove on. My angel had been right on top of things! But my Father God already had sent one of His children to rescue His daughter in distress. He sent two people to assist me. Should we ever doubt our wonderful Lord? I think we know the answer to that. "I will love You, O Lord, my strength. The Lord is my rock and my fortress and my deliverer; my God, my strength, in whom I will trust; my shield and the horn of my salvation, my stronghold. I will call upon the Lord, who is worthy to be praised; so shall I be saved from my enemies" (Psalm 18:1–3, NKJV).

Chapter 26

Stories of Faith

Most of us know the obvious regarding faith. We all have faith in some things. We have faith that a chair we choose to sit in will hold us up. We have faith that an airplane, automobile, or train will be safe, so we get in them trusting them to take us where we want to go. We all have faith! My mother had faith in the Lord Jesus Christ, and she read the Word of God and prayed. However, one thing that always puzzled me when I was growing up was that she always kept her driver's license renewed. I could not understand that. She had never driven anywhere in her life that I could remember. When my mom turned nineteen, she bought a car. She gave birth to six children after marrying my daddy three or four years later, and she drove for many years. A few years later, when serious heart disease made her unable to do anything stressful, she was unable to drive for many years. In fact, she rarely left the house. Then when I was nineteen, I became ill with rheumatic fever. Both my mother and my grandmother had rheumatic fever that left their hearts impaired. Because of my mother's serious heart disease, the doctors were very concerned for me and kept me in the hospital for a couple of weeks. I was on complete bed rest for a time. They did everything they could to make sure I didn't follow in her, or my grandmother's, footsteps and end up with some type of heart disease. So imagine my surprise one day when she showed up in my hospital room to visit me. She didn't drive herself there; a friend of mine brought her. But that was just a miracle to me to have her there. What a delight! After I returned home, the doctor's orders were for me to be on complete bed rest for quite a while. Our gracious God had given my mother renewed strength, and like many mothers, she was not going to be kept down when her daughter needed her. I just wonder how many prayers she sent up to the Lord during that time. Well, she got answers! The next thing I knew, one day she got her purse and the car keys, drove to the grocery store, shopped, and drove herself home! On another afternoon, she got caught up in big traffic when the nearby university was having a home football game. That did not deter her. She had never driven a car with power steering or automatic shift. But she learned and did great until I got well. When I became well enough to be up and around again, that time for her had ended. She had become very ill again. I have no doubt that God in His mercy and grace gave her a special gift because of her faith. It was that faith in Him that kept her renewing her driver's license faithfully year in and year out for so many years and for no visible reason. It even touches my heart today. I had a mother who had faith, but not faith in an inanimate object or ordinary person; she knew in Whom to place her trust. Although she would tell me sometimes what specific issues she was dealing with, I don't ever remember hearing her complain when her health failed, and she was no longer up and around. I'm sure she knew that the Lord had given her a special blessing of His supernatural strength for such a time as that. "Now faith is the substance of things hoped for, the evidence of things not seen" (Hebrews 11:1, NKJV).

Faith the Size of a Mustard Seed

When I began speaking for the Christian women's organizations, church groups, etc. to give my personal story, I always made sure that I had my outline and notes in front of me—highlighted just right—so that I could glance down and know exactly what I was to say next. It almost became so fixed in my mind that I could turn the page without checking. However, I definitely still took those notes to the podium with me. Then there came a time when it seemed the Holy Spirit was telling me that I was depending on those notes and not on Him. It also seemed He was saying to leave them aside and trust in Him. That was not what I wanted to hear! However, I came to the place where I submitted myself to Him and left the notes on the table when I got up to speak for approximately thirty plus minutes. As it turned out, it was no problem! He gave me the words I was to say each time I went to speak to give my personal story in that format. Everything still went well for a very long time. That is . . . until one day. I was in the middle of my story in front of a big crowd of ladies when suddenly I went blank! After a few seconds, I explained that I needed to take a short break, and I exited the podium and went to a little room right behind the stage. I was just beginning to try to figure out what happened, when the chairman of the group came in, along with my hostess from the night before. We all prayed together. Nothing! Still blank! I excused myself and walked across the hall to a little room alone where I prayed: "Lord, I really need You to fill my mind up again with my testimony so I can go back out there and finish this. You know You will be the One to have egg on Your face if You don't because I can walk out this door and never see these people again." I can't believe I said that! But bless His precious name; He heard and answered me. Suddenly, my personal story was scrolled across my brain as though I had never missed a beat. Remembering this brings tears to my eyes even now.

The three of us walked back in, I went back to the podium, and completed my talk. I believe at least one person accepted Christ that day. One thing I know for sure, He gave me a test of my faith that day and, thankfully, I placed my trust in Him, and I passed.

After that, He kept opening doors for me to speak, and I kept speaking the truth of the gospel of Jesus Christ and what He could do through an ordinary housewife like me. I had faith enough to know that He could do it, and I depended totally on Him. I can also assure you that I never went to the podium without notes again! Perhaps it was a setup from the beginning from the evil one who knew he would trap me one day. But God allowed it, even so. ". . . greater is He who is in you than he who is in the world" (1 John 4:4b, NASB). Our God reigns!

Chapter 27

Fulfilling the Great Commission

O ne thing we can be sure of and that is getting our prayers answered if we are praying according to God's will. 1 John 5:14–15 (NASB) states, "This is the confidence which we have before Him, that, if we ask anything according to His will, He hears us. And, if we know that He hears us in whatever we ask, we know that we have the requests which we have asked from Him." Matthew 28:18–20 (NASB) states this: "And Jesus came up and spoke to them saying, 'All authority has been given to Me in Heaven and on earth. Go therefore and make disciples of all the nations, baptizing them in the name of the Father and the Son and the Holy Spirit, teaching them to observe all that I commanded you; and lo, I am with you always, even to the end of the age.'" Therefore, if you know that He is calling you to do work in the area of reaching people for Jesus, then you can be sure that He will be with you in a special way to enable you to accomplish what He has called you to do.

Only a couple of years or so after repatriating to the United States, I was listening to Dennis Rainey's program, "Family Life Today," on a local Christian radio station. We were approaching the Christmas season, and the guest on Dennis Rainey's program that day told a story: She said she felt led by the Holy Spirit one Christmas to enlist a few friends to do a Christmas luncheon for some of her neighbors. After praying about it, she was convinced that it was the Lord, so she set about enlisting her friends' assistance, and they joined her in that endeavor. They decorated the house beautifully and prepared a sumptuous lunch. She had invited a Christian speaker to give her testimony to tell the ladies about Jesus Christ, how they could know Him, and what He would do for them too. It had been a great success! While listening to the program, I had the distinct feeling the Holy Spirit was speaking to me that it was also His plan for me during the upcoming Christmas season, which was already upon us. I began to pray and seek Him on this for confirmation. The more I prayed, it seemed He was saying that it was not to be at our house, but it was to be held in the home of an acquaintance of mine just down the street. This lady was a new acquaintance, someone who had attended a Bible study that God had me leading a few houses from us. Not only was she a new acquaintance, so was everyone else in the neighborhood since we had moved into a totally new section of the city upon our return from Asia. I knew she was an extremely busy person, but that was about the only thing I knew about her. After praying for a time, there seemed to be no way around calling to tell her that I believed the Lord had this plan for the two of us to enter into. After introducing myself, I explained that it was my belief that the Lord wanted us to have a community outreach luncheon or dinner in *her* home, similar to the one the lady had described on Dennis Rainey's program. Soon after I began explaining the reason for my call, it became apparent to me that she was weeping. Somewhat puzzled, it seemed that my call was upsetting her, so I apologized and attempted to get off the phone. She assured me that was not the case at all. She went on to explain that she had recently been to their house in Florida where she was doing her homework for the

Bible study we were doing. That particular week, as a part of the homework, we were to do a prayer walk where we would focus on talking to the Lord about issues we needed Him to help us with. She had done her prayer walk while walking on the beach. As she walked, she cried out to the Lord that she wanted Him to help her move out of their big house. She explained that she never liked being in such a large house. Also, one of her daughters didn't like it because she felt uncomfortable in bringing her friends there. As she continued to cry out to the Lord about that, suddenly, He called her by name and said, "I gave you that house and I want you to use it for My glory!" In speaking with her, she had immediately thought back to that experience with Him in Florida, and she was overcome with emotion that He was beginning to show her very quickly some of His plans. As we spoke further, we thought perhaps it should be a dinner for men and women to attend. Our husbands concurred, and we enlisted other ladies in the community to assist in the planning and development to bring this event to fruition.

The team did an excellent job of getting things done. Invitations were printed and issued, and people responded overwhelmingly. When the people arrived, they found a beautifully decorated Christmas gala in that lovely home and on the grounds of that estate. The music was lovely and the dinner superb. We had enlisted a wonderful, humorous, local Christian dentist as our speaker, who gave his testimony of how God had brought him to Himself and what He had done for him since. Then, he gave everyone an opportunity to pray to receive Jesus Christ as their Savior. We also offered invitations to Bible studies if anyone wanted to attend. It was such a success that we decided to have it annually, which we did for a few years. We were blessed one year to have Dennis Rainey come speak, since it was his program that the Lord had used to plant the seeds. We also had the popular evangelist, Jay Strack, one year. We just thanked God and praised Him for the privilege to serve Him in that way.

~ Author's Note ~

We should remember to use our time, our talents, and our money for God's kingdom work as He calls us to do. Yes, if you feel God is speaking to you regarding some issue, and you really need to know that you are being heard and can depend on God to enable you, then search the scriptures for one of His commands or promises. When you find a scripture command or a promise that you believe He is giving to you for some particular thing in your life, stand on it until you see it come to fruition. Just make sure that you are not claiming one that is not for you in that particular situation. The best place to check for confirmation is with God Himself in prayer . . . and wait. Also, don't forget to ask other godly people to pray for God to give them a word of confirmation for you. That is why it is so important for us to stay in fellowship with Him and to get to know His ways. That is an investment none of us will ever regret. Jesus has commissioned us to go and make disciples, so let's just do it—with His enabling and in His timing.

Once, at the small international church we attended in Hong Kong, the even smaller group in women's ministry decided to have an outreach luncheon to attract unbelievers, so they could hear about Jesus Christ and understand how to come to know Him personally. I explained that in the United States we have found that having a fashion show as a special feature draws in many secular people, even men, that otherwise might not be inclined to attend. The idea was accepted immediately by everyone, so we began the task of selecting a date for the event and a five-star hotel with a lovely ballroom where the event would take place. The Lord blessed us by leading us to a lovely lady from Brussels, Belgium. She and her husband agreed to come. My husband and I invited them to be our guests in our home for a few days, which cut out a huge expense for a hotel. However, we still had the expense of the plane ticket. We found a clothier to do the fashion show for us, which was a big accomplishment. By now, the cost of this event was growing higher exponentially. I told the ladies that we normally used ladies of Christian women's organizations or ladies in the church to be models for events like this. But they wanted professional models. And so it was. When we "passed the plate" and asked for people to participate, the need was met. At the end of the day, the event was an incredible success. The ballroom was filled with lovely ladies, from various religious beliefs, dressed to the nines with the most amazing jewelry. We were so blessed to be a part of it. Everything went off without a hitch. Then they listened attentively to hear an ordinary housewife, who was called for such a time as that, tell them the story of Jesus Christ and how He had given His life to pay the penalty for their sins. They learned that day that they could have the most Perfect Jewel one could ever receive—Jesus Christ as their Lord and Savior and an eternity with Him in heaven. They learned that it is a free gift; all they had to do was reach out and receive it by faith.

Later on, we had another similar outreach dinner. We invited many very successful business people to attend, and again we held it at a five-star hotel ballroom. We did what we believe was a good thing in service for the King of kings; we brought people in who might have never known the good news of Jesus Christ. What they do with that is between them and Him. One attractive component of people in countries where little, if anything, is known about Jesus Christ is that when they *do* understand what Christianity truly is and receive Jesus by faith, they are inclined to really be sold out for Him. Many have come from very dark religions, and once they realize what a wonderful blessing it is to be out of bondage to the devil, they fall in love with Jesus. He becomes preeminent in their lives, which is what He expects from all of us! Give Him all the glory and praise.

In many countries, there are so few Christians, and yet in the USA, the majority of people say they are Christians and don't live it. It is very confusing to believers in other countries. They think we are a nation of believers three thousand miles wide but only three inches deep. We are a nation spoiled with the abundance of God's blessings. Yet we are a nation of people who have lost our way. We must individually and collectively discover where we stepped away from our Father God and our love and respect for Jesus Christ as our Savior and what He has done for us. Then, we need to go to Him, confess and repent, accept His forgiveness, get back to the basic doctrines of the Bible, pray for all the saints, and ask our great God to restore us. Please join me in dedicating our time, our talents, and our money to the Lord. "If I shut up the heavens so that there is no rain, or if I command the locust to devour the land, or if I send pestilence among My people, and My people who are called by My name humble themselves and pray and seek My face and turn from their wicked ways, then I will hear from heaven, will forgive their sin and will heal their land. Now My eyes will be open and My ears attentive to the prayer offered in this place!" (2 Chronicles 7:13–15, NASB).

Either we are unaware of our wicked ways (as a nation), or we are not interested in changing them, which is a very scary thing. If we don't know, then we need to ask Him. And when He shows us, let's repent, turn away from our wicked ways, and cry out to Him to heal our land. I know He will be faithful to do as He has promised. Dr. Adrian Rogers stated in a sermon titled, "When God says NO," that God will never hear us as long as we are a nation that continues to kill babies. There is scientific evidence that it is NOT just a blob of tissue; it is a baby. That, along with SO many other immoral issues, is rampant in our nation, and many people in the church just seem passive. Here's another Adrianism: "Sin will take you a lot further than you want to go, it will keep you a lot longer than you want to stay, and it will cost you a lot more than you want to pay!"[8] Point well taken! And I am including myself here. It is time for us to surrender to God and allow Him to bring us where He wants us to be. He demands preeminence in our lives. "while we were yet sinners, Christ died for us!" (Romans 5:8, NASB). Apathy, prayerlessness, and complacency must be repented of and forsaken.

Restore us to You, O LORD, that we may be restored; renew our days as of old, unless You have utterly rejected us, and are exceedingly angry with us! (Lamentations 5:21–22, NASB).

Have You Yourself, O God, rejected us? And will You not go forward with our armies, O God? Oh give us help against the adversary for deliverance by man is in vain. Through God we will do valiantly; and it is He Who will tread down our adversaries (Psalm 108:11–13, NASB).

The Lord nullifies the counsel of the nations; He frustrates the plans of the peoples. The counsel of the Lord stands forever, the plans of His heart from generation to generation. Blessed is the nation whose God is the Lord, the people whom He has chosen for His own inheritance! . . . Behold, the eye of the Lord is on those who fear Him, on those who hope for His loving kindness (Psalm 33:10–13, 18, NASB).

---

[8] Adrian Rogers, *Adrianisms: The Wit and Wisdom of Adrian Rogers, Volume One* (Bartlett, TN: Love Worth Finding Ministries, 2007) 114.

Our soul waits for the Lord; He is our help and our shield (Psalm 33:20, NASB).

He it is who reduces rulers to nothing, who makes the judges of the earth meaningless (Isaiah 40:23, NASB).

Chapter 28

God's Ways of Meeting Our Needs

Ayear after our return to the United States, my father-in-law passed away. Not long afterward, my mother-in-law was diagnosed with scleroderma crest variant, a very serious, incurable autoimmune disease. She began to require someone to be with her day and night except for short periods. She was blessed to find a very good lady to stay with her, plus others who filled in on weekends. She had two adult children and their families living in the same area, so they began taking turns staying with her as needed. Everyone made sure her every need was met as best they could. We lived several hours away from them, so we were not always made aware of her daily needs. However, we did make frequent trips there to see about her.

My in-laws had lived on a beautiful lake for many years, and everyone wanted to go there to visit. They both seemed to have the gift of service and hospitality. Even in her eighties, my mother-in-law found it difficult to be on the receiving end of things. She hated to disrupt people's lifestyles even though she was so ill. One day my husband said we should go to Mobile, Alabama, to check on our motor yacht on which maintenance was being done. Since we had no other engagements, it seemed on the surface to be a good plan to both of us. As I was enjoying my devotional time with our Lord one morning that week prior to leaving on our trip, it seemed the messages to me in Joshua were speaking directly to me. When I read about where they "went up into the hill country," it seemed the Lord was speaking to me that we were to go to see my mother-in-law. She lived in the "hill country" of east Tennessee. As I continued my quiet time with the Lord, the feeling would not go away. I called my husband at work and told him. He said, "Call Mama and tell her we are coming home this weekend." Thank God for husbands who listen when God speaks to them through their wives. But with that comes a huge responsibility for us wives to make sure we *really* are hearing from the Lord. When I hung up with him, I called his mother. When she answered the phone, I could tell that she was crying. Many times through the years if she became emotional about something, she would always say, "Don't mind me; I'm crying one minute and laughing the next," which was very true. But this time it was different. She said, "Oh, I was just crying out to the Lord. I don't have anyone to stay with me this weekend, and I don't know what I will do. I just can't stay by myself anymore!" It seemed that her sons and their families had other plans, preventing them from coming that weekend, and her helpers were unable to stay with her. I'm certain the family did not know of this, or they would have changed their plans or contacted us to see if we could come. But God had a different way of providing for her that weekend. What a blessing it was to her when she heard the plans He had for her, that we were coming to spend the weekend with her. She was so grateful at how amazing our God is. Of course, we were only too happy to go be with her. What an incredible boost to our faith, and hers, to see Him work in this way to meet her needs. Just thinking about how He concerns Himself with our daily needs is awesome! "And my God will provide all your needs according to His riches in glory in Christ Jesus" (Philippians 4:19, NASB). Thank You, dear Lord, for Your goodness and Your incredible generosity. We know Your resources are limitless, and You don't withhold any good gifts from Your children.

We did go very happily to be with her according to the Lord's leading that weekend, and we continued to do whatever we were able in the future until the Lord took her home to be with Him. While completing all the necessary arrangements with the family following her funeral, my husband was going through her desk. He found a precious gift. Sometime in the years past we had given her a Christian booklet to read. As the writer drew the message to a conclusion, an outreach prayer was given that you could pray inviting Jesus Christ into your heart if you had never done so, or if you just wanted to make sure. At the bottom of the page was a place to sign and date it. There was her signature and the date of her prayer.

Chapter 29

A Path Through the Waters

On our thirtieth anniversary, my husband and I had plans to depart from a maintenance yard/marina in Mobile, Alabama, on our Hatteras Motor Yacht and head to a marina on the Tennessee River. He had dreamed of owning a Hatteras because, in his mind, it was considered the Rolls Royce of boats. She had been docked there since May of that year having her interior upgraded, as well as some items of maintenance. We would be journeying across Mobile Bay first, which was known for having quick storms pop up, maybe similar to the Sea of Galilee. After navigating our way across Mobile Bay, our path would wind upriver through the city of Mobile proper, right by the shipyards where large ships came in for maintenance. Major cruise lines docked in that area as well. It was a wonderful alley of unusual sights for those of us who lived inland and rarely had the occasion to see all this boating and shipping activity. It was very interesting to see the flags on all of the freighters and cruise ships.

From the Mobile Harbor, our compass heading was northward up the Tennessee Tombigbee Waterway, much of which was actually cut through farmland to allow commercial and pleasure craft egress from Mobile Bay to the Tennessee River, thereby saving days of travel time for the boating traffic using it. Our final destination for that journey was the marina on the Tennessee River. Five days and four nights of arduous tasks and long days lay before us before arrival, assuming all went well. Since departure time was quite early, and our interior designer was expected to arrive shortly, there was very little "quiet time" with my Lord. When I opened my Bible, several verses jumped into my heart. Although I don't recommend that as a way to find a Word from the Lord, it sometimes turns out to be just what is needed for the occasion. "But now, thus says the Lord, your Creator, O Jacob, and He Who formed you, O Israel, 'Do not fear, for I have redeemed you; I have called you by name; you are Mine! When you pass through the waters, I will be with you; and through the rivers, they will not overflow you . . . I am the LORD, your Holy One, the Creator of Israel, your King,' thus says the LORD, 'Who makes a way through the sea and a path through the mighty waters . . .'" (Isaiah 43:1–2a, 15–16, NASB).

Deep inside my heart, I knew that my Lord had just given me a promise of protection. With that also came peace in my heart for the crossing. I scanned my devotional for the Word of the day: "Hold your tongue!" The weather was picture perfect, the scenery and sights blissful. It was so relaxing that we just enjoyed each other and God's world. Just as we had planned, we reached our first day's destination, early—Lady's Landing.

There were no overnight land accommodations so people stayed on their boats, yachts, or whatever their modes of river travel. They had the most unbelievable service; they served the food to us on our yacht. Because it was our anniversary, they treated us to a decadent chocolate cake to accompany our meal. They even had candles! Everything was served in first-class fashion on silver trays, etc. I had changed into a long summer sundress to make the occasion even more festive. What a magnificent day and evening it had been! With everything being so beautiful, why did the Lord impress upon me to, "Hold your tongue!"?

Several hours into the trip from Mobile, we began to experience problems with our tachometer and synchronizer, which meant more work and concentration for my husband the captain, who was the primary helmsman. My duties were more mundane: helping in the twelve locks,[9] handling the lines docking, being the backup helmsman, being the legs for all the things the captain needed, cooking, cleaning, and laundry, etc. Suffice it to say, by the time we arrived at Lady's Landing and finished our meal, we were ready for rest and sleep. Regarding the maintenance issue that I mentioned, my husband had contacted the maintenance yard. They had given him quite a bit of instruction to attempt to rig up a "fix" for the problem we had encountered. All that being accomplished, we "held our tongues" and went to bed. The next day's journey was to be the longest of the trip, so departure time would be prior to daylight.

He arose earlier and let me sleep in—till four thirty or five in the morning! Just as it was almost time to depart, he returned to inform me that the engines would not start! Unfortunately the "fix" he was instructed to do the night before did not work. So, we needed to wait for help to come from Mobile, which happened quite early that morning. However, by the time the maintenance was completed, it was much too late for us to attempt to make that long day's trip. We spent a second night at Lady's Landing. Now we were beginning to understand why the Lord gave me that verse regarding "Hold your tongue!" If you have been wondering where to find that verse in the Bible, here is the actual verse: "Set a guard, O Lord over my mouth; keep watch over the door of my lips"

---

[9] A "lock" in water transport is "a device for raising and lowering boats between stretches of water of different levels on river and canal waterways," accessed April 23, 2014, http://en.wikipedia.org/wiki/Lock_(water_transport)

(Psalm 141:3, NASB). The title of the day's devotion—"Hold your tongue!"—was so much easier to remember so that became my paraphrase for that verse. Certainly, the Lord knew of the beauty we would enjoy that day, seeing His lovely creation of deer, wild turkeys, egrets, blue heron, and other memory-making wonders of His. However, He also knew of all the frustrations ahead of us, not just on that day but for the rest of the trip: the early departures and long days, dealing with the river culture, the constant concerns of traveling on the water, and going through the twelve locks. Great is His faithfulness! What a wonderful Lord we serve. The rest of that trip went beautifully. The weather was friendly and whether we docked at a marina in the evenings and ate out, or anchored and ate dinner on board, all was well on that trip. The Lord had gone before us and made the rough places smooth (Isaiah 40:4) all the way to the marina and the Tennessee River!

Chapter 30

The Divine Refiner at Work

The following is a story told to me by Harry, a good friend to my husband and me through the years. As Harry and his wife began their day, many years ago, they had no idea they were about to be catapulted into experiencing the treasures of God's excellent greatness in a new and profound way.

In 1977, Harry and his wife were newlyweds living in a small mobile home on a college campus attending Bible college. There was a furnace in their mobile home that had a small eight-inch porthole with a hinged door. In order to light the pilot light, that little hinged door had to be opened. Early one morning, as he opened that small door and attempted to light their furnace, something strange happened. Even though there was no hint of it, apparently gas had leaked in. There was a flash of light and a loud explosion. A ball of fire came out of that porthole and hit him in the chest, arm, and neck, literally blowing him against the opposite wall! His wife rushed him to the hospital. They packed him in ice and attempted to keep him as comfortable as possible. Harry told me, "It was really bad! The doctor, without question, set up an appointment after the fifth day for me to receive skin grafts. Due to God's gracious gift of healing, they never had to proceed with the skin grafts. On day seven, the doctor was truly amazed. Underneath that black, charred skin was pink skin—healing!" Harry said that they knew many people were praying Proverbs 15:29: "The LORD is far from the wicked, but He hears the prayers of the righteous" (NASB). Obviously, the Lord did hear and in His mercy and compassion, healed Harry of those horrible burns and restored him to health. "Beyond that, unbelievably, people who we still do not know until this day, paid our hospital bill! Why my wife and I were so blessed in this particular way, even to full recovery and then some, we do not know. But we do know WHO did it! His name is Jesus, the great physician. We give Him all the glory and honor. Even since then, God has saved me from other near tragic events. It is apparent that God has me here for a purpose. Good health is a blessing! Each day is a miracle from God. It is my prayer that my life will count for Him," Harry said.

Harry has been a blessing to my husband and me. I know that he and his wife live their lives for Jesus. He has gone on extended international mission trips devoting his time, his talents, and his money to the Lord. One extended mission trip that I remember he made was to Kosovo to help rebuild an area there. His is a remarkable story, and it is a marvelous report of the Body of Christ working together in prayer, and in other ways, bringing glory and honor to God and blessings to all involved.

***

I am reminded of the story of Peter. When he was in prison, with Herod about to send for him to be executed, there was no doubt that Herod was serious. He had just slain James, the brother of John, with a sword. Knowing that it pleased the Jews, Herod had Peter seized, and ordered that four squads of soldiers protect him. Herod was a powerful man on earth. But the body of believers had met together to pray to Almighty God. (Read the rest of the story in Acts 12.) God's purpose for Peter at that moment in time was to miraculously set Peter free so he could continue in the Lord's work. What happened to Herod? "So on a set day Herod, arrayed in royal apparel, sat on his throne and gave an oration to them. And, the people kept shouting, 'The voice of a god and not of a man!' Then immediately, an angel of the Lord struck him, because he did not give glory to God. And he was eaten by worms and died. But the word of God grew and multiplied" (Acts 12:21–24 KJV). Obviously, we can see here that it is a good thing to give glory, thanksgiving, and praise to God for the wonderful things He does in and through us. Romans 8:28 states, "And, we know that God causes all things to work together for good to those who love God, to those who are called according to His purpose" (NASB). Every day, and everything in it, can become something good for us as believers, according to the Word of God. These blessings are sent to sanctify us—perfecting us and purifying us. "Count it all joy, my brethren, when you encounter various trials, knowing that the testing of your faith produces endurance. And let your endurance have its perfect result, so that you may be perfect and complete, lacking in nothing" (James 1:2, NASB).

If you don't understand what He is attempting to teach you, then do as He says in James 1:5–8, "But if any of you lacks wisdom, let him ask of God, who gives to all generously and without reproach, and it will be given to him. But he must ask in faith without any doubting, for the one who doubts is like the surf of the sea, driven and tossed by the wind. For that man ought not to expect that he will receive anything from the Lord, being a double-minded man, unstable in all his ways" (NASB). So, we need to praise God, give Him thanksgiving, and pray for His wisdom, grace, strength, discernment, and endurance until he sees fit to lift the trial. In addition, we should be watching and waiting for what the Divine Potter wants us to know while He is sculpting us. If you are not yet saved, you will suffer here and for all eternity.

> Some time ago, a few ladies met to read some scriptures, and while reading Malachi they came upon a remarkable expression: "And He shall sit as a refiner and purifier of silver" (Malachi 3:3, KJV). One lady's opinion was that it was intended to convey the view of the sanctifying influence of the grace of Christ. Then she proposed to visit a silversmith and report to her friends what he said on the subject. She went and, without telling the silversmith the objective of her errand, asked to know the process of refining silver, which he fully described to her. "But sir," she said, "do you sit while the work of refining is going on?" "Oh, yes, madam," replied the silversmith. "I must sit with my eye steadily fixed on the furnace, for if the time necessary for refining is exceeded in the slightest degree, the silver will be injured." The lady at once saw the beauty, and comfort, of the expression: "And He shall sit as a refiner and purifier of silver." Christ sees it needful to put His children into a furnace. But His eye is steadily intent on the work of purifying, and His wisdom and love are both engaged in the best manner for them. Their trials do not come at random; the very hairs on our heads are numbered.
>
> As the lady was leaving the shop, the silversmith called her back and said he had more to say on the subject—that only he knows when the process of purification is complete. He knows it when he *sees his own image* reflected in the silver. When Christ shall see

His own image in His people, His work of purifying
will be accomplished (author unknown).

Only God can make gold or silver out of human beings. He
created Adam out of dust and Eve out of one of Adam's ribs. He
created us, and He knows just how much to temper us before we
experience burn out and become useless to Him. "In this world you
will have tribulation, but take courage; I have overcome the world"
(John 16:33, NASB). Until the decision is made to follow Jesus, you
are serving the enemy! Scriptures say we cannot have two masters.
We must choose. When we choose Jesus, we are promised that He
will not put more on us than we can bear without providing a way
of escape. He knows, too, that He has suffered and endured, as
Jesus the man, more than we can ever imagine, and He did it for us.
Blessings abound evermore! Look for them. God is working in our
lives even when we are totally unaware and do not feel that He is.
"When He has tested me, I will come forth as gold" (Job 23:10b,
NKJV).

Chapter 31

Another Miracle of Jesus

We had followed the sun to a warmer spot to escape the cold winter weather we were having. Although the Florida Panhandle is definitely not as warm in the winter months as southern Florida, it is usually much warmer than Tennessee. It seemed our boat, the *Morning Star*, was there just waiting to welcome us aboard. She was tucked away at Bay Point Marina, a part of a lovely resort right on the bay. It was a haven for yachters at the time. We had been blessed to host guests, friends, and family on the *Morning Star*, but this time it was just my husband and me. A big storm with really high winds blew in and settled in for a day and a night. The boat was safely tied with strong lines, and it could sustain almost any wind, so we didn't feel any danger in staying there. We were docked at the very end of the dock right by the channel, which we preferred. However, the wind was blowing so fiercely and slapping the tide on the side of our boat so hard that it made it extremely noisy inside. There was no way I would get any sleep until the winds died down, and they were not projected to do so anytime soon. My husband and I decided to leave the boat, drive to another city, and find a nice hotel.

As we neared San Destin, Florida, approximately forty-five minutes up the coast from Panama City Beach, my husband said that the San Destin Hilton might be a better place to stay. We checked in and enjoyed such a lovely evening that we decided to stay an additional night. The next morning, my husband decided to take a walk, leaving me in the room to do some prayer time and Bible study. Soon after he left the room, housekeeping showed up to clean the room. Since I still was not dressed for the day, I just sat there on the settee and continued to read the Bible. Soon, she and I began to chitchat.

As the Holy Spirit of God revealed the words for me to say to this dear lady, she became very interested in the message He had for her that day. She began to weep and expressed her reasons for her sorrow. It was my privilege to be able to talk with her about her spiritual condition and explain God's gift of salvation—that it is available to all of us through Jesus Christ. She seemed very sincere in praying and asking Jesus to come into her heart right then. Hallelujah! What a Savior! I later contacted her from time to time to disciple her.

On one occasion when I was back in San Destin with a friend, we delivered a Bible and materials to her, for which she seemed very grateful. We prayed for a miracle in her relationship with her husband, and once when I called her, he spoke with me on the telephone. He indicated that he, too, had received Jesus as his Savior. However, at that time, his wife hadn't noticed any fruit—that there was a true heart change. In situations like this, one must not jump to the conclusion that the confession wasn't real. We must remember that not everyone has a "Damascus Road" experience like the apostle Paul and others have had. Sometimes it takes longer for some to begin to grow spiritually.

Once a heart turns to God, our Lord can do amazing things. I always remember 1 Peter 3:1–4: "In the same way, you wives, be submissive to your own husbands so that even if any of them are disobedient to the word, they may be won without a word by the behavior of their wives, as they observe your chaste and respectful behavior. Your adornment must not be merely external—braiding the hair, and wearing gold jewelry, or putting on dresses, but let it be the hidden person of the heart, with the imperishable quality of a gentle and quiet spirit, which is precious in the sight of God" (NASB). Our great God is still able; after all, He is sovereign. Looking back on that day of high winds and noisiness on the boat, can't you just see Father God orchestrating all of it in order that one soul might come to know Him? Perhaps two? Perhaps one marriage saved? And perhaps more as they live out their lives for Him? What a mighty God we serve. Only He knows. We must take advantage of those wonderful opportunities He provides. He has certainly blessed me so many times to have this privilege of seeing Him work through this ordinary person. Imagine the times He is working where we don't see or hear Him speak to us.

Chapter 32

Never Alone

O ne day my mother-in-law told me, "I tell all of my friends not to bother trying to talk to God. You have Him tied up!" She was kidding of course. The beauty is that He is able and willing to be there for all of us all of the time. We never need anyone to mediate for us. When He died on the cross that day, the temple veil was torn right down the middle. We can now go straight to Him, in Jesus' name, to the Holy of Holies, IF we have given our lives to Him. How or when He answers, we don't know for sure, but sometimes He answers yes right away. What a delight!

We had many blessings with boat trips, ministry opportunities, etc. Now retired, my husband was able to take the *Morning Star* to Nova Scotia with some friends. He left her at a great marina in Hampton, Virginia, so he could come home for a while. He really wanted me to go with him and spend the summer on the boat "island hopping" in Chesapeake Bay, which we did. We stayed six weeks. We also had friends come travel with us. We had so much fun! Reflecting, as much fun as it was, it was truly a God-thing that kept me going. I wasn't feeling well during that time, so when we returned home, I went to my cardiologist.

He told me I wasn't getting enough oxygen to my brain. I became more and more fatigued and began having difficulty breathing. I had already been to the famed Cleveland Clinic in Ohio and had a procedure there. My cardiologist ordered a barrage of tests. I was diagnosed with Primary Pulmonary Hypertension (PPH). This is a heart-lung disease, for which there is no cure, and because of my age and specific other illnesses causing fragility in my body, I was not a candidate for a heart-lung transplant. Having also been diagnosed with another very rare incurable heart condition— impaired left atrial compliance due to scarring—about the same time at Vanderbilt Hospital in Nashville, Tennessee, I figured that pretty much cinched it for me and my future unless our Lord God decided to perform another miracle healing. So far, that has not happened.

With PPH, there were times when I knew down deep in my heart that it was God and God alone Who could bring me through the storm. These storms can be very turbulent at times and, frankly, I cannot imagine *not* being a child of God. There are episodes when it seems each heartbeat will be my last, but God sees me through it all, and I remain here today for a time and for His purposes. It's very obvious to me, and to most Christians on the front lines, that the enemy of our souls is always attempting to bring us down, but especially when we are the most vulnerable.

I had heard the enemy speaking lies into my mind while I was very ill and battling physically, and he had attempted to take over my mind. Usually he would tell me I was not really God's child, or I was such a bad person, or that Jesus isn't the only way to the Father, etc. He uses discouragement, oppression, and depression when he can. Of course, he will delude us at times, appearing as the angel of light with good news, when he really is just attempting to lead us astray. What we thought was the Holy Spirit was actually the enemy acting as the counterfeiter. One day when I was extremely ill, he seemed to present himself right in the forefront of my mind, consuming me with the demand that I worship him. All praises to the Holy Spirit Who lives within me, He kept me very calm. I recall saying something like, "I believe in the Lord Jesus Christ! He is my Lord and Savior, and He has taken my sins to the cross, paid the penalty for my sins there with the shedding of His perfect blood, and He has given me His righteousness so that I stand blameless before God the Father." Immediately, the enemy fled!

> He has delivered us from the power of darkness and conveyed us into the kingdom of the Son of His love, in Whom we have redemption through His blood, the forgiveness of sins. He is the image of the invisible God, the firstborn over all creation. For by Him all things were created that are in Heaven and that are on earth, visible and invisible, whether thrones or dominions or principalities or powers. All things were created through Him and for Him. And He is before all things, and in Him all things consist. And He is the Head of the body, the Church, Who is the beginning, the firstborn from the dead, that in all things He may have the preeminence" (Colossians 1:13–18, NKJV).

***

Another time, my battle with the enemy included a day of daunting physical battles with my health. At some point I cried out to the Lord, asking Him to please come to my rescue. "Can't You do something? Do I have to take this from him and suffer so much physically as well?" I quoted a scripture from Psalm. "Then they cry out to the Lord in their trouble, and He delivers them out of their distresses" (Psalm 107:6, NASB). As soon as I cried out to Him, it was as if He reached down, grabbed me, and brought me right up in front of His face, where He kept me for hours. I was totally consumed to overflowing with His loving and powerful Presence and His all-encompassing sufficiency! Nothing else mattered! It totally filled me up. All around me was His powerful, loving Presence and the realization that I needed nothing else. As the time passed, it was as if He allowed my mind to drift, first to my husband. Then, it was as if He said, "No! Don't go there! I am sufficient!" Several times as the day waned, that happened, and each time He reminded me strongly that my needs were all met in Him and Him alone. Yes, He uses other people and things to fulfill His purpose, but it is all through His grace because of Who He is. It was such an incredibly wonderful time that lasted nearly all day. I pray that memory will never go away. One day we will be with Him face to face in heaven. "And He said to me, 'My grace is sufficient for you, for My strength is made perfect in weakness.' Therefore most gladly I will boast in my infirmities, that the power of Christ may rest upon me. Therefore, I take pleasure in infirmities, in reproaches, in needs, in persecutions, in distresses, for Christ's sake. For when I am weak, then I am strong" (2 Corinthians 12:9–10, NKJV).

***

One day during another terribly rough morning, I sent a text to my prayer partner in Texas, who, at the time, was away from her home city visiting a son in San Antonio. There was no response from her, and as the day wore on, it became apparent she hadn't received it. However, late in the day, she phoned me to say she had just realized my message. But the Lord had done a beautiful thing for me that day. She told me that during the time I had originally sent that message, the Holy Spirit had laid me on her mind and heart so heavy that she was praying continually for me during that time, even though she had not received the text. He had alerted her in His own way. He has done this on other occasions since then. Isn't He wonderful? Hallelujah! So remember—when He puts someone on your mind and you don't know why, just start praying until you can speak to them to find out what is going on. Even then, you may never find out what it is all about until you see Jesus face to face.

***

At some point my body became extremely fragile and weak. Then I contracted some type of flu bug. As my body seemed to grow more ill, for a couple of days and at least one night, I seemed to slip into a semiconscious state. I was barely aware that my husband came in to my bedroom to encourage me to drink or eat something; it felt like I was suspended somewhere. One night after midnight, still in this state, suddenly I became aware of praise music going up to the Lord. Amazingly, even though I was in that horribly ill place, I knew it was coming from deep, deep down within me. That much I knew! It wasn't something that I heard with my ears. Upon the realization that praise music was emanating up to the Lord from my spirit, God's perfect peace began to flow through my entire body, and I relaxed from what seemed to have been a most terrible war for my life. Perhaps I slept after that; I cannot say. However, the next afternoon, even though I was still very ill, my body became a little stronger, and I began to be able to bring the event of the previous evening to my mind. As it all began to replay, I quickly thought, *It could not have been me initiating those praises to the Lord.* It's not that I don't normally sing praises to the Lord, because I do all the time, it's just that on that particular night I had not been cognizant of my surroundings enough to initiate praise songs. As I relayed that story to some friends, they surmised that I had heard angels singing. (There is a well-known pastor who has a wonderful series of messages about angels, and he said there is nothing about angels singing in all of the scriptures, but there are incidents about them rejoicing.) But no, it wasn't like that. I didn't hear it with my ears. It was coming from my spirit deep within me. My conclusion was that it was the Holy Spirit. I believe that He was singing praise songs to the Father through my spirit, since I was unable to do so. 2 Chronicles 20:22 sums up what God told His chosen people to do when they were under siege. Earlier in that chapter, it was noted that the people proclaimed a fast and prayed for the Lord to deliver them. He responded by telling them that the battle was not theirs, but God's. Then, He instructed some to go out singing and praising. That verse tells us that "When they began singing and praising, the Lord set ambushes against . . . (the enemy—my interpretation) so they were routed" (2 Chronicles 20:22, NASB). I believe that is what happened that night. I believe that when our Father God heard the singing and praising, He set ambushes against the enemy that was attempting to take my life before His planned time. While I was unable to do so, the Holy Spirit of God did it for me and through me.

For the next few days, part of Psalm 23:4 came to my mind: "Yea though I walk through the valley of the shadow of death, I will fear no evil . . ." (Psalm 23:4, KJV). A week or two later, a couple of friends came to visit us. The husband, who happened to be a pastor of a local church, sat in the chair nearest me. We had been visiting for some time, and as time passed, I thought it would be good to mention my experience with the praise music and get his thoughts. I had sent up an arrow prayer to the Lord early on regarding whether I should mention it to him. He told me, "I don't know if you are dying now, I can't speak to that, but this verse comes to me, 'Yea though I walk through the valley of the shadow of death, I will fear no evil . . .'" I excitedly said, "That is the same verse the Lord gave me in the days that followed that time!" In my heart, it was confirmation that indeed I had been walking in the "valley of the shadow of death," and I feared no evil for He was with me!

A few days later, a dear friend was speaking to me about some issues, and I told her my experience with the praise music. She gasped and said, "That is the same scripture I have been praying for you for weeks!" She believes the Holy Spirit had been leading her to pray that verse for me because He knew I would need it. Although she knew I was very ill, she had no idea about the severity of my illness. We were both so totally blessed with how the Lord had led us through our lives. It was yet another confirmation.

There are a lot of statistics out there that tell of the average life span of those with PPH. I have lived a couple of years past my prognosis. As my cardiologist said, no one really knows how long I will live except God. In the meantime, I am being taken care of by my Lord through my husband, who has given himself to the Lord and to me during this time like nothing I could have ever imagined. He has such a servant's heart for me. God shows His love to me through him every day as He makes sure my needs are taken care of. There are times when my husband is ill and needs to be in bed himself, but he gets up and serves me. Sometimes I call him Radar because he reminds me of the character Radar who served the colonel on the television series *Mash*. Sometimes I can just think of something I would like to have, and my husband suddenly appears with whatever it is. Sometimes he just shows up with something wonderful before I have even thought of it.

I'm reminded of a time when I was very ill when I asked the Lord, "Where are You? It feels like You have left me!" He quickly responded, "I haven't left you. Every time your husband serves you, that's Me." We are so very grateful for friends and family around the world who pray for us; some of them pray every day. Some pray many times a day. What a priceless gift that is! Thank You, Lord! No one knows the time or place that will be his or her last day on earth. The message is to be ready to go with Him when He calls. We have our choice of heaven or hell. He says that He alone is THE way! "Have I not commanded you? Be strong and courageous! Do not tremble or be dismayed, for the Lord your God will be with you wherever you go" (Joshua 1:9, NASB). How grateful I am to Him for that promise.

Despite all those previous situations and the beautiful resolutions, there came a time when the enemy came against me unlike any time before. My appetite had diminished, and I had lost a lot of weight. I was seriously ill, weak, and vulnerable. Without the graphics, just know it was ugly! Because of circumstances, I was unable to listen to praise music, sermons, TV, or even read my Bible. All I could do was pray and cling to the scripture verses I had memorized, along with praise songs, night and day.

A verse kept coming to my mind: "When the enemy comes in like a flood, the Lord raises up a standard against him!" He did that for me! One by one the Lord tapped people here in this country and in countries around the world to engage in prayer for me, many people I didn't know. It was amazing!

My pastor friend said that's a sure sign you are saved because the enemy wouldn't bother you otherwise. He also agreed that the Lord had raised a standard for me. It's like the Roman army that stood shoulder to shoulder when fighting and nothing could penetrate the lines, unless someone like a Jonah runs away from what they are called to do.

After weeks of warfare, I was delivered from that. It's imperative we remember to be armored up with the full armor of God and stand firm (Ephesians 6:10 and following). Although it felt like the Lord had left me at times, He had not. He sometimes allows the enemy to sift us like wheat as He did Peter. He stood aside and allowed my faith to be tested for a time. But He promises we are never alone. And He is faithful! (Isaiah 26:3–4).

Special Stories

In the Lives of Ordinary People

A Story of God's Grace

Pam's Story

Far too many years passed before I could tell this painful part of my life. Now it is time, and I pray that God will use it for His glory and for the good of others in some way. I was born in Bude, Mississippi, where I grew up with wonderful hardworking parents, a brother, and a sister. There was a lot of love in that household. Additionally, our extended family of aunts, uncles, and cousins were very close; we had so much fun together. We were also surrounded by good friends. I had lots of girlfriends and boyfriends. My mother made sure our home was a hospitality home with plenty of good cooking. Homemade ice cream was big at our house. I realize now how blessed I was to have that environment. I knew that I was loved; I knew that I was safe; and we had fun! Those are some of the most incredible gifts any child can receive. Looking back, I don't think I would have changed a thing at home. However, one negative thing was that we attended a very dry church, but I learned that the Holy Spirit can work in a desert.

When I was twelve years old, I accepted Christ as my Savior during a revival. The church became a big influence in my life, even though we did not have a lot of in-depth Bible teaching like we have today. As I reflect now, I know that I received enough spiritual foundation there to enable me to go through some very tough situations not too much later in my young life. That rather enchanting life took a rather dramatic change at an early age for me in my mid-teens.

One weekend prior to the Fourth of July, my parents, an aunt, and an uncle went to the coast and left my cousin and me in our brothers' charge. However, they didn't keep good tabs on us, so we went cruising for guys at Hoppers, a drive-in restaurant in Baton Rouge. At that time in Mississippi, you could obtain your driver's license at age fifteen, and I was the designated driver. My cousin knew one guy, who was our age and knew we were coming, who had a brother that was twenty-one. He told his older brother that we were about eighteen. Little did he know that I was only fifteen at the time.

The next day we spent quite a bit of time at a man-made beach, and we had a really great time together. Although I had lots of guys I could date, since he was older and more mature, I was very intrigued with the older one. All too quickly the weekend was over and we returned to Bude. However, my thoughts were still on the older guy. I was so excited that I had met him. Even though I returned home thinking that I would probably never see him again, he called me a couple of weeks later and wanted to come and see me. Somehow I mustered up the courage to tell my parents. When they discovered how old he was, they were very hesitant but decided we probably would sneak around if we really wanted to see each other. So they gave permission. He had completed his military obligation and was in college at LSU, loved to hunt, and could communicate with my parents so much better than any of the other young men I had dated. He really impressed them. We spent every weekend together for the next nine months. Finally, my parents decided we were getting too serious, which we were. It had been my privilege to be in homecoming court twice at school, and during those few months I received seven "Who's Who" honors. So, my parents thought I was limiting myself. They had very high expectations for me and did not want me to settle for this man who seemed to have become my safety net. For one thing, he didn't make the demands on me that I felt they were requiring. As a result of their concerns, we decided to run off and get married.

Since I had always been very respectful of my parents up until that time, it was very difficult for me to tell them what we had done. So we kept it a secret for a short time, and I just continued attending high school. I told one friend, then she told another friend, and before we knew it everyone knew, including my daddy. When he told my mother, she was so upset that she missed two days of work. Prior to that, she had only missed one day of work and that was to give birth to my baby sister. My new husband and I thought we had better give them some cooling off time, so we went to Baton Rouge for the weekend.

The next week I came back home and returned to school. People could not believe that we had done it, and quite frankly, it was surreal to me. We knew we had done wrong, but we were not ready to cave in and get the marriage annulled. Although we had seen each other every weekend for nine months, marriage was extremely difficult. We discovered we did not know each other; we had just barely scratched the surface. Although I had come from a very loving family background, he had come from a dysfunctional one. My new husband was determined to prove to his daddy that he could make something of himself. Therefore, our unspoken goal between us was to see him finish his education and have a career in aviation as he had dreamed. I was a senior in high school during our first year of marriage. Our daughter laughs and tells people that her dad had to sign her mother's report cards. It is the truth!

For the next four years, he attended college full time, got up at four in the morning to study, and began classes at seven. After classes, he taught ROTC at LSU at the airport until seven or eight o'clock. He also worked full time, and when he possibly could work it in his schedule, he was also working on his flying ratings to make himself more marketable. It is difficult to imagine anything more stressful. He just needed someone to believe in him, and I was that someone. Somehow, at that young age, I knew that this man was an intelligent, hardworking achiever who could accomplish anything he set his mind on. Fortunately for me, the State of Louisiana's school credit system was different, so it only took me a half a semester to finish high school at the age of seventeen. With our schedules, we had very little time together. We saw each other for supper on Saturday nights, but that was about it.

During the next few years, I worked as a receptionist, and then I was hired as a dental assistant where they did on-the-job training. It paid quite well, especially for someone with limited skills. Not too long afterward, I became pregnant. I carried the baby for four months, but I was bleeding the entire time. One doctor, who treated me with blatant disrespect, told me that it was just a cyst on the cervix that was causing the bleeding. He also told me I had made a big mistake in getting married so young and messing up my life. My mother decided to take me to her doctor, who informed us right away that I would lose this baby. Because money was tight, we had to live with some of my husband's alcoholic relatives for a while. Then we were able to move in with another cousin of his. Unfortunately, they were having marital problems, and though I was weak from the continued bleeding, it became my duty to babysit their two boys. Soon afterward I began cramping really bad and had to be taken to the hospital. It was just a few short hours later that I miscarried. When the doctor came in to speak with my husband, he brought with him a glass cylinder that held what looked like a bunch of grapes. The doctor explained that he had heard about this very rare pregnancy, although he had never seen anything like it in his entire career. It is called a *hydatid mole*. It is a weird genetic happening in some extremely rare pregnancies. They performed a suction curettage (D&C) and life went on.

We went to live with the cousin who had introduced us until we were finally able to rent an apartment in a two-story house with no air conditioning . . . in Louisiana . . . in the summertime. It was so steamy. The floor was so uneven we could roll a lead pipe from one side of the house to the other. But it was our place. We paid $57 per month and $2 for water. A week after the D&C, the doctor had me return for him to cauterize the cyst. Having never even heard the word *cauterize* before, I certainly did not know what to expect. He did it without anesthesia, and it was brutal. My cousin, who drove me there, heard me screaming while she sat in the waiting area. Because of continuing menstrual problems, I changed doctors. It seemed important to me that he know about the type of miscarriage I had. However, he received the news in a very flippant way. He just put me on birth control pills that helped initially, but soon things began going downhill again. I knew something was wrong, but I just didn't know what. Life became pretty rough. I ended up finding a new doctor, and one weekend I became very ill and hemorrhaged blood clots as large as my fist. My husband rushed me to the hospital for what we thought would be another D&C. My doctor took some chest X-Rays and told me I had walking pneumonia. When the tissue samples came back from the lab, he told me I had cancer! He said it was a very rare and very fast-growing cancer. Arrangements were quickly made for me to fly to Houston, Texas, to be treated by a doctor whose specialty was this type of cancer. I was in the hospital for six weeks.

My husband went across the street to the Baylor University library and did some research on the type of cancer I had. I was thankful for that because it helped us to be able to speak more intelligently to the doctor and understand more about the treatment and the testing. I was allowed to go home to Baton Rouge for six weeks to recover before returning to Houston for my next treatment as an outpatient. During our stay in Houston, we'd stay on a street known as "prostitute row." We had to. It was what we could afford. While getting my treatment, I would see other patients getting their treatments. Some of them had so many treatments that the doctors needed to start using the veins in their scalps. We knew that was our next stop. During this time, I had begun to make deals with the Lord. I was trying to hang on with "faith the size of a mustard seed" that the Lord spoke of in Matthew 17:20 (NASB). He said if we had even such small faith, we could move mountains and that nothing would be impossible for us. Yet, there was no evidence there to back up my faith. All the indications pointed to the fact that I would not be coming out of that place alive. At that time in our lives, there had been no Bible study, and I was not attending church because I was too sick. Thankfully, there was enough deep down inside me that I was able to draw from what I had learned years before. My husband made a deal that when the next round of treatments were over, we would return to Baton Rouge again.

A few days after returning to Baton Rouge, I became very ill with ulcers in my mouth. My physician at home spoke with my doctor in Houston about my symptoms and upcoming cancer treatment. I returned to Houston for two weeks. My mom and dad were able to come down and visit me. My mom fixed me special meals, and it was so wonderful to have my parents show their love in that way.

Suddenly one night a thought came to me that I know came from the Lord. *If these are bad cells, then I must have some good cells.* So I began envisioning the good cells eating the bad cells. I had not heard of that before; however, now there are studies that show that the mind emits endorphins that help with the healing process. God was so good to give me that. At night, I would go to sleep envisioning my good cells moving around inside my body chewing away at the bad cells. The Lord increased my faith by giving me this as a picture of the healing process. The next thing we did was begin to think of ways to make me laugh, which is also well-known now as part of the healing process. We would laugh about my losing my hair, and my husband would say he would just introduce me as Yul Brynner's sister. Mom and Dad would tell me real-life stories about things that happened at home, and we would laugh and laugh. We did a lot of laughing. After several months of treatment, it looked like they had gotten all of the cancer, but later on it looked like it had reappeared. I was devastated. More for my family than for me. I could see what all of this was doing to them. But we had to go on.

The doctors tried an experimental drug that cleared up my mouth ulcers, but there were still dormant cells in my body that needed to be taken care of. With the exception of lying on my right side for thirty minutes and then my left side for thirty minutes, I had to lie flat on my back for two weeks. At that point, my kidneys began having problems, and I ended up with a bladder infection. It felt like it was all too much for me. I began talking about suicide. I told one of the nurses that I just wanted to die. I was ready to give up. I had lost hope. They sent up a student psychologist who diagnosed me as being immature and under pressure. With all the stuff we had been through since our marriage at such a young age, I was continuing to struggle with low self-esteem. This just added to it. I had decided that I would tell my husband that it was time to pull out all the tubes, remove the catheters, and just let me go home to die. When my husband showed up, he looked so tired; I just couldn't tell him. Instead, I asked him to lay beside me on the bed. I never told him I wanted to die; I knew he needed me too much.

I had been through a litany of things, but still the cancer kept returning. Interestingly, my world didn't cave like I expected. I wasn't nauseous, and I didn't have any ulcers in my mouth at all. I was beginning to feel pretty well. The doctors knew there was a dormant cell somewhere, but they couldn't find it. It had been about a year since this horrible situation began.

One day I decided to walk outside. I remember that beautiful autumn leaves were falling, and I was admiring God's handiwork. The sun was shining. I began a prayer: "Lord, You know our hearts better than we know our hearts, but if I know my heart, I'm ready to go whenever You want me. I'm ready to die if that's what You want. I totally submit to Your will. I am really not afraid to die. If anything, I'm more fearful to live on." He knew that I was sincere. At that moment, it was like He put His hand on my chest, and somehow I knew I was healed. I knew in my heart He was saying that I didn't have any cancer left in my body. I knew deep down inside without any doubt that the cancer was gone. About that time my husband arrived and I said, "I just want you to know that I am cured." He said, "I know, baby, we're going to beat this." I responded, "No, you don't understand; I really am cured." I could tell he wasn't convinced, so I just kept my conversation with God to myself for a while. After my next set of X-Rays, the doctor said, "I've never seen anything like this in all of my life. There is not a trace of the cancer there in your lungs, not even a trace of scar tissue. Your lungs were coated with scar tissue, and there is no trace of it now." I looked at my husband and said, "I told you!" Both of them were totally baffled. The doctor went on to say, "On top of that, you weren't sick from the last treatment. I would have put money on your being sick. We are going to give you another round to be on the safe side." So I went through another round of treatment. Still, everything was negative. You have to stay negative for one year for them to agree that you are clear. And I did. My deep thanks and all praise goes to our Lord that well over thirty years later, I'm still cancer free!

The blessing is that God enables us and gives us the tools we need. He is the only One we can depend on, and He will always be there for us. Thankfully, my husband, my parents, and others were there for me. God is a God of second chances.

~ Author's Note ~

It is such a blessing to see how He provided for them at such a time as that in their very young lives. How great is our God! It is a blessing every time I think of her story. God does indeed allow us to go through "fiery trials," but He always sees us through.

"Beloved, do not be surprised at the fiery ordeal among you, which comes upon you for your testing, as though some strange thing were happening to you; but to the degree that you share the sufferings of Christ, keep on rejoicing; so that also at the revelation of His glory, you may rejoice with exultation" (1 Peter 4:12–13, NASB). We have choices about how we respond to any type of trial. We can receive it without whining, murmuring, and complaining and turn to God for His strength and His grace, wisdom, etc., or we can turn away from Him, become embittered by it, and be miserable and make others miserable around us. I suggest the former. I love the fact that Pam, who knew little about how to live "in the Spirit," did turn to God in those tough days and dug deep within to the Holy Spirit Who had lived within her from the day she accepted Jesus as her Savior. He was there for her and provided for her in that tough battle. He delivered her! He is there for you, too, even if you haven't invited Him into your heart yet. Just go to Him now and tell Him what you need and that you want Him to take over your life. He will come in and He will guide you through the storms of life. It will not always be easy, but it will be worth it. You will never make a better decision for your life. "I am the Vine, you are the branches. He who abides in Me, and I in him, he bears much fruit; for apart from Me you can do nothing" (John 15:5, *NASB*).

Naming the Morning Star and Other Things

For many years, my husband had wanted to purchase a larger boat, something for us to travel and live on when we had time. He especially wanted it for our retirement years so we could take long trips. Four years after our return from Hong Kong, we began searching for just the right boat. He wanted a cruiser or a motor yacht. Even though we purchased the boat after our return to the States, we started thinking about it and praying about it while still in Hong Kong.

One morning, before he departed for work, my husband asked me to spend time with the Lord to determine what type of boat we should purchase. In questioning the Lord about just the right boat, I received no response. I reminded the Lord that my husband had asked me to get answers from Him. Knowing that He wants us to be in submission to our husbands and thereby be pleasing to Him because of our obedience to Him, I appealed to Him on that basis to give me something to tell my husband that evening. Almost immediately I sensed the Lord leading me to turn in the Bible to the book of 2 Peter and begin reading, which I did. However, as I read, I was somewhat frustrated; Peter was indeed a fisherman, but the subject of the first chapter was nothing about boats. I was a little frustrated but continued to read. As I began reading verse 19, it seemed to resonate in my spirit. When I read the words "MORNING STAR," they appeared not only to be in bold print, but they were on stilts, lifted high off the page as well. Then the Holy Spirit spoke clearly to my spirit that "MORNING STAR" was to be the name of our boat, whatever type we bought. So when my husband returned home that evening, I told him about my time with the Lord. We both knew in our spirits that even though our boat was yet to be purchased, we had the name all picked out by the Lord Himself. "And so we have the prophetic word made more sure, to which you do well to pay attention as to a lamp shining in a dark place, until the day dawns and the *morning star* arises in your hearts. But know this first of all, that no prophecy of Scripture is a matter of one's own interpretation, for no prophecy was ever made by an act of human will, but men moved by the Holy Spirit spoke from God" (2 Peter1:19–21, NASB).

Our God has a purpose and a plan for each of us, and I believe that He is more willing to reveal to us what that is than we could ever imagine. He is interested in the minutest things in our lives, just as much as the important things. Nothing is too small for Him to consider or too large for Him to handle. It is important that we take everything to Him, and then listen and look for His answers. Hearing from Him takes a surrendered heart that is cleansed and ready to know and do the will of God. We aren't perfect, so keeping a short list with Him is good. When we sin, we must confess and repent right away. We must read and study His Word, ask Him to reveal Himself to us through the written Word of God, ask Him questions, and be prepared to follow what He says. I would suggest that you write down your questions in black ink, and then write down His answers in red ink. He may or may not answer immediately, so be patient. Sometimes He may speak by not speaking, which may mean He wants you to wait or He's saying no. Also, be on the alert for the answer to come through some other source—a godly person, circumstances, in another quiet prayer time with Him, or through the reading of His Word. It is all a part of teaching us to look to Him for our needs to be met, learning from Him, and leaning on Him. He doesn't always speak to us in the same way. There's no record of two or more burning bushes! Moses was the only one to encounter Him in that way.

In reading the New Testament, we see that He heals in different and strange ways as well. It is His desire that we fellowship with Him, trust Him, and listen for Him. It is about our growing up in Christ Jesus so that we are no longer babes in Christ, but more mature believers willing to give up a part of our busy lives to spend time with Him. It is also the difference in having His power and His enabling in our lives to accomplish His mission for us and through us. We have His promises to us in His Word that we will always have His presence, but we desperately need His power to know and do His will. A wise person told me years ago that he believed that the Holy Spirit of God is always speaking to us in some way. The question is, are we listening? Sometimes He chooses to whisper to us when we are very busy, so we must always be listening no matter what. God is so good about pointing out directions to us when we need them.

A parent may tell his child no regarding something the child really wants to do. Usually, it is not because they are attempting to prevent the child from having a good time; they are simply protecting their child from potential harm. So it is with our loving Father God. If He says no, it is because He has something better for us. He doesn't always override our wills, but He does use circumstances quite often to block our paths. When He does, we can choose to fight with Him, or we can relax and thank Him for His divinely providential plans. It isn't wise to go ahead and force those plans to work without His blessing. You may get your way, but you might live to regret it for a very long time. Disobedience to God is very costly. Dr. Adrian Rogers had this to say: "Sin will take you further than you ever wanted to go. It will keep you a lot longer than you wanted to stay, and it will cost you a lot more than you ever want to pay."[10] Sometimes, we simply run ahead of Him and make plans that are not of Him, according to Isaiah 30:1 that says, "'Woe to the rebellious children,' declares the LORD, 'who execute a plan, but not Mine, and make an alliance, but not of My Spirit, in order to add sin to sin'" (NASB). Seek Him and wait on Him. He knows everything about us. He created us, and He certainly knows what is best for us. "O LORD, You have searched me and known me. You know my sitting down and my rising up; you understand my thought afar off. You comprehend my path and my lying down, and are acquainted with all my ways. For there is not a word on my tongue, but behold, O LORD, You know it altogether" (Psalm 139:1–4, NKJV). Of course, He knew the name for our boat! But we had to wait a couple of years before we purchased it.

---

[10] Adrian Rogers, *Adrianisms: The Wit and Wisdom of Adrian Rogers, Volume One* (Bartlett, TN: Love Worth Finding Ministries, 2007) 114.

Powerful Firsthand Account

A line of severe thunderstorms swept across the United States on February 5, 2008, producing powerful tornadoes over a period of two to three days, causing mayhem for everything in their path. This dangerous weather episode caused severe injuries and even death to several people. Along with it came the destruction of homes, businesses, and churches. In its aftermath, the people shared a common thread of grief, posttraumatic stress, depression, and concern about how to pick up the pieces and go on with their lives. After surviving such an event, you will most likely never be the same; you will better appreciate your life, family, and friends; and if you haven't before, hopefully it will encourage you to surrender your life to the Lord Jesus Christ. When my husband and I were in that tornado, we were not living for the Lord. Read Heather's account of her tornado experience. I believe you will be blessed.

Powerful Firsthand Account from a Christian Perspective: Heather's Story

I was in the February 5 tornado that hit Union University. Around 5:30 p.m., I was studying at Books-a-Million and had planned on riding out the storm there. After a few phone calls from concerned friends, I decided to return to campus. The weather began to change. It was stormy, but it felt like just an ordinary, frustrating tornado drill. I was stressing that I wasn't going to get much studying accomplished. About two minutes before the tornado hit, my roommate ran into our room and said, "Get in the tub, now!" My roommates and I headed to the bathroom along with three girls from upstairs. Our ears began popping from the pressure change. The lights went off. Hail pounded our building. I was almost in the tub when the tornado hit. It sounded like a thousand trains. The noise was incredible. I felt my legs being pulled up by the force. Then, everything collapsed. A wall pressed down across my back, and my legs hadn't made it into the tub yet. They were pinned between a wall of debris and the edge of the tub. One of the girls had her cell phone and thankfully could move enough to call 911. My mind began thinking irrationally. My initial thoughts were: *Every student on campus is either dead or trapped like we are. This is where I am going to die. No one will ever find us. We will be here for days and we won't last that long.* Somehow, though, I had the presence of mind to begin to think more clearly.

In the darkness, we accounted for each other and tried calming each other. I assessed my situation. My legs were pinned, but I felt no pain. Breathing was my biggest issue. I only had a small pocket of air and my whole body was compressed. I began to think what death would be like. I just thought I was going to pass out and then I would be with Jesus. That thought allowed me to remain calm and not panic about the process of my death. At that point, it sounded like someone next to me was breathing her last breaths. I had no idea who it was, but I called out Julie's name and she responded. My heart sank. I told Julie to breathe, not talk. I was positioned on top of her in such a way that if I moved, she either couldn't breathe or it caused her excruciating pain. I cannot begin to describe the fear in my heart that this precious person was possibly going to die underneath me. I prayed aloud. I quoted scripture. I found another friend's hand, and she prayed as well. After realizing this could possibly be the night of my death, I was able to move on and focus on simply breathing. At one point, I had to tell Julie I was out of breath and couldn't pray out loud any more, but I assured her that I was still praying in my heart and mind. This was not me being strong, brave, or courageous; it was the power of Christ in me. He guided me in my thoughts. He helped me to focus on breathing, praying, and encourage Julie to breathe. The whole experience was terrifying but God was in the midst of us. I recall just crying out, "God, You are here. Give us strength." One of my friends calmly said, "Heather, it's going to be okay." God spoke to me through her in that moment. I had an overwhelming sense of peace—we were either going to join Christ in heaven, or He was going to sustain us and leave us here on earth for a little while longer.

When the rescue teams arrived, they heard muffled sounds under the pile of debris that used to be my dorm room. There was fifteen feet of rubble on top of us. The rescue team had to remove the debris piece by piece by hand. Julie's breathing was erratic, and she was in and out of consciousness. As rescuers neared our tub, it was terrifying because the debris shifted and pressure increased. Several of the girls were screaming. Finally, light broke through. Unfortunately, Julie wasn't doing well. I couldn't move because it hurt her, and she couldn't breathe. Her neck was exposed and in danger of being broken if the rescuers slid the debris off. She told me that I had to tell them where she was. The rescue workers told us not to scream and panic because they thought we were in pain each time we did. Then, I saw one of the firefighter's face. I screamed at him, "I am not panicking. You have to listen to me! There is someone stuck under me and if I move, she can't breathe. Her neck is exposed, so you can't slide the debris. You have to lift it!" When they lifted off the main piece, for the first time in forty-five minutes, we could breathe in fresh air. They got the other girls out and Julie and I were left. They tried to get me next, but my legs were still pinned. So they got Julie out. A firefighter came and held my torso and head. He kept telling me, "We're going to get you out of here." It took a lot of maneuvering and strength on the part of the rescuers because I couldn't feel my legs enough to pull them out myself. As it happened, a 2 x 4 next to my right knee—between the edge of the tub and mass of debris—kept just enough of the pressure off of my legs so that I didn't completely lose blood flow to my lower extremities. It saved my legs. We were rescued. We sustained only minor physical injuries. I was taken to the emergency room because I had passed out from shock. Afterward, I only had a slight limp and pain from strained back muscles.

As I reflect over that Tuesday night, I see the Lord. I cannot explain our survival and the fact that there were no fatalities, other than it was God. The destruction and chaos of Tuesday night was incredible. The amazing power, strength, grace, and love of Jesus Christ is the only explanation I have to offer. In the midst of the chaos and rubble, He knew how each board, brick, piece of metal, or chunk of concrete was placed, and He protected us. I have struggled in the past with my faith, wondering if I were truly saved, wondering what my last thoughts would be. Well, now I know. My last thoughts were: God has me. Either way, I am okay. I will either join Him in heaven, or He will save me for yet a little while longer here on earth. I lived through a tornado.

There are sounds and feelings stored in my memory that are terrifying and paralyzing at times. My dear friend almost died underneath me. I still struggle to come to grips with that. I struggle to sleep because there are so many vivid images and feelings when I shut my eyes. However, I find hope in this: God knew, as I lay pinned at that tub, that I would make it out. He is the One responsible for getting me out. He already knows what each and every second of the next few weeks, months, and years hold for me, my friends, and my family. Knowing that gives me hope; it keeps me going. He sustained me through Tuesday night, and He will continue to sustain me in the days that follow. "We are hard pressed on every side, but not crushed; perplexed, but not in despair; persecuted, but not abandoned; struck down, but not destroyed" (2 Corinthians 4:8–9, NKJV).

I should not be alive today, but I am because He still has plans for my life here on earth. He is good. If you don't know Him, you need to. He loves you. He wants a relationship with you. I pray that through my story you have caught a glimpse of Who He is and that you felt His love, His sovereignty, His strength, His grace, and ultimately, His salvation.

A Story of a Little Girl's Faith

Joanna's Story

We know that God never allows anything to come into our lives by accident, and it never comes without a purpose. We need to remember a passage from the Psalms, "Weeping may last for a night, but joy comes in the morning" (Psalm 30:5, NASB). However, we do well to remember that "night" that is spoken of in this passage may be quite lengthy and different from a normal night because with the Lord "a day is like a thousand years and a thousand years is like one day" (2 Peter 3:8, NASB). Gratefully, my "night" was much shorter than that, although at times it certainly seemed to be a thousand years. Still, I made a decision to wait for my joy—whatever length of time it took. According to the scriptures, Jesus says, "In the world you will have tribulation; but be of good cheer, I have overcome the world" (John 16:33, NKJV).

I have certainly had a platform from which to praise God in the time of troubles. I have grown, and I have been stretched. You might say that I became a minor celebrity in my little community of Frog Jump, Tennessee, at the age of six, and a more precocious child could not be found. My memorable record in the archives of not only our town, but those surrounding it, was the result of an accident. It had been a momentous day already since it was day one of the first grade, and I had just had a chance meeting with a little tow-headed boy by the name of Richard. After school, and completely against parental advice, my brother and I decided to cross our one busy highway to entice our best friends to come over to play with us. Because of the roar of the cotton gin nearby, which happened to be located next to Jones Cash Grocery, it was impossible for me to hear the sound of impending danger. The impetuous youngster living inside my little body on that exciting day probably was subconsciously thinking nothing could harm me. As I began darting across the road, suddenly I turned to see the monstrous frame of the bug-spattered front end of a loaded eighteen-wheeler tractor-trailer truck barreling down upon me. At the wheel was a man whose judgment was impaired by spirits, but they certainly were not holy. He failed to maintain proper control of the truck, crossed over the wrong side of the road, and plowed over my dainty, young body. To make matters much worse, because of his disorientation, once he stopped the truck he incorrectly thought he was on top of me, so he backed up. The initial impact damaged my left hip and right leg, but in the process of reversing, he backed over my right knee again, crushing it and completely destroying the growth plate above my knee and damaging the one above my ankle. The flesh was stripped from above and below the knee, leaving torn skin dangling over a broken and twisted ankle. To believers and followers of Jesus Christ, there is no doubt that Satan used this man's weakness for alcohol to snuff out or destroy my young life at such a tender age. However, he failed to consider what our living, Almighty Jehovah God can do through a surrendered heart. Even though we certainly cannot entirely understand *why* such tragic things are allowed, we do know the *Who* that will always be there for us. Somewhere I read: looking on the bright side of life will never cause eyestrain. So early on, I chose to let this make me better rather than bitter.

I was rushed one hundred miles away to Campbell's Clinic in Memphis, Tennessee, where the ambulance driver waited all night to take my little corpse back home to Frog Jump the next morning. But our great God had other plans. The first miracle was that I lived. Even though the doctors explained to my parents that amputation was necessary to save my life, their broken hearts could not imagine their precious little girl walking around the rest of her life like that. So they asked the doctors to at least try to save my leg. The second miracle—the doctors saved my leg. They said that I would probably never be able to walk on my leg or use it, but they were wrong again. They had to literally make me a knee. They took skin grafts from all over my body to cover the bones and turn my ankle the proper way. Back in 1949, I was probably the first bionic person. The third miracle—not only did I learn to walk on my leg, but I rode horses and a host of other things as well. My dear mother always told me, "If you can't do something one way, do it another. You and God can do anything you want to, if you want it bad enough." Although almost everyone thought I was way too young, I am convinced that I was precisely the right age. It is my understanding that it was a toss-up for a while whether my family would invest in a tombstone or a pair of crutches for me.

Fifteen weeks of concentrated medical attention, combined with my youthful and normal healthy resiliency, I was issued back to the world as badly damaged goods. Fortunately, I was able to finish the first grade with a home-bound teacher, so I began my second grade with all of my classmates, especially that little tow-headed boy with the name of Richard. It was tough at times when some of the kids at school would make fun of my leg. On those days, I would go home crying to my mother. She would gather me up in her arms as Jesus does, and say, "Honey, you just make them look at your face and not your feet. It is what is on the inside that counts, not the outside. If you would just ask Jesus to come into your heart and let others see Jesus in you, you would be truly beautiful." It is amazing the influence of a parent in the life of a child.

At the young age of eight, I invited Jesus to come into my heart to change me into the person He wanted me to be, and I asked Him to help me get through this life. He did come into my heart, and He has done all that I desired and so much more. He has also filled me with joy! It was about this time that the desire came into my heart to be a missionary to faraway places like Russia. When those thoughts penetrated my mind, I would cry out, "Lord, how can I ever go to faraway countries? It's hard for me to walk anywhere." (I had to walk on a five-inch built-up shoe.) But the God of the universe said, "Wait." I don't believe there is anything wrong with asking God why things happen. Jesus asked God His own "Why?" question on the cross. God is big enough to answer our questions in His own timing and in His own way. The Lord tells us, ". . . if you have faith the size of a mustard seed, you will say to this mountain, 'Move from here to there,' and it will move and nothing will be impossible to you . . ." (Matthew 17:20, NASB). My mother gave me a little mustard-seed necklace, and I knew that I had more faith than that. I also knew that my "mountain" was my crippled short leg. So, I started praying for my miracle. Sometimes I would pray almost all night that the Lord would give me two pretty legs. I believed it so much that the next morning I would throw back the covers, fully expecting to see two pretty legs, the same length, overnight. It didn't happen like that, but I never gave up hope, and I never gave up on God. I just waited.

The problem with certain people never getting their prayers answered is that they don't continue praying until they receive God's final answer on the situation. They simply become discouraged and give up. I have heard it said, "Pray, believe, and receive." Or "Pray, doubt, and do without." God WILL answer our prayers. It just might not be the exact way we prayed it would happen, or certainly not on the time schedule we prayed for. But His ways and His timing are always best for us. Sometimes His answer is no because He knows what we are asking for is not His best for us. Jeremiah 29:11 states, "'For I know the plans I have for you,' declares the LORD, 'plans to prosper you and not harm you; plans to give you hope and a good future.'" I really believed God had assured me that He would one day heal me. When you get a Word from God, it totally changes your life. While I waited, I also continued to pray, love the Lord, smile, and walk after Him the best I could. There were difficult days. Some people did not understand at all and some just pitied me. But then there was Richard. We became sweethearts and remained sweethearts all through elementary school, high school, and college.

After being sweethearts for almost fifteen years, we felt we knew each other well enough to get married, so we did. Then, we found out that we didn't know each other at all! But with God, all things are possible. After many, many years, we are still together, and we are still in love. Uncle Sam called Richard to Norfolk, Virginia, for four years. While there, God gave us our fourth and fifth miracles. He gave us two little girls, both born with two pretty legs. I began to think that perhaps this was God's way of answering my prayers. I knew that my being handicapped had certainly caused me to lean on Him a lot more than I probably would have had that horrible accident never taken place. Certainly, if that were the case, my life has been a much better one by living for Him from such a young age. I had definitely accepted the fact that if He never did anything else for me, that I would serve Him and give my whole life to Him. I still had a desire to go on mission trips to Russia, although I was still unable to because of my short leg and platform shoe. I also knew that Jesus had said, " Delight yourself in the Lord; and He will give you the desires of your heart" (Psalm 37:4, NASB).

Praises to our God, our sixth miracle came. After forty years of waiting, God chose to use a Russian doctor to provide the answer to my childhood prayer of faith. Through research, in

God's perfect timing, we discovered that at almost the same time I was injured, Dr. Ilizarov, in Russia, had, by God's grace, begun perfecting the limb-lengthening procedure. Incredible! He found that if a limb broke and was set, the bone would grow back together. But if a limb needed to be lengthened, one could break the bone, drive steel pins through the skin and bone to connect steel rings on each side of the break. Then, by placing rods with screws between them, one could control the growth of the bone. I had to turn those screws four times a day to tease the bone apart, but my leg grew an inch every twenty-one days. When the scriptures say that we "fellowship in the sufferings of Christ Jesus," I believe these types of trials may begin to give us insight into that. Of course, there are many more sufferings where people are actually tortured and put to death for their belief in Him.

After we prayed and believed this to be God's answer to our prayers, we could not get approval from our insurance company to cover what they called "experimental and investigative surgery." For two years we tried, but the insurance company continued to decline coverage. Even a local television station covered the story with the hope that pressure on the insurance company would cause them to change their minds, but to no avail. Personally, I believe the insurance company's refusal hurt more than my predicament. At some point, with encouragement from the doctors, we took a huge step of faith by putting our feet into our own Jordan River of sorts. Richard, the girls, and I felt the Lord had told us to drive the fifteen hundred miles to Baltimore, Maryland, and just leave the rest to Him. First Samuel says, "To obey is better than sacrifice," so we obeyed, and God rewarded our obedience in His perfect timing.

When we arrived there, the hospital staff asked who our insurance company was. We told them and didn't say anything else. Amazingly, in about ten minutes, they came back saying that precertification had shown up on their computer. We all looked at each other and almost shouted! We knew that was a real miracle of

God and confirmation of our obedience. Dr. Dror Paley performed the ten-hour procedure. The lengthening device was put on, and I settled in for physical therapy. Six days later we received a call from our insurance company stating they were unaware how the precertification showed up on the computer, and they were not paying for the surgery. So, we did.

At age fifty, my leg grew five inches in three and a half months. They straightened my knee and flexed my ankle, which had been frozen for forty years, so I could walk with both feet flat on the floor ... or even in heels! What a miracle from God! We hired an attorney to fight the insurance battle and fifteen months later, we received word the insurance company would pay for the procedure, not only for me, but for others who needed it as badly as I. And they would pay the rest of my bills, including my attorney's fees, with enough left over to take care of my last checkup trip to Baltimore.

The Lord fulfilled my childhood missionary desire by allowing me to tell of His wondrous deeds at our church, other churches, schools and conferences. One other wonderful gift was that I went on a mission trip, along with 165 others from our church, to Romania. Romania is on the border of Russia, part of the former Soviet Union. Through this mission effort, nearly two thousand people made spiritual decisions for the Lord, and through God's inexplicable workings, we were able to get a Romanian child, who had leukemia, into St. Jude's Children's Research Hospital in Memphis, Tennessee, where she was treated and healed. Incredibly, God used a Russian doctor to answer an American child's prayer of faith, and He used an American doctor to answer a Romanian child's prayer of faith. Is anyone like our wonderful God? For many years, God gave me a very tangible platform from which to speak—five inches to be exact—and I chose to use even that dais to praise Him long before He lengthened and strengthened my leg. What have I learned from my experiences? I believe the Lord has shown me His faithfulness. He has taught me about waiting on Him for our good and His glory, and to never give up if you know that He has given you a Word from Him about anything. "I press on toward the goal for the prize of the upward call of God in Christ Jesus" (Philippians 3:14, NASB).

Agape Love and "Gloria"

Many years ago an invitation was extended to me by our women's ministry director to hold a two-night seminar on the topic of love and forgiveness. This presentation was to be held in the chapel of the church we were attending at that time. It was to be a part of their ongoing weekly sessions aimed primarily for working women from across the city. It was a subject the Lord was already speaking to me about. He knew I needed much more in-depth research. As I began preparing for this assignment, I began praying for an outline. Finally, an elementary outlined popped into my head: "Who, What, When, Where, Why, and How?" I sought input from my husband and asked him to pray about the outline for me. He came up with the same answer! Doesn't that make you smile when you see how God works sometimes? Now the research began.

While at the hair salon one day, the Holy Spirit prompted me to ask the shampoo lady if she had anything to contribute on the subject that might be included in this seminar. For her privacy, I have decided to call her Gloria. She said she would think about it and let me know. A little later she came to me in the salon and whispered to me, "I do have something that I would like you to know about, but I prefer not to speak about it here at the shop. If I could please have your home phone number, I will call you." Of course, I agreed. She called a couple of days later. What she told me was one of the most amazing acts of love and forgiveness of a human being that I have ever known. It blessed not only me and the ladies attending the seminar but others around the world who received tapes of the seminar.

Gloria had known pain, hurt, and anger all through life in one form or another. A few years earlier her sister had been killed by a former boyfriend. Neither Gloria nor her sister was a Christian at the time. Sometime later, after her sister's death, Gloria accepted Jesus Christ as her Savior. Prior to that, she explained that she had harbored anger, hatred, malice, resentment, bitterness, and unforgiveness in her heart toward her sister's killer. Later on, after Gloria was saved, He began to make her a whole a new creation— from the inside out. Only then was she able to forgive the former boyfriend who had murdered her sister, as Christ had forgiven her. Jesus said, "I am the way, and the truth, and the life; no one comes to the Father, but through Me" (John 14:6, NASB). So unless her sister prayed and invited Jesus into her heart just before her death, she will be forever separated from His Presence in heaven for all eternity and from Gloria, as well. Because now, Gloria's eternal home is with Jesus in heaven. She told me that she simply had to leave that knowledge with our holy and just God to give her peace to live with that understanding. As I think on this, obviously that is what we all must do in similar situations when our loved ones die without our knowledge of their having made peace with God. Now that Gloria had become a new creation in Christ Jesus, her heart's desire was to bring her precious daughter up properly.

Sometime later, when she met someone and came to believe that he was a good man who would help make a family for her daughter, she married him. All was going well to her understanding; they seemed to be making a good home together . . . or so it seemed. Her new husband was a hard worker and became an over-the-road truck driver. Both of them worked very hard to have some of the nicer things in life. All certainly seemed to be going well until one evening when Gloria received a message that someone had found her husband in a neighboring state, the victim of an assault. He had been hit on the head and was suffering from amnesia. He did not even know who he was and was generally confused about everything. Gloria went to him immediately and brought him home.

Over time she was able to nurse him back to health, but only temporarily. Gradually, his mental health began to decline again. For a time he would be aware of who she was and what was going on around him, but he would not remember any of that the next day. Eventually though, all short- and long-term memory vanished. He was non compos mentis—not in his right mind. Gloria was able to provide excellent care for him at home for quite some time, but eventually he needed more care than she was able to give. Sadly for her, the time came when she had to commit him to a nursing home. All of this required a tremendous commitment on her part spiritually, financially, emotionally, and physically. In addition, she still had a young daughter at home who needed her very much. The love her and her husband shared made it all a little easier and worthwhile. One day, quite unexpectedly, her world fell apart.

Knowledge came to her that this man, whom she was so devoted to, had attempted to sexually abuse her young daughter—his stepdaughter—while she was in her early teens. This was quite some time prior to the assault on him. Somehow the attempt on her daughter was foiled, and for that she was grateful.

~ Author's Note ~

Molestation doesn't necessarily mean rape; it means to attack or interfere with a person sexually without their permission. It is a very serious offense, even if there was no penetration.

According to psychologists, it's something that most people never get over for the rest of their lives, unless there is divine deliverance.

Gloria was filled with anger, hurt, and unforgiveness because of this man's actions against her daughter. She was in a terrible dilemma. She was still responsible for his care. Nothing had changed in his need of her to provide for him. Yet, how could she continue as if nothing had happened? There was no need to ever mention it to him because he would not remember it anyway. She thought, *How can I stop providing for him? I am God's child. What does He expect from me in this awful situation?* She sought the Lord in prayer and in His holy Word. She knew she could not cope with this on her own.

Day after long day, month after month, and year after year she spent time with him, caring for him with money and energy that she needed for herself and her child. Only now she carried the extra burden of the knowledge of what he had done to her daughter. Still, as she studied the Word of God and sought the Lord regarding this colossal burden, she found that not only did God require her to forgive him in her heart, but as she interpreted the Word, He required her to continue to love him and provide for him. She said, "In Matthew 6 in the Lord's prayer, it says, 'Forgive us our trespasses AS we forgive those who trespass against us' (emphasis added). I know if I don't forgive him, God won't forgive me. And I know that I have so much that needs to be forgiven, and if I don't forgive, God is just not going to forgive me. God commands us to forgive and we're to exemplify His characteristics. 'And we know all things work together for good to those who love God and are called according to His purpose' (Romans 8:28, NASB). God blesses those who love Him and follow His example. We're to focus on the eternal prize. It is only through God Who has given me the heart that I could do this. He has given me a heart to love. I didn't want anything to prevent me from knowing God. Know who you are in Christ Jesus. I am a royal child. This life is but a vapor. I can't have hatred and bitterness because God doesn't allow that into the kingdom. I love God more than anything in the world. And I know that unforgiveness also hinders prayers because then I have sin in my heart."

There is an addendum to Gloria's story. When I first met with Gloria, her husband was still in the nursing home. Just a short while later, she found out that her husband had AIDS. She then had to be tested. She was HIV positive. Gloria continued to be the same sweet person that I had come to know. Shortly afterward, her husband died. By this time, she had left the job at the salon and had entered a different career. All seemed to be finally going well for this dear lady but not for long. The next time I spoke with her, the news had again been very difficult. Now, she had full-blown AIDS. She had good days and bad days and, still, Gloria only pointed out the positives. She still praised God and gave Him the glory.

> "Ah, LORD GOD. Behold, You have made the Heavens and the earth by Your great power and by Your outstretched arm. Nothing is too difficult for You" (Jeremiah 32:17, NASB).

> "I know that You can do all things, and no purpose of Yours can be thwarted" (Job 42:2, NASB).

> "Call to Me and I will answer you and I will tell you great and mighty things which you do not know" (Jeremiah 33:3, NASB).

With a heart turned toward God like that of Gloria, we, too, can experience and understand more fully about His agape love. Then, maybe the footprints we leave can also be those of a spiritual giant.

> *Love protects, trusts, always hopes and prevails;*
> *For as God's word tells us, "love never fails."*
> *So don't keep records of wrongs you may suffer;*
> *Remember, love others with the love God offers.*[11]

---

[11] A portion of a poem written by Joyce Morton, based on 1 Corinthians 13.

A Lady's Encounter
with an Angel

When my youngest son was three, I began experiencing severe back pain. My other boys were twelve, fifteen, and seventeen. I went to a doctor who prescribed tranquilizers, pain pills, and a little pill called Decadron, which I did not realize at the time was a potent steroid. I became a prescription addict. My mother-in-law convinced me that God could heal me, so read scriptures about healing. I also prayed that He would watch over my little boy.

Several years passed, and I had just given up. I started having severe abdominal pain, and an ultrasound showed that I had a blocked kidney. God impressed upon my mind that the medication was damaging my kidneys. I agreed to have one of my kidneys removed, and I became determined to get off all medication. When I told my doctor, he told me that if I did that I would be in really bad shape. He said that when you take steroids your adrenal glands stop functioning. I was determined.

I was informed that medication disrupts the brain's chemistry; the result is severe depression. Bottom line, I had come to the point that I had lost my desire to live. I frankly felt that God had forsaken me, and I mistakenly believed that my family would be better off without me. So, I attempted to overdose. When I was found, I was taken to the hospital where I stayed in a coma for several days. Naturally, a psychiatrist was called in. They administered shock treatments, and I began to recover.

After I returned home, I had to have someone with me because my mind was fuzzy. A couple weeks later, the most incredible thing happened. I was awakened by what I believed to be an angel from God. He spoke to me and said, "I have healed you!" I just cried for joy. I awoke my husband to tell him, and we rejoiced together. That was more than twenty years ago. The back pain and terrible depression disappeared and has never returned. Through it all, I have found that God is faithful; He *does* answer prayer, and He still does heal spiritually, physically, and emotionally. I praise God!

A Granddaughter's Witness

While living in Hong Kong, we met a couple with three lovely children in the church we attended. Very quickly Marie and I became really good friends. That friendship has developed through the years and so has the friendship with her husband, Daniel, and each of their children, who call us Uncle and Aunt. In addition to our friendship, Marie and I became prayer partners early on. We soon discovered that when the Lord was speaking to one of us about an issue, it was highly likely that He was speaking to the other about the same. Because we bring those things together to Him with like minds, He has allowed us to see incredible results to our prayer requests.

Daniel's dad, Ben, was a nonpracticing Jewish gentleman from Germany, who assumed much of the teachings of German philosopher Friedrich Nietze. Daniel, Marie, and their three children were all Christians, and when they had opportunity to do so, they planted seeds of Christianity through words of testimony and scripture verses regarding salvation through the gospel of Jesus Christ. On occasion, he did attend church with them where more seeds were planted about Jesus Christ. Still, there seemed to be only a moderate amount of genuine interest in Christianity. Marie and I began to pray together and beseech the Lord for the truth of Jesus

Christ to be made known to him. Quite a long period of time went by and we saw no results.

Sometimes we find specific promises in God's Word that pertain to our specific prayer. Then we pray and wait, trusting in Him to bring it about in His timing and in His way. When praying for certain things, especially unbelievers, we as believers like to pray this passage from 1 John 5:14–15: "This is the confidence which we have before Him, that, if we ask anything according to His will, He hears us. And if we know that He hears us in whatever we ask, we know that we have the requests which we have asked from Him" (NASB). Regarding praying for unbelievers, we also learn from the Lord that it is not His will that any should perish, but that all should have eternal life. "The Lord is not slow concerning His promise, as some count slowness, but is patient toward you, not wishing that any should perish but for all to come to repentance" (2 Peter 3:9, NASB). But He will not force Himself on anyone. Each of us has to make that decision.

Ben was a gentle man who enjoyed the arts, and he continued practicing law into his eighties. Then misfortune struck. He was diagnosed with lung cancer and a massive brain tumor, which became more and more acute over time. He went through many treatments, but his life was slipping away. The time came when he slipped into a coma. Gratefully, the family was able to keep him at home with private nurses administering medication, and near the end, morphine, to attempt to keep him as comfortable as possible. He began writhing in pain and thrashing about on his bed, moaning from the unchecked suffering he was enduring. One night about ten o'clock in the evening, Daniel told Marie he was going to visit his dad prior to going to bed that night. Their young teenage daughter, Jodie, said she wanted to go with him.

When they got there, Daniel spoke with the hospice nurse, but Jodie went directly to her grandfather's bedside to console him. He was nonresponsive. Jodie sensed the Lord leading her to speak to him about his need of the Lord Jesus Christ as his Savior, so she did just that. She became aware that he had suddenly quit thrashing about and had become very still, listening intently to her, it seemed. She went through the plan of salvation and explained to him that even though he was unable to speak and was in a coma, she believed he could hear and understand her. She informed him that he could speak to the Lord in his spirit and tell Him that he needed Him and wanted to be forgiven of his sins and receive Jesus Christ as his Savior. Surprisingly, as she spoke to him, Jodie noticed a tear forming in one of her granddaddy's eyes and watched as it slid down his cheek. She believed the Lord was doing His work within her granddaddy's heart at that very moment. Daniel and the nurse joined them. Jodie read some of the Psalms to him before they left his bedside.

After returning home that evening, they all went to bed. Sometime right after Marie had dropped off to sleep, she was awakened with the thought that she could hear angels' praises. Although she had never heard them before, somehow she believed she had the assurance in her spirit from the Lord that they were rejoicing over Ben. Only a short couple of hours later, they were awakened by the nurse's call informing Daniel that Ben's earthly journey was over. He had slipped out to be with the Lord sometime earlier. What a time of rejoicing that was! How can we be sure that Ben was saved since he never spoke audibly again? We believe his response—tears—spoke much louder than words. Once we receive Jesus as our Savior, He enables us to have special discernment and insight, among other gifts, so that deep within our spirits we can understand certain spiritual truths. Unbelievers cannot discern spiritual things. We must first open our hearts with a willingness to receive Him as our Savior. John 9:31 states, "We know that God does not hear sinners; but if anyone is God-fearing and does His will, He hears him" (NASB). We believe God responded to Ben's faith in Him during the last few minutes of his life and welcomed him into the family of God.

> ". . . Jesus, remember me when You come into Your kingdom. And, He said unto him, 'Truly I say to you, today you shall be with Me in Paradise'" (Luke 23:42–43 NASB).

> "I will lift up my eyes to the hills; from whence comes my help? My help comes from the LORD, who made Heaven and earth" (Psalm 121:1–2, NKJV).

From Weeds of Woe to Flowers of Faith

Jackie's Story

My husband and I have known Jackie (pen name) and her husband, for many years. They are a lovely couple who have walked the walk of faith for quite some time. Like with all of us, God takes broken people who surrender themselves to Him and puts them back together so that they are better, lovelier, and useful to Him for His glory and for our good.

***

How many of you remember the nursery rhyme, "Mary, Mary, quite contrary. How does your garden grow?" Well, by nature, I'm quite contrary and my garden is a mess. Are any of you gardeners? Those of you who share my passion for gardening know that the first step to a productive and beautiful garden is excavation. You have to dig out the old, poor soil and put in some rich, loamy soil if you're going to have a pretty garden, right? It seems that nothing but weeds will grow in unprepared soil (think of a handful of weeds). But prepared soil produces beautiful flowers (think of a beautiful spring flower arrangement). I'm still under extensive excavation. God is still tilling and amending my soil, and He's still teaching me to pull weeds when they sprout up. God wants to change all of our sun-scorched lives into a well-watered garden.

You must know that flowers of faith don't grow overnight. Some days I feel as if there should be a "Danger! Keep out!" sign hung around my neck. Do you wonder if your life will ever become anything useful or beautiful like a garden? Does it seem as if no matter what you try to plant in the garden of life only weeds come up? Philippians 1:6 (NKJV) says, "Being confident of this very thing, that He who has began a good work in you will complete it . . ." and Philippians 2:13 (NKJV) continues, "For it is God who works in you both to will and to do for His good pleasure." And "His good pleasure" is to make me look more and more like Jesus.

For the first thirty-nine years of my life, I looked like anything but. The only religion I was ever exposed to as a child was a joyless, frightening list of dos and don'ts devised by well-meaning men who thought that's what was necessary to keep you out of hell. The church my father grew up in, and the one we went to when we went, believed children should be still and quiet and just listen. There was no Sunday school, no programs of any kind, let alone for children, and no music. It was boring, and I stopped going just as soon as I could. Church was sort of hit and miss from then on. I only went if I had to. I was more into partying. I didn't have time for church, and I didn't think I needed what they were selling. It took many years and much heartache to show me differently.

In the late seventies, weeds of woe were entangling the garden of my life to the point that it looked like a neglected lot in the inner city. Do you remember the seventies? They started with the energy crisis and got worse as the decade progressed. The Vietnam War was still playing prime time in the nation's living rooms, and we saw our country defeated for the first time in a war that caused almost as much divisiveness as our Civil War. There were massive layoffs in the work force, double-digit inflation, and interest rates at 20 percent. Then came Watergate, followed by the Iran hostage crisis. Added to these national maladies were my personal adversities. The near-death of my dad added despair to the tangle of weeds overtaking my life. Then came the death of Elvis Presley. For me, it was the sober reality that death is an inescapable fact. The accumulative effect of all these woes was the death of my sense of security and invincibility. Coupled with personal financial problems, the weeds of discontent and dissatisfaction invaded my orderly garden of well-being like kudzu.

By the end of the seventies, I knew that something was seriously wrong in my country and in my life. But I still couldn't see that the source of these spreading weeds of woe was my own sense of disillusionment. I tried about every off-the-wall form of occultism there was from reading horoscopes to transcendental meditation, but I couldn't uproot those weeds. They just kept growing and spreading no matter what I tried. At the same time, new weeds of disrespect and disgust for my husband were springing up like dandelions in April. It became obvious that he had a serious drinking problem. He was losing interest in his family, his friends, and his business. They could no longer compete successfully with the invasive, choking, tendrils of alcoholism. Let me illustrate. We have a tall pine tree in our yard that was damaged by an ice storm a few years back. The storm stripped a lot of its limbs off, so we planted a wisteria vine at the base to help fill in the gaps. That vine is now larger than my leg, and it is wrapped around and around that poor pine all the way to the top. Unless uprooted and destroyed, it will bring that tall pine tree down some day. That's what happened to my husband. The choking vine of his addiction wrapped itself around him like that wisteria vine wrapped itself around that pine. By the time he realized his drinking was out of control, his abuse of alcohol was threatening to bring him down. If he was to live, and we were to survive as a family, his addiction had to be uprooted. It was killing him, and it was killing our life together. As my life became more and more entangled in the weeds of the worries of the world, God began to use these troubles to drive me to a point of desperation, so dire that I would search for a solution. But I knew of no "Weed-be-Gone" for the soul and spirit.

During this time, *by chance*, I bought a copy of *The Late Great Planet Earth*. It scared me to death! But it also got me thinking that there might be something to this "God business." There had been a previous incident in my life that had also piqued my interest in God. I mentioned earlier that my father had almost died. Well, while I was keeping vigil at what we all thought would be his deathbed, a miracle happened. He came out of the coma and lived. I was convinced his recovery was the result of my mom's believing prayers. I had never given credence to the power of faith in a person's life until I saw it demonstrated so dramatically through my mother. God got my attention, at least for the moment, when my father recovered. While all this was going on, we were in the process of selling our house and moving to the country. I thought that perhaps a simpler lifestyle was the answer. I was trying to weed the garden of my life with the hoe of human reasoning. I never gave God a thought in my decisions. I was entirely too busy for God, but He wasn't too busy for me. He's never too busy for anyone. He was patiently out searching for His lost sheep, and He sent one of His children into my life.

The woman who finally bought our house was impressed in her spirit "to stand in the gap" for me in prayer, though it was ten years later before I knew of His divine intervention at just this juncture in my life. In His infinite grace and mercy, He moved me right into the middle of a nest of Christians. My new neighborhood was full of them. They kept inviting me to church and Bible study. I'd tell them I didn't believe in all that "Jesus stuff," but no matter how rude and ugly I was to them, they kept loving me and coming back for more. I couldn't figure them out, but I knew they had something I didn't have—joy and peace. The Lord used two of them to begin to convict me of my need for the joy and peace I saw in them.

Finally, things got so bad I decided I might as well give God a try. I'd tried everything else. So I began reading the Bible, really because I didn't know where else to turn, and that's just where God wanted me. It was then that the first seeds of faith were sown in my heart. Romans 10:17 declares, "Faith comes by hearing and hearing by the word of God" (NKJV). When I got in the Word, God's Spirit began to speak to my spirit. I read verses like Romans 3:23, "For all have sinned, and come short of the glory of God" (NKJV), and "There is none righteous, no, not one" (Romans 3:10, NKJV). I had always thought you had to live a good life in order to be acceptable to God, but I slowly began to realize that God loves us and accepts us just as we are. Jesus' death on the cross made that possible. We come in faith, and by His grace, He accepts us. Jesus said, ". . . him that cometh to me I will in no wise cast out" (KJV).

On June 11, 1981, He gently gathered me to His chest. I met the living Lord Jesus Christ and nothing has ever been the same since. I repented. I did a complete 180-degree turn around, which is all repent means: "to turn from." I surrendered all I knew of me to all I knew of Him. I turned *toward God* and started trying to go His way instead of my own sinful way. God's revealed truth in His Word took me from despair to delight, from hopelessness to happiness, from judgment to joy, from a spiritual vacuum to victory in Jesus. I felt as if a thousand-pound burden had been lifted off my shoulders. I felt as if I were floating on air. For the first time in my adult life, I felt clean, pure, and forgiven. It was, and still is, the most glorious experience I have ever had. I fell head, heart, body, and soul in love with my Savior, Jesus Christ. Best of all, I experienced His unfailing love and His total acceptance of me just the way I am. I realized He had been waiting with open arms for me to walk into them all my life.

God had begun a good work in me, which He will complete until the day of Christ Jesus, as Philippians 1:6 says. I joined a local Bible-believing, Christ-honoring church and was faithful in attendance. I studied God's Word and prayed. I read the Bible straight through three times in three different translations. I was so starved for truth, meaning, and purpose in my life. God's Word showed me all three and I couldn't get enough. As I prayed for understanding, God, Who delights to show His truth to those who seek to know Him, gave me understanding of His Word. I saw that not only had I been mercifully and miraculously saved, I had also been sealed by the Holy Spirit, as gloriously promised in Ephesians 1:13, guaranteeing my inheritance in Christ Jesus as a child of God. I was forgiven for all my sins: past, present, and future. I was accepted in the Beloved. I was seated in the heavenly places in Christ and reconciled to God through faith in Him. I had been granted access into the throne room of Almighty God where I could commune with Him, my heavenly Father, face to face. It was mind-boggling and spirit expanding. I had been granted everything pertaining to life and godliness in Christ Jesus (see 2 Peter 1:3). Immediately, I began praying for my husband's salvation.

He wanted nothing to do with my newfound faith. He said that was fine for me but not to bother him with it. So I tried not to. I didn't read my Bible or any other Christian literature around him. I was sensitive to his lack of understanding of what had happened in my life. I knew I was saved. God's Spirit bore witness with my spirit that I was His child. So I just tried to live a changed life in which he could see the difference Jesus was making in me. I read in Matthew 17:20 that if I had faith as small as a mustard seed, I could move mountains. Jesus went on to say in that verse, "Nothing will be impossible for you" (NASB). I chose, then and there, to believe that what God says in His Word, He means. The first seeds were being planted that would take root downward and bear flowers of faith upward. However, before you can have flowers, you must prepare the soil, remember? God, the Holy Spirit, led me to verses such as Genesis 18:14, "Is anything too hard for the LORD?" (KJV). And where Jeremiah said, "Ah, Sovereign LORD, you have made the heavens and the earth by your great power and outstretched arm. Nothing is too hard for you" (Jeremiah 32:17, 27, NASB). Then in verse 27, the LORD replied, "I am the LORD, the God of all mankind. Is anything too hard for me?" I was certainly beginning to think not. Verses like Isaiah 59:1 (NIV), "Surely the arm of the LORD is not too short to save, nor His ear too dull to hear" just reinforced my growing faith. If I just kept praying, God could, and would, hear and no one was out of reach of His arm. God was amending the hardened soil of my heart by helping me believe, by faith, that He could do anything. I knew if He could save a sinner like me, He could surely save my husband.

After those first flowers of faith began to grow in the freshly amended soil of my heart, our great and gracious God started showing me new and wondrous things in His Word:

> "For God so loved the world that He gave His only begotten Son, that whoever believes in Him shall not perish but have eternal life" (John 3:16, NASB).

> "The Lord is not slow in keeping His promise, as some understand slowness. He is patient with you, not wanting anyone to perish, but everyone to come to repentance" (2 Peter 3:9, NIV).

These, and other verses, showed me that it was not God's will for anyone to be lost. Those glorious truths were like sunshine that grew more flowers of faith in the newly weeded and cultivated garden of my life. I realized that God loved my husband even more than I did and wanted him to come to the knowledge of the truth. God was tilling my garden in preparation for sowing more seeds to grow more flowers of faith. Now let me ask you again, how does your garden grow? Is it full of the rocks of human reason? Is its surface soil so hard that the water of the Word cannot penetrate down to where the seeds are to be sown? Is it so overtaken by the weeds of the worries of this world that the S-O-N-light of God's promises can't warm its soil and cause the seeds to germinate and grow flowers of faith? Have you come to the realization, as Hosea 10:12 says, "that it's time to break up your unplowed ground; for it is time to seek the LORD, until He comes and showers righteousness on you"? God tells us in Isaiah 58:11, "You will be like a well-watered garden, like a spring whose waters never fail" (NASB). But you will never be that well-watered garden whose "fragrance may spread abroad," as the Song of Songs says, until you have the faith that can wait on God without wavering. At this point, I must ask you, do you know the God of the Bible as your heavenly Father? Do you know Him as the Holy One, Who imputes His righteousness to you when you come to know Him as Savior and Lord? Do you know Him as the Shepherd of your Soul Who only wants what is best for you? Do you believe the Bible is the unchangeable, everlasting Word of God? Luke 1:45 says, "Blessed is she who has believed that the Lord would fulfill His promises to her!" (NIV). Do you believe God waits to be gracious to you? Do you believe Jeremiah 29:11, "'For I know the plans I have for you,' declares the LORD, 'plans to prosper you and not to harm you, plans to give you hope and a future'" (NIV). This is the litmus test: do you believe that what God says in His Word, He will do? I did, as I prayed for my husband's salvation, and I still do. I pray that you too believe that what God says in His Word He will do. Hebrews 11:6 says, "For without faith it is impossible to please God, because anyone who comes to Him must believe that He exists and that He rewards those who earnestly seek Him" (NIV).

Examine yourselves before the Lord. Be honest with Him. He knows the truth anyway. Tell Him if your faith is anemic. Ask Him to give you a verse that will feed your faith with the nutrients of His promises. Then search His Word for a special rhema word to you, and He will lead you to one that will nourish your soul and spirit. A *rhema* word is *a word from the Word*. It is a word that God gives you personally, which pertains to some circumstance in your life that you are seeking God's face about. When God leads you to a scripture promise, claim it for your particular situation. Stand on it. Pray it back to Him. He loves that! Never give up. For example, when I was praying about whether to take on a project I knew I was totally inadequate to tackle, the Lord led me to Isaiah 41:9b–10 which says, "I said (meaning God said), You are My servant; I have chosen you and have not rejected you. So do not fear, for I am with you; do not be dismayed, for I am your God. I will strengthen you and help you; I will uphold you with my righteous right hand" (NIV). The minute I read that, I knew it was the Lord's Word to me to take on the job. It was as if God's voice had spoken the promise in that passage directly to me. It gave me the faith and courage to attempt the assignment because I knew it was His plan for me at that time.

God gave me some great and precious promises from His Word for my husband's salvation, but He had to settle something with me first. He led me to 2 Corinthians 12:9, "My grace is sufficient for you, for My power is made perfect in weakness" (NIV). When that verse was impressed upon my heart by the Holy Spirit, I knew that no matter how bad things got, I was to remain with my husband and be faithful in prayer for him. I was to love him just the way he was. It was amazing how God gave me the grace to love him more than I ever thought possible. I was not to preach to him or nag him about his drinking. There was to be no neglecting my growing garden of faith, or giving up on it, just because there were still weeds everywhere! God showed me that I had sown many of those weeds myself. It was my responsibility to dig them up and destroy them. Every garden has weeds, but by constant vigilance, they can be eliminated. And by constant, believing prayer, God will change your circumstances. Zechariah 4:6 says, "'Not by might nor by power, but by My Spirit,' says the LORD Almighty" (NIV).

Whether you have a husband who is already saved, or you are praying for his salvation, you must remain faithful to your ministry task. Make no mistake. It is God first, then your husband, not your children, your parents, or anyone or anything else. Remember this: YOU CANNOT CHANGE YOUR HUSBAND, WIFE, OR ANYONE. *ONLY GOD CAN!* It is your job to lift him to the throne of grace in prayer, "that we may obtain mercy, and find grace to help in time of need" (Hebrews 4:16, KJV). God works to change people, their attitudes, and their circumstances through your prayers.

God led me to scripture that became rhema word pertaining to my husband's, our son's, and my brother's salvation. Don't give up because God doesn't answer your prayer when you think He should. His timing is always perfect! He may need to teach you some lessons, as He did me, while you wait. It was seven years and seven days after my own salvation before my husband was saved. There wasn't a day during that seven years that I did not pray for him. God honors persistent faith. And He desires consistent faith. I still pray for him every day.

Since his "new birth," we have been tending our garden together. There are still weeds of woe to contend with among our flowers of faith, but we know that "He gives strength to the weary and increases the power of the weak" (Isaiah 40:29, NIV). And we have reaped a wonderful harvest: our son and his wife have both made professions of faith. Faith has a deep, strong taproot planted in the Word of God that is present in every season of your life. If you choose to believe what God says in His Word, even though faith's roots are sometimes hidden from the view of others, God will see.

My prayer is that God will bless you with an abundantly growing garden full of these fragrant flowers of faith ". . .to the praise of His glory . . ." (Ephesians 1:6, NASB). Before God can make your life like a garden of fragrant flowers you must, by faith, accept Christ as your personal Savior. You now know how the Lord has taken the weed-infested, empty lot of my life and is making it into something beautiful that He can use for His glory. I have good news for you. He wants to make something beautiful out of your life also. The same Lord Jesus Christ Who loved and accepted me is waiting to show you right now that He loves and accepts you too.

The Amazing Story of Vivienne

My husband and I had the privilege to live near, attend church with, and get to know on a more personal level Vivienne, her husband, Levi, and their family during the four years we lived on Hong Kong Island. Even though we are now thousands of miles apart and on different continents, our hearts are still close, and we stay in touch frequently by e-mail and occasional phone calls. They are a lovely family, and her story is an another amazing account of God fulfilling His promises and showing His sufficiency.

***

My name is Vivienne, and many people wonder about my name. My mother loved Vivien Leigh, the actress, so she named me Vivienne. Later on, I grew up, met, fell in love with, and married Levi. We live in Hong Kong. My husband, Levi, and I have two sons. While the older son chose to study at Harvard, our younger son studied medicine in Hong Kong, to follow in his father's footsteps. He is now married, and he and his wife have a baby. God has blessed me with a lovely family. We are very close, and it is very difficult sometimes with so many of them living so far away and in many different countries. But we try to see each other as often as possible.

One year after Christmas vacation, our older son and I traveled back to Boston where we could continue our visit and also visit with several other relatives who lived there. Five days prior to my returning to Hong Kong, several of us were in a very serious automobile accident. It was on January 24, 1998, the second day of the Chinese New Year. Several family members from Hong Kong were also visiting in Boston, so we decided to go pay tribute to our grandmother by visiting her cemetery. As my aunt was driving along the street, suddenly, for what seemed no apparent reason, the car began to accelerate on its own. As it gained speed, the car began to veer furiously toward the left, causing it to mount a fairly wide median. When I saw the car racing toward a tall street light in the center of the median, I reached out and grabbed the steering wheel and helped pull the car back on the road. Meanwhile, my brother shouted at my aunt to apply the brake, and he leaned forward to attempt to disengage the cruise control, which he thought kicked in. He also tried to switch the engine off. Unable to do either, he returned to his seat, buckled his seatbelt, and shouted for his wife and daughter to do the same. The thought flashed through my mind to unbuckle my seatbelt to assist my aunt with the brake. Fortunately, the next thought came, reminding me that it would be unwise. Instead, I went for the gearshift, hoping to stop the car. I pushed it into park, I pushed it into low gear, and then I pushed it into reverse in order to break the speed or ruin the engine. Nothing happened. Even though I repeated the motion two and a half times, incredibly nothing changed. As I glanced back outside the car, I saw that we were approaching the end of a bridge and hurling directly toward a busy T-intersection. Expecting those cars to ram into our right side, I sank low into my seat, covered my head with my arms, and screamed. After bracing myself for the crash, I did not observe how the car crashed, but I believe I was the first to become cognizant of what was going on around us. I realized that the seatbelt was extremely tight across my chest, so much so that it was causing me difficulty in breathing, and I had pain in my back. Unable to breathe properly, I became frightened. I cried out twice to the Lord Jesus Christ for help. Then I just closed my eyes and gasped for air. In that moment, I recalled reading a story in Billy Graham's book, *Angels*. It was an account of a Chinese peasant woman carrying a baby on her back while going into the foothills to cut grass. She met a tiger, and in her fear, she, too, cried out to Jesus for help. She knew to do this because a year before a missionary had told her about Jesus helping those in trouble. In her case, the tiger, instead of attacking, suddenly turned and ran away. Psalm 91:11 says, " For He will give His angels charge concerning you, to guard you in all your ways" (NASB).

I believe God and His angels did take charge because, very shortly, I heard two male voices, and one of them said he had a knife in his car so he went to fetch it. I don't know how many people carry knives in their cars, but this one was strong enough to cut through my seatbelt effortlessly. I was pulled out of the car and placed on the ground under a tree. As I lay there gasping for air, a very kind, well-dressed gentleman knelt by my side, assuring me the other passengers appeared to be okay. I didn't know at the time that his definition of okay only meant they were still alive. This gentleman accompanied me until the paramedics took me to the hospital. I do not know who that gentleman was, but I am so very grateful for his kindness. Additionally, I am very grateful for the firefighters and all others who were involved in the rescue operation.

At the hospital, I was informed that my X-rays revealed four broken ribs, a punctured lung, and a blowout fracture on one of my vertebrae. In simple words, I had broken my back, and some of the bone fragments were lodged in my spine. I was told that I needed emergency surgery and that I was being transferred to another hospital. The time had come for me to inform my husband,

Levi. He would be very angry if I went into surgery without his knowledge, so I finally told the doctor in charge that my husband was a doctor and that I needed to notify him.

We awakened Levi at approximately 5:00 a.m. Hong Kong time. With God's help enabling me to "live above my circumstances," he never suspected that I was injured as I calmly broke the news to him that we had been in a car accident. He asked if anyone was hurt. When he found out that surgery was necessary for me, he said, "You don't need surgery; who said you needed surgery?" Knowing that I could never out-argue him, I handed the phone to the doctor in charge, and she explained my condition to him. At once he agreed that I, indeed, needed surgery without delay. He promised that he would take the first plane over from Hong Kong, which he did. Somehow prior to leaving for the twenty plus hours' journey to Boston, he managed to contact my surgeons and arranged for them to keep my sister in San Francisco informed. He also contacted our pastor, requesting that prayers be sent to our Lord on our behalf. Our younger son was left alone in Hong Kong to deal with the uncertainty of my condition and to be the contact person there for all of our other family members and many friends.

I was transferred to Beth Israel, a teaching hospital for Harvard Medical School. Upon arrival, the resident doctor explained the procedures of my operation. I was told that I would be operated on in the front and in the back and that fragments would be taken from my hip for a graft—the most pain I would experience would be from my hip. I thought that I might be paralyzed because of the bone fragments in my spine. Although the doctor reassured me otherwise, he kept poking needles into my legs and asking, "Do you feel this? Do you feel that?"

However, later on there was a sudden switch of doctors; a different team operated on me. Instead of being operated on in the front and back and having a fragment removed from my hip where most of my pain would be, these surgeons used a new technique using one incision on the side and a donor bone to insert into my vertebrae, sparing me the pain in my hip. In the two-volume text book called *Spinal Surgery*, published in 1997, there is an article written by an orthopedic surgeon in California who is one of the pioneers of this technique. Nine days after the surgery, we found out that the author of this article was in Boston at the time . . . and he operated on me! God's amazing goodness and faithfulness.

Levi spoke to the attending physician, whose first words were, "We almost lost her." I had almost died due to complications during the surgery. A very uncommon severe bleeding condition called Disseminated Intravascular Coagulation (DIC) had developed, and I bled a total of eleven liters of blood, which is more than two and a half times the total blood volume in my body. The amount of blood was equivalent to twenty-four units or twenty-four bags of donor blood. Thanks be unto God, my surgeon was extra alert, immediately diagnosed the problem, and began treating it. Fortunately, my last memory of anything prior to surgery was being wheeled into the operating room.

After an eight and a half hours of surgery, I awakened in the intensive care unit. Although I could not open my eyes due to the swelling, I recalled having visitors. Family and friends were there to see about me. I knew that many prayers had been lifted up on my behalf, precisely when the bleeding condition placed my life in jeopardy. How precious is it that God has a way of protecting those who trust in Him, even moving other members of the body of true believers to pray in times of great danger. After six days in recovery, my doctors gave me the okay to travel back to Hong Kong.

Word finally reached me, approximately ten days after the accident, that according to police reports and our lawyer's investigation, somehow our car had struck a road sign as we drove over the median. It hit a mound of snow, which then launched it eight feet into the air and impacted a tree on a second median. Unbelievably, it then crossed over a third divider to hit four parked cars in front of a school cafeteria before coming to rest. Two large glass panels of the cafeteria were shattered. I thank God that, although the accident happened at 11:30 a.m., no children were in the cafeteria and no one else was injured. The distance between the first island of impact and the final point of impact was approximately four hundred feet. At least two of the parked cars were deemed total losses. All five passengers in our vehicle were injured, but we all survived.

As I reflect on the events of the accident, and those following, I have no doubt of God's presence throughout. Even before I cried out to Jesus for help, when I was strapped in the car, God intervened with His protection. I believe that God had placed a boundary of protection around us. Before we crashed, I had expected the cars traveling on the road perpendicular to us to ram into our right side. I still don't know how we avoided them. In my mind, I imagine we may have been thrown over them. At any rate, God not only protected us, but them as well. That was just the beginning of God's provision for me in my desperate hours and days of need.

Lately, one of my favorite hymns has been "Great Is Thy Faithfulness." "All I have needed, Thy hands have provided. Great is Thy faithfulness, Lord unto me." How true that is! God's faithfulness provided me with what I needed. Even in my most uncomfortable days in the hospital, I had a wonderful sense of peace and joy. John 3:16 says, "For God so loved the world, that He gave His only Begotten Son so that whoever believes in Him shall not perish, but have eternal life" (NASB). First John 5:13 says, "These things I have written to you who BELIEVE in the name of the Son of God, so that you may KNOW that you have eternal life" (NASB, emphasis added). So I have the insurance and the assurance of His Word that He is bound to fulfill, for God cannot lie. I pray that you have secured this insurance and assurance too. Jesus' death on the cross paid for our sins IN FULL. You will

NEVER be short of your salvation if you put your faith and trust in Him. If you haven't secured this insurance, don't wait and think you have plenty of time to secure it. When I left my aunt's apartment that morning, I certainly had no idea that within less than an hour, I would be carried off to a hospital by ambulance and would be so close to death on three different occasions. God has a purpose for our lives. His highest purpose for our lives is for us to have eternal life with Him. All He requires is for us to come to Him with a sincere and repentant heart. Better than any earthly insurance, God can guarantee you a place in heaven with Him and insurance for eternal life.

Most of my life I have attended church, and in the recent years have attended Bible studies. What I have learned about God from the Bible, I experienced personally during this accident, and I believe God revealed Himself so clearly to me. From Genesis all the way through the Bible, God reveals Himself and His promises to us so that we may know Him and experience His power and His presence while we are on this earth. That is my hope for you. Surrender your life to Him and find His ultimate purpose for your life. "Not to us, O Lord, not to us, but to Your name give glory, because of Your lovingkindness, because of Your truth" (Psalm 115:1, NASB).

Psalm 23:4 states, "Even though I walk through the valley of the shadow of death, I fear no evil, for You are with me, Your rod and Your staff, they comfort me" (NASB). I walked through the valley of death during this trial, but I know His promise is true. He *did* walk with me, and He *did* comfort me. His promises are most assuredly true. And I say, "Yay and amen!" Thank You, dear Lord, for the blessings You gave all of us.

Prevented Death, Provided Life

Tom was a real blessing to his wife, Mary. She often spoke of her gentle giant as just so. When he met with others, their perception was the same. He was a burly giant who loved his Lord, Jesus Christ. His desire was to be a dedicated and selfless provider for his family. He worked with a light, gas, and water company where he, on occasion, found himself in less than desirable surroundings.

On one particular day, he found himself in just such a place. The owner of the house met him at the door, and Tom quickly observed that this man's massive stature matched his own. Troubleshooting and repairing the problem led Tom to the attic of the house. He began his work and was well into it when he heard the other man enter the attic with him. Still intent on his work, he didn't even acknowledge the man's presence until a few moments later. At the precise moment of God's perfect timing, Tom asked the other man, "Do you know my Lord Jesus Christ?" At the question, the owner gasped, to which Tom turned his head and looked around. When he did, he saw the burly man with a wrench in his hand, drawn back and ready to deal a fatal blow to Tom. With Tom's question ringing in the burly man's mind, the homeowner crumbled and brought the weapon down without incident. What followed, amazingly, was Tom communicating the love of the Lord to this massive man in the state of the affairs of his life relating to the Lord Jesus Christ. Before their time together was over, Tom had the privilege of introducing this man to the Lord. It turned out that the owner of the house had entered that attic with the intention of murdering Tom that day—for no apparent reason. But God had a different agenda, and it was carried forth. He had a plan for good and not evil. He saved Tom's life and provided a changed heart and eternal life and light for the man who had known only darkness prior to that day.

Our God is faithful! But He needs His children to be soldiers on the front lines, filled with the Holy Spirit, trained, ready, and obedient. Imagine what that scene would have looked like that day, and on into eternity, if Tom had been too busy with his "day job" to care enough to tell the other gentleman about God's Son, Jesus, and the plan He had for the man's life. As it turned out, Tom left that place with a new brother in Christ Jesus whom he would spend eternity with. Hallelujah! What a mighty God we serve! "Trust in the Lord with all your heart and do not lean on your own understanding. In all your ways acknowledge Him, and He will make your paths straight" (Proverbs 3:5–6, NASB).

There was a time when I acknowledged to the Lord that it was my desire to speak to any service personnel, delivery people, etc. who came to my house regarding where they stood spiritually. It was my desire to give them a booklet that told them about Jesus and how they could come to know Him. Recently, I asked a young man who frequently delivered oxygen canisters if he was a Christian. He was. So I asked a favor of him. I gave him a booklet and asked him to read it and then pass it along to anyone he thought might need it. It is up to the Lord what happens with these people spiritually, but it is up to us, if we belong to Him, to be willing to be a messenger for the Good News of Jesus Christ.

God Working in the Hinterlands

Miranda had not been in her assigned country very long before she became quite ill. Because of the lack of medical assistance in her area, she flew to a well-known hospital in another country in the same general area. After her initial consultation with the doctor, her ultrasound had revealed many gallstones, and he recommended that she have additional tests. He then advised her to meet with him two days later to schedule the surgery. The clinic performed numerous blood tests, an ultrasound, and a nuclear scan. While waiting for her appointment, she developed severe abdominal pain and a high fever. Her daughter took her to the emergency room, where they admitted her to the hospital.

While in the hospital, she received antibiotics and pain medicine. The doctor called in a specialist, and he ascertained that a stone was stuck in the bile duct. This would require immediate surgery. In preparation for the surgery, the doctors ordered more scans, put her under general anesthesia, and inserted a probe with a camera down her throat to examine the ducts and the first part of the small intestine. To their amazement, they could not find a single stone in the gallbladder, ducts, or elsewhere. The stones had just disappeared. They concluded in their report that she had passed the binary stones and told her to have a follow-up ultrasound in four months. They told her that if her pain returned to come back to the hospital. She did not have to go back. "My Father told me in His letters that there is nothing too difficult for Him, and when the going gets rough, and it will, I have an experience that will forever cause me to take my Father at His Word."

Miranda's Daughter

Miranda's daughter had been treated for ten years for high blood pressure. She kept fainting. She began having heart problems, and her heart rate dropped to 38–48 beats per minute. She also had severe occurrences of AV heart block where her natural pacemaker stopped working. It was a really frightening time. They were a half a world away in a city of millions of people with inadequate health care. But God . . .

She was admitted to a heart hospital in their area, but there was nothing they could do for her there. So she was flown to the same country where Miranda went with her gallstone problem. While at the airport, her daughter had another fainting episode, and their medical escort lost her pulse for about four seconds. She was taken to a clinic there at the airport, and the hospital sent an ambulance. Once at the hospital, the cardiologist told her she might need a new pacemaker. Miranda said, "God visited her and healed her. He has totally healed her of everything, including the high blood pressure she had for ten years. She has been off meds for almost four weeks and her blood pressure is 118/64. Before, two days off meds and it would be 195/115. I am amazed at WHO we serve!" God had also done a work in her daughter's spiritual heart.

More from Miranda

One Sunday, Miranda's son took an overdose of heroin. He shot pure, undiluted heroin into his arm, and his body immediately stopped moving. It was like someone had unplugged his power. His girlfriend kicked him out of the car, and started hitting him on the chest as hard as she could. She did this about twelve times, but there was no response. He was blue! Just then, a couple came running up. The girlfriend tried to call 911, but her phone wouldn't work. The lady called 911 and the husband did CPR. The couple was Christian. The paramedics were there in about two and a half minutes. They started an IV and continued the CPR. Then they injected some medication in him. Her son said the first thing he heard in the darkness was, "He is back. He is back." When he woke up, there was a tube in his chest, and the medics were saying over and over again, "We got him back." He also saw his little son through the crowd and heard him saying, "My daddy turned blue." Miranda's son said that immediately he had an overwhelming love for his children. The time from the overdose until he returned was seven minutes.

On the ride to the hospital, the paramedic told him that he was a miracle. He said, "Son, 90 percent of the people who go through what you went through die; the other 10 percent are brain dead. You are a miracle! Don't waste your life, Son; you have been given a second chance." He recalled that the whole time he was in the hospital, doctors and nurses were coming to his room and telling him what a miracle he was. Children's Services got involved and for a time, he was not allowed to be with his children. He was glad that they did. He had to get drug tested regularly and had to do outpatient rehab.

Since then, things have been going much better. He now wants to spend his life serving God. Miranda said, "What is so amazing is that very Sunday, I was doubting Dad's [God's] love for me, and prayed through tears, 'God, if You are real and You love me, please show me in a real and meaningful way.' That day, some four hours after I prayed that, He saved my son, even though He didn't spare His own. I will never doubt God's love, power, and sovereignty again."

~ Author's Note ~

Miranda, like most of us, was in a continuous battle with the devil. Remember, God wants control of our minds and so does the devil. Thankfully, it says in Revelation, "And they overcame him because of the blood of the Lamb and because of the word of their testimony, . . ." (12:11, NASB). We, as His children, have been given authority over the devil and his cohorts, but sometimes we forget and allow him to cause us unnecessary pain. He sometimes stands by and watches over us as the devil brings things into our lives to "sift you like wheat" (Luke 22:31, NASB). I personally love where the Lord Jesus told Peter (also called Simon), "Simon, Simon, behold, Satan has demanded permission to sift you like wheat; but I have prayed for you, that your faith may not fail; and you, when once you have turned again, strengthen your brothers" (Luke 22:31–32, NASB). It is precious to know that the Lord Jesus Christ personally looked at Peter and acknowledged the fact that he would be sifted like wheat but that Jesus had already prayed for him, that his faith would not fail. He is still the same yesterday, today, and forever.

Obedience Is Key

For many years, as my husband traveled around the globe on business, sometimes he would tell me how impressed he was with some place and that he would really like to take me there some day. But those occasions were rare. In his career, he visited five continents and too many cities to remember. One year, while coming back from a business trip to South America, he needed to stop off at Paradise Island in the Bahamas, where he stayed at The Atlantis Resort. That evening he called me, very excited, to tell me about the resort. He was in awe of the aquarium there. It held the largest number of fish known, with the exception of the ocean. After much prayer, we happily made reservations and began to eagerly await the day of departure. Just prior to our day to depart, we learned there were three hurricanes in the area. Each of them was large enough to ruin our plans. Two in particular looked rather menacing and gave us an unsettled feeling. We went back to the Lord to inquire of Him. Of course, we had been in that horrific tornado, an uneventful earthquake, and several typhoons in Hong Kong, where our high-rise building swayed in the wind—literally! I felt that we should not go, but my husband felt the Lord was saying that we were to trust Him and go, that He wanted us there on mission for Him. My husband assured me that IF one of the hurricanes did hit the little island, we would be in that fabulous hotel, and since it had been recently built, it would withstand any hurricane, just as our high-rise building did in Hong Kong. I knew that if he believed so strongly that the Lord was sending us, then we were to go.

We arrived there safely and watched the weather reports frequently. We had prayed the whole way there. My husband began praying specifically about each storm. Since we were particularly interested in two of them headed toward us from the southeast, he asked the Lord for one to turn north over the ocean and the other one to dissipate. As we prayed and waited on Him, He used us to bring the gospel of Jesus Christ to people He had already lined up for us right there on the resort and downtown Nassau. I shared the gospel of Jesus Christ with a lady named Carol, and although she came close, she just wouldn't embrace it. (I was reminded of another lady who went through a six-week Bible study with me but refused to accept Jesus. She admitted that if she had all the evidence that she needed and she knew in her heart it was true, she still would refuse to surrender her heart and life to Jesus.) That broke my heart. I pray that she has since accepted Him, or will, before Jesus comes.

One evening while having dinner, we began a conversation with our waiter to see if he knew about Jesus. The waiter's name was Emmanuel, so we asked if he knew what his name meant. He quickly and proudly exclaimed, "God with us!" Emmanuel was a lovely young man, and we enjoyed chatting with him. Each time he came to our table, a little more information would come forth. Somehow he learned that we were from Tennessee. We were pleasantly surprised to hear Emmanuel say that he would love to come and meet our pastor because he had seen him on television and loved him. As we left him that evening, Emmanuel had one request: that we ask our pastor to pray for him. As God would have it planned, some friends of ours from another country were coming to see us soon and wanted to have a little private time with our pastor. As it turned out, I was delighted to know that he invited me to sit in on the session. After introductions were made and we were settling in, a perfect time presented itself for me to inform our pastor of Emmanuel's love for Jesus, and for him, and about his request for our pastor to pray for him. He was so touched by this young man's request that he immediately asked that we stop right there and pray for him. Emmanuel would be so pleased. Included in this small meeting was a young college student. As we sat visiting with the pastor, he suddenly turned to the young man and asked him where he was spiritually. In what seemed to be a very few short minutes, he explained how to come to know the Lord, and the young man accepted Jesus Christ as his Savior that day. What a blessing to be there for that! We may not know until we get to heaven what that trip to the Bahamas was really all about, whatever happened to Emmanuel, or any of the others we made contact with while we were there. But God knows, and that is sufficient for us.

He commands us in the great commission in Matthew 28 to "Go." So, we were obedient, trusted in Him, and went. He proved Himself to be entirely faithful to us. We enjoyed beautiful weather, a wonderful vacation at a most interesting resort, and safe flights. And lest you think our faith to be so strong, consider this story.

A few years ago, we met a couple through boating in Mobile, Alabama. They were Bible translators and their "home" at the time was Papua, New Guinea. There were back in the US on furlough for a few months building support and visiting families and friends. Since they needed living quarters when they went into tribal areas to learn the different dialects, they believed the Lord provided the answer through the purchase of a thirty-foot sailboat. A few months later, they sailed across the Pacific Ocean, eventually arriving in Papua, New Guinea. It took several months for them to arrive because they would have to sail out of their way to various islands to replenish supplies before getting back on course. In addition, she was diabetic and insulin dependent. Later, they told us that not one time on their journey did they encounter a thunderstorm. Not once! Imagine that! They dealt with some pretty high winds at times, but never a thunderstorm. Can you not just envision our Lord directing the wind, the waves, the thunder, and the lightning, just so that tiny little vessel would have safe passage from Mobile, Alabama, through the Gulf of Mexico, through the Pacific Ocean, and on to *His* destination for them! Do you get my point? That's faith!

That story really blesses me. I have been such a chicken at times. It's faith like theirs that should encourage us all to trust the Lord and just go when He says go.

Jan's Story

It was May 1990. My Bible study that day was in the book of James chapter 5. As I read verses 13 through15, they jumped off the page at me. It says in part, "Is anyone among you suffering?" "Yes!" I said aloud. "That's me! I'm suffering, and I have been for nearly sixteen years." A disc in my lower back was deteriorated and the vertebrae had fused together. That part of my spine had no flexibility, and it felt like I had a brick back there. When I read those verses, I became excited because it was just as if God had spoken directly to me through His Word. Right then, I claimed those verses as my own, believing this was His promise to me if I would do what He said.

The following Sunday I went to a deacon and personal friend of my husband and me. I explained what I had read and what I wanted him to do for me. In front of the church, he laid his hands on me and prayed. Two months later, I was getting ready for work and had a Christian radio station on, as was my custom. I was in my bathroom putting on my makeup, bending slightly into my makeup mirror. The minister on the radio said he wasn't going to preach but felt he needed to pray because there were many out there hurting. I agreed. As he prayed, I was slightly bent, but I felt what had to be the bones of my lower back separate. I knew that

I had been healed, that my gracious heavenly Father had answered our prayers, and that He had allowed me to know exactly when He healed me. I blurted out that I had an arthritic finger also. He healed that too! Now I have complete freedom of movement with no pain in my back and hand. What a mighty and merciful God!

Eight years later, we had moved to another town. Over a period of several months, I had begun to feel discomfort or pain on my left side—in my shoulder, hip, leg, and ankle. The pain had worsened to the point where I thought I needed to see a doctor. All the while, that verse in the book of James chapter 5 kept running through my mind. I thought it would be selfish of me to ask God for yet another miracle. After all, where in the Bible were two miracles given to one person? I realized it was God's decision as to whether or not He would heal me. I discussed it with my husband, and we shared this with our close friend, who was also a deacon in our church. They prayed, and our friend laid his hands on me, asking God for healing and for God's will to be done in my life. That night I went to bed with pain, but woke up without it. Once again, God had shown his abundant mercy and love to me. Thank You, Jesus! "Trust in the Lord with ALL your heart; do not lean unto your own understanding. Acknowledge him in ALL your ways and HE will make your paths straight!"(Proverbs 3:5–6, NASB, emphasis added). "Now unto Him that is able to do exceedingly abundantly above all that we ask or think, according to the power that works in us, and to Him be glory in the church by Christ Jesus throughout all ages, world without end. Amen" (Ephesians 3:20–21, NKJV).

Divorce and Forgiveness

Margo's Story

All of my life I believed that divorce was wrong; it just did not happen in Christian families. I grew up in a time when divorce was a shameful thing. It was wrong, not just in God's eyes but also in the eyes of man. It was WRONG, bad, and just plain AWFUL. And when it did happen, it was mostly to the young and immature. I thought that usually at least one or the other spouse was not a Christian, and God's Word did not seem be a standard in the home. I am a Christian; I trusted Christ as my Savior in my teens and have had a deep personal relationship with Him since then. Of course, I'm not saying that I have never erred or failed Him, and myself, by sinning. But I know that He is my Redeemer and He forgives me when I sin, if I come to Him with a repentant heart and ask for forgiveness. I know that God hates divorce. He says so in the Bible (Malachi 2:16). God hates it, and, as a believer, so do I. I never expected to be writing a message about divorce from a personal experience. However, I have walked the dark valley of divorce.

I have experienced the pain of rejection by the person I loved more than any other. I know why God hates divorce. I do not dare try to explain why I was allowed to go through this experience.

But I do know that He walked every step of it with me and carried me when I was too weak to go on. He comforted me when the pain was too great to bear. He sent friends and loved ones to show His tender love and care, to pray with me, to bring forth the scriptures, and He gave me hope. Jeremiah 29:11 states, "'For I know the plans I have for you,' declares the Lord, 'plans to prosper you and not to harm you, plans to give you hope and a future'" (NIV).

All through the Bible we find that God hates divorce, that divorce is man's way not God's way. My belief is even stronger today than it was when I first went through the divorce. He hates SIN, but He loves me and He loves my former husband. In His Excellent Greatness, over the past years, He has shown me a new awareness of His Presence in my life. He has shown me that His promises in His Word are true. He promises, "My grace is sufficient for you, for My power is made perfect in weakness" (2 Corinthians 12:9, NIV). He continues to be with me and guide me. Am I happy about the divorce? No! Am I joyful in my life? YES! I have peace that surpasses understanding and joy in my heart. And I know that my Lord and Savior, my Shepherd, is watching over me and walking with me daily.

Several years ago a friend passed along a phrase to me, and it stuck in my mind. "Nothing happens to us that isn't Father-filtered." That is a great source of comfort to me because it tells me that He is aware of all of my circumstances, and that He is with me in all of my trials. In the New Testament, we are told that He clothes the fields, He knows the number of hairs on my head, and He knows when every sparrow falls. Then He states how much more He loves us. He was present with me in the pain and darkness; He is present with me in my healing. I know that through the pain, the dreams dashed, the hopes vanquished, the sorrow, the hurt of failure, the plans that will never come about, He, in His Excellent Greatness, has provided me with a love that no human can provide. He loves each of us as if there were only one of us.

He always has time for us. He will never reject me for any other. Divorce tears away our earthly home, but God has promised me a home with Him forever. John 14:2 tells us that He goes to prepare a place for us. His Word is truth, so if He says that, then it's true.

There is another aspect to this thing called divorce. Divorce hurts more than just the two people whose lives are ripped apart. Someone has said that when two people put aside what God has joined together, it is like tearing two pieces of paper apart that have been superglued together. Both are severely damaged! It hurts entire families and friends of the couple. It makes for awkward relationships with most of the people who know the couple. But the deep hurt and pain that the rejected spouse deals with brings about real need for forgiveness. First comes the element of blaming, which is a natural human instinct for survival. The experience of healing is necessary to become a thriving and vital person again. We cannot move forward without dealing with our hurts and disappointments. We need to look deeply and honestly at every aspect of the hurt. Perhaps you are angry with your spouse who left, with yourself, and maybe even God for letting it happen. The Lord showed me that if I wanted to be spiritually healthy again, I must go further than accepting the fact that my husband left me. Just as I had to accept being rejected by the one person I loved and trusted most on this earth, I had to forgive him, even if he never asked for forgiveness from me. In my quiet time one morning, I read, "Forgive and you will be forgiven" (Luke 6:37, NKJV). The words jumped off the page! The human side of me rebelled. I thought, *No way! I don't need to be forgiven; I wasn't the one who . . .* I lay back for a few minutes. With tears in my eyes, I asked God to show me all the areas in my life that I needed forgiveness. I asked for forgiveness for my part in the divorce. Then, after many more tears, I said, "Lord, I know that You want me to forgive him. I know that I have talked to You and my friends about this." I proceeded to give excuses for my husband's leaving: I was tired all the time from my rheumatoid disease, I wasn't as attractive as I used to be, I didn't always please him, etc. God said to me, "I did not ask you to excuse him. I asked you to forgive him." It took some time, but I prayed, read scriptures, read books on forgiveness, and sought prayer with Christian friends. But still, I need His help. He told me, "My child, I am helping you. Whom do you think led you to those scriptures, books, and friends who could help you understand?" I wept and forgave my husband. Does that mean that I never have a "relapse" in my thinking, never feel the hurt, or never wish things had turned out differently? No, but it means that when I have negative thoughts, I come back to God and ask His forgiveness.

The Lord then moved me to forgive the woman who my husband had the affair with. I just told the Lord that I would work on that later. He let me know that I would get my peace *later*. I didn't feel I had it in me. He promised me that if I let Him, He would enable me to forgive. And He did.

When we go through the storms, dark voyages, times of utter despair, or when things seem totally hopeless, we can only find true peace and relief in the Lord. It comes when we allow the Holy Spirit, the Comforter, to come and dwell in us. It comes when we accept His love and His promises. After all, He sent His Son, who was willing to die for our sins, into this world that we might have life to the full. The Bible tells us that in this world we will have trouble (John 16:33). Our Savior, Jesus Christ, Who has overcome the world, can restore the joy in our lives, if we let Him, no matter the circumstances. His amazing grace has indeed proven to be sufficient, just as He promises in 2 Corinthians 12:9.

I pray that whatever pain you are facing, you will turn to the Lord and His Word; He is waiting for you there and wants to show you His Excellent Greatness. "Let your light so shine before men, that they may see your good works and glorify your Father which is in heaven" (Matthew 5:16, KJV).

Nothing, Lord, is too hard for You.
You made the earth, the sky so blue
You made the trees
With the leaves to flutter in the breeze
So, I know that nothing, Lord, is too hard for You.
You made the darkness of the night
But You also made the day with all its light
The sun and moon that shine so bright
So, I know nothing, Lord, is too hard for You.
You made the snow and the rain
You allow the tears and the pain
You cause joy to come into our hearts again
So, I know that nothing, Lord, is too hard for You.
You came to me when I was so sad
When everything in my world seemed so bad
And You restored my joy and made me glad
So, I know that nothing, Lord, is too hard for you.

~ Author's Note ~

Many theologians have covered divorce in-depth and have come out with varying conclusions. Scripture states, "For the Lord God of Israel says that He hates divorce!" (Malachi 2:16, NKJV). Divorce is not His plan for us. Our great God prefers we follow His commandments, which are not suggestions, for both men and women in marriage relationships and in our other daily lives. The New Testament outlines the biblical basis for divorce. However, that is not a commandment; we have been taught that it is simply an option when there is a pattern of continual, incessant, unremorseful unfaithfulness on the part of a spouse. Yet, it is amazing what God has done in some of these circumstances. Moses gave permission for divorce because of the rebelliousness of the people's hearts—not a good foundation for going against the Most High God. And how many of us have not been in rebellion to Him in our lives? It still does not give us a pass. What we do with the circumstances we find ourselves in is what is important. I know there are spouses who have stayed in relationships for years and years with a spouse who is abusive emotionally, verbally, sexually, and physically, and they refuse to change. Some are ill and have no place else to go. It is a very difficult situation, especially if the abusive spouse is highly thought of in the community and by other family members, so there is no support system for the victim. While I certainly don't recommend that someone stay in an unsafe relationship, I know of those who stayed and developed an intimate relationship with the Lord, to where others could see Jesus in them. They allowed those tough situations to make them into beautiful saints of God. They allowed God to be their "husbands" as He promises in His Word. It seems to me that it is best to seek a place of refuge from abuse if that can be arranged but if not, then the Lord is definitely there for you at all times. Go to Him continuously for your spiritual, physical, and emotional strength. He may not change the plight you find yourself in, but He can change you. Pray in faith, and ask others to join you, that God may change your spouse and protect you and your marriage. May God bless you!

If you wake up one morning and discover that the person sitting across the table from you has gone in a different direction and you have nothing in common, seek God immediately and ask Him to restore the two of you. Or if like so many people in this time of no-fault divorce, you suddenly realize you have no love for this person and begin to think perhaps there would be someone better for you, seek God immediately and ask Him to restore your love and respect for that person. If your heart is completely surrendered to Him and His perfect will for you, before you know it, you will find love returning to your heart for that person. Our great God cannot be kept in a box; He is totally limitless. He is much more interested in seeing our marriages saved than we are. He appreciates a heart that is willing to die to self and live for Him. If you have a willing heart and will give Him time, He will take all the broken pieces of your heart and do amazing things that you could never think of.

Many of the problems in today's society can be laid on the back of our pride and narcissism, which is arrogance, selfishness, and self-absorption. Our age of instant gratification and Cinderella-type expectations for marriage in the United States is a large part of the cause of marriage failure. When things go wrong, or if our mate doesn't meet our needs exactly right in our eyes, then we are ready to dump that one and go on to another. There is no relationship that doesn't take work! What matures us and our marriage relationship is overcoming trials—together. We will all fail each other at varying times throughout life. No one will meet our expectations except our relationship with Jesus Christ. And He certainly doesn't always jump when we first cry out to Him either. That is also how we grow closer to Him, by sticking with Him when He takes us through the fire. Marriage is a picture of Jesus and the Bride of Christ.

God first began to lay it out for us way back in the book of Genesis. He stipulated that when a man and woman get married, they are to leave their families and cleave to each other. Someone once drew an analogy that said: it's like we are superglued together in God's sight when we are married. If divorce happens, it destroys both the man and the woman so that they are damaged forever in some ways. Imagine then, too, what happens if children are involved; they may forever see things differently regarding marriage, divorce, and remarriage. Please do not think that I am being harsh and uncaring! I do not want anyone to misunderstand. There are situations where it seems divorce is the only way or certainly legal separation. However, for a couple I knew, it only took one member of the marriage to stay focused on God and His promises in His Word to see Him create a miracle and bring their spouse to repentance. After long-term counseling sessions and much dating, they were restored and remained together, very much in love and serving God. He is a God of love, forgiveness, and restoration, and He will work miracles for us and through us IF we allow Him to. It may not ever be perfect, but life on earth never will be perfect. This is the time of trials and tribulations. When Jesus comes, all things change for good for all eternity IF we have surrendered our lives to Him.

All that being said, although God hates divorce (see Malachi 2:16), if divorce has already happened in your life, remember He is a God of love, compassion, and forgiveness. If you have already gone through divorce without biblical grounds, then you need to seek God for His forgiveness, then you need to confess, repent and, where possible, be restored to your former spouse. He can redeem the time. In Joel 2:25 (NASB), He states, "Then I will make up to you for the years that the swarming locust has eaten. . . ." If your former spouse is already married and living in that relationship, it is too late. If you are a believer and your former spouse is not, then don't be reunited. It's better not to be reunited with an unbeliever. If it is too late, then go forward with the Lord at the helm of your life from where you are now. He still has a plan for your life; however, it just might not be for remarriage. Don't compound the problem by remarrying out of His will. If you already have, then the above verse still holds true for you too. Confess, repent, etc. God makes known to us His thoughts on the subject of how we are to be yoked. If we run ahead of Him, we make choices sent to us by the counterfeiter before God reveals His prized selection for us. We are NOT to be unbiblically yoked or bound together in marriage or business partnerships or anywhere else where partnerships are formed. The Word of God begs these questions, "Do not be bound together with unbelievers; for what partnership have righteousness and lawlessness, or what fellowship has light with darkness? Or what harmony has Christ with Belial, or what has a believer in common with an unbeliever?" (2 Corinthians 6:14–15, NASB). We obviously must be in the world and associating with unbelievers, but we certainly do not need to be intimately associated with them through unbiblical partnerships. Sometimes we end up being unequally yoked because we have become a Christian after we are married and our spouse has not. If there is no biblical basis to divorce or no abuse to cause you to leave, then it is our responsibility to stay there, pray for our spouse, and live our lives according to God's plan until that spouse comes into the kingdom. If they do not, then that's between them and God. If they decide to leave, then God's Word says to let them go, and you will be free.

Scripture teaches us to dress modestly and to lead a gentle and quiet life. The years of the sexual revolution from the sixties to the years of the feminists and humanists, integrated with the alcohol and drug culture, have caused homes to break up with alarmingly high statistics in the Christian Evangelical community. Women are often left to raise their children, many husbands become absentee dads, and children with no male Christian leadership are left to repeat the mistakes of their parents. Society does not determine God's will on the matter. God's will determines what a society should do. A nation that follows God's will is blessed. We need to surrender to the Lord Jesus Christ, and allow Him to bring revival so that our families and our nation can be restored to our Savior. "If I shut up the heavens . . . and My people who are called by My name humble themselves and pray and seek My face and turn from their wicked ways, then will I hear from heaven, will forgive their sin, and will heal their land" (2 Chronicles 7:14, NASB). Let's all please ask the Holy Spirit of God to shine His holy spotlight into our hearts so that we can see our wicked ways, confess and repent of them, so He can bring about the healing that we so desperately need in our homes and in our land. Today can be the first day of a new surrendered life to Christ Jesus.

"I love the LORD, because He hears my voice and my supplications. Because He has inclined His ear to me, therefore I shall call upon Him as long as I live" (Psalm 116:1–2 NASB).

"Husbands, love your wives, just as Christ also loved the church and gave Himself for her . . ." (Ephesians 5:25, NKJV).

"You husbands, in the same way, live with your wives in an understanding way, as with someone weaker, since she is a woman; and show her honor as a fellow heir of the grace of life, so that your prayers will not be hindered" (1 Peter 3:7, NASB).

"In the same way, you wives, be submissive to your own husbands so that even if any of them are disobedient to the Word, they may be won without a word by the behavior of their wives" (1 Peter 3:1, NASB).

In the sight of God, men and women are equal. However, someone has to be head, just as in any business arrangement. Men and women have strengths and weaknesses, and we complement our spouse if we love and respect each other as is pleasing to the Lord.

Husbands and wives, read Ephesians 5:22–33 and 1 Peter 3:1–17. There are some very stern commandments here, and in other parts of the Bible, regarding marriage and divorce for all of us. It should serve as a great caution to those of us who have either suffered through our parents' bad marriages, bad marriages with our spouses, or see what's happening to those we love. We really need to be careful how we counsel others, as well. Seek the Lord and be sure you are following His lead. We will be held accountable before the Lord. On a couple of occasions after my husband had given me a decision on something, I have gone to the Lord and asked what He wanted me to do. His answer came quickly in those situations: "I want you to listen to your husband!" There was a time that God had told Abraham to listen to his wife and do all she said. Another time, he listened to her when he should not have. Husbands, you will be held accountable not only for yourselves, but for your wife and your family, as well. Check out who the Lord God held responsible in the Garden of Eden with Adam and Eve. All that being said, we are told in the book of Lamentations that God is still faithful to us. "The LORD'S loving kindnesses indeed never cease, for His compassions never fail. They are new every morning; great is Your faithfulness" (Lamentations 3:22–23, NASB). He knows that we are all capable of any sin. He is waiting with outstretched arms to welcome us back, if we will just listen and learn, run to Him, and confess and repent. Our gracious

God is still able to do miracles in the lives of ordinary people. "God's plan is to take ordinary people with ordinary talents, do extraordinary things through them and give glory to Himself"[12] (apply to 1 Corinthians 1:27–31). *GREAT IS THY FAITHFULNESS, O LORD!* Thank You for Your great love to us! Forgive us of our iniquities as individuals and as a nation, O Lord, and bring back Your glory to us. Thank You, dear Father God. We can surely pray this in the name of Your Son, Jesus, the Christ. Amen.

---

[12] Adrian Rogers, *Adrianisms: The Wit and Wisdom of Adrian Rogers, Volume One* (Bartlett, TN: Love Worth Finding Ministries, 2007) 57.

New Year, Renewed Faith

Joy's Story

It was January 1, and I was having morning Bible study and prayer when I came across a verse of scripture that caught my attention. It listed all the terrible sins I thought I would never be caught doing. "But the fearful and unbelieving and the abominable and murderers and whoremongers and sorcerers and idolaters and all liars, shall have their part in the second death" (Revelation 21:8, KJV). Heading that whole list of sins was the sin of FEAR. For years, I had been so fearful, and now I was having to deal with this.

My husband traveled extensively, but I had not been anywhere because I was afraid to fly. As God began to speak to me through His Word, I ran to the family room where my husband was reading the newspaper. "Guess what! I'm going to fly," I announced. He couldn't imagine what had come over me! Then I shared with him the verse and how God had spoken to me through it.

One day in December, I received a letter. It informed me that I had been chosen, along with thirty-seven other women from all over the United States, to be a part of a conference that was to be held in Dallas, Texas. They would be sending me my airline ticket in the next letter!

On January 19, I stood in line at the airport to receive my boarding pass. I was seated next to a lovely lady from Columbus, Ohio. I began to tell her about the conference I was going to attend in Dallas and that it was my first time flying. "I'm going to that same conference," she said, "and nearly every time I fly, it is with a first timer." As the plane took off, she held my hand. Tears were streaming down my face. But they were not tears of fear. Do you see what God had done? He had gone before me and placed me beside a lady who was going to the same conference, and who had a heart for a first-time flyer. I learned that day that He can remove all fear! "So do not fear, for I am with you; do not be dismayed, for I am your God. I will strengthen you and help you; I will uphold you with my righteous right hand" (Isaiah 41:10, NIV).

~ Author's Note ~

It was my privilege to meet Joy many years ago during one of my speaking trips to Ohio. She is a very gracious and lovely lady; she was certainly not someone I would have thought to have a fear of anything. To me, she looked like a swan on a pond—appearing as if she had everything under control. However, if you look at swans' feet under water, you will see that they, too, are paddling as fast as they can. We all have issues we are working on, or should be working on, with the Lord. Whether it's fear or other issues, we must allow our Lord to remove them step by step: first, to rid ourselves of the strongholds of the enemy and get out of bondage, and second, to enable us to grow more intimate with Him. Even King David had fear! In the Psalms, we are told, "I sought the

Lord, and He heard me; and delivered me from all my fears" (Psalm 34:4).

In Isaiah 44:8 it says, "'Do not tremble and do not be afraid; have I not long since announced it to you and declared it? And you are My witnesses. Is there any God besides Me? Or is there any other Rock? I know of none'" (NASB). Joy was learning to walk in faith. All believers will be given opportunities to take a step in faith. If we desire to grow more like Him and desire a more intimate relationship with Him, we will follow in that challenge. Think of Abraham when he offered up Isaac, or what Esther did by offering herself to King Ahasuerus in order to save her people. The scriptures are full of stories about people taking a step in faith. Remember, Jesus is fully man and fully God. Scripture tells us that in His manhood, "Although He was a Son, He learned obedience from the things which He suffered" (Hebrews 5:8, NASB). An Adrianism says, "Glance at your problems; gaze on God!"[13]

---

[13] Adrian Rogers, *Adrianisms: The Wit and Wisdom of Adrian Rogers, Volume Two* (Bartlett, TN: Love Worth Finding Ministries, 2007).

Epilogue

Many years have passed since the birth of that little girl on a farm in the Deep South. Many experiences have occurred to shape and form her thinking. We see that good and evil does indeed travel on parallel tracks, something that I have seen up close and personal all through the years. The battle surely continues in everyone's life because the Lord our God wants to control our minds, and Satan wants to control our minds too. But all praises to God our Father!

Initially, God is simply our Creator. Once we accept His Son, Jesus, we become His children. He, then, is our Father. If we have been born again spiritually, the victory is already won by Him through Jesus Christ our Savior. Jesus died on the cross for our sins, and by the shedding of His perfect, unblemished blood, everyone can partake of that wonderful gift of His salvation. Dr. Adrian Rogers once said that when Jesus died on the cross, God dropped the A-Bomb on the devil (paraphrased). Time is running out. When you study the Bible and watch the news, you can see that the end-times truly are upon us. I truly believe the Rapture of the church could be at any time now. If you do not believe rapture is in the scriptures, read 1 Thessalonians 4:16–17 (NASB), "For the Lord Himself will descend from Heaven with a shout, with the voice of an archangel, and with the trumpet of God. And the dead in Christ shall rise first. Then we who are alive and remain shall be caught up together with them in the clouds to meet the Lord in the air. And thus we shall always be with the Lord." The words "caught up" here means rapture, coming from the Latin Vulgate verb *rapio*. If you have never surrendered your heart to Jesus Christ and accepted Him as your Savior, please do it now. You need to get settled as to who your daddy is. Once this life is over, you no longer have that choice. The following is simply a story that has floated around on e-mail for many years:

Who's Your Daddy?

> A seminary professor was vacationing with his wife in Gatlinburg, Tennessee. One morning they were eating breakfast at a little restaurant, hoping to enjoy a quiet, family meal. While they were waiting for their food, they noticed a distinguished looking, white-haired man moving from table to table, visiting with the guests. The professor leaned over and whispered to his wife, "I hope he doesn't come over here."

> But sure enough, the man did come over to their table. "Where are you folks from?" he asked in a friendly voice.

> "Oklahoma," they answered.

> "Great to have you here in Tennessee," the stranger said. "What do you do for a living?"

> "I teach at a seminary," he replied.

"Oh, so you teach preachers how to preach, do you? Well, I've got a really great story for you." And with that, the gentleman pulled up a chair and sat down at the table with the couple.

The professor groaned and thought to himself, *Great! Just what I need—another preacher story!*

The man began with, "See that mountain over there? (Pointing out the restaurant window). Not far from the base of that mountain, there was a boy born to an unwed mother. He had a hard time growing up because everyplace he went, he was always asked the same question, 'Hey boy! Who's your daddy?' Whether he was at school, in the grocery store, or drug store, people would ask the same question, 'Who's your daddy?' He would hide at recess and lunchtime from other students. He would avoid going into stores because that question hurt him so badly. When he was about twelve years old, a new preacher came to his church. The lad would always go in late and slip out early to avoid hearing the question, 'Who's your daddy?' But one day, the new preacher said the benediction so fast that he got caught and had to walk out with the crowd. Just about the time he got to the back door, the new preacher, not knowing anything about him put his hand on his shoulder and asked him, 'Son, who's your daddy?' The whole church got deathly quiet. He could feel every eye in the church looking at him. Now everyone would finally know the answer to the question, 'Who's your daddy?' This new preacher, though, sensed the situation around him and, using discernment that only the Holy Spirit could give, said the following to that scared little boy: 'Wait a minute! I know who you are! I see the family resemblance now. You are a child of God!' He patted the boy on his shoulder and said, 'Boy, you've got a great inheritance. Go and claim it.' With that, the boy smiled for the first time in a long time and walked out the door a changed person. He was never the same again. Whenever anyone asked him, 'Who's your daddy?' he would just tell them, 'I'm a child of God.'"

The distinguished gentleman got up from the table and said, "Isn't that a great story?"

The professor responded that it really was a great story.

As the man turned to leave, he said, "You know, if that new preacher hadn't told me that I was one of God's children, I probably never would have amounted to anything!" And he walked away.

The seminary professor and his wife were stunned. He called the waitress over and asked her, "Do you know who that man was—the one who just left that was sitting at our table?"

The waitress grinned and said, "Of course. Everyone here knows him. That's Ben Hooper. He's the former governor of Tennessee!"

This story is true—sort of. Ben Hooper was the former governor of Tennessee, and he was born out of wedlock. The part about the preacher is not true. Ben Hooper was actually the son of a physician, who refused to marry his mother because he was engaged to another lady. Ben Hooper was illegitimate; people made fun of him because of what his parents had done. He got into a lot of scrapes with other boys. His mother died and he ended up in an orphanage. Finally, somewhere along the way, his daddy and his wife rescued him and brought him to live with them. So, he knew who his daddy was. Everyone in the community where he lived had known that all along. The beauty of Ben's life is that he apparently gave his life to the Lord around age fifteen, was baptized, was a member of a Baptist church, and lived his life for the Lord from then on. He was a child of God and did begin to bear resemblance to his heavenly Father.

We are not automatically a child of God if we are baptized when we are infants, or if we are baptized later in life, or even if we grow up with Christian parents. We must *choose* to surrender our lives to Jesus Christ and follow His teachings, then we are to be baptized. By the way, baptism means immersion. The scripture tells us that Jesus came up out of the water. Baptism doesn't save us. Baptism is simply an outward sign of an inner change in one's heart. It represents the death, burial, and resurrection of Jesus Christ. It is important that we get baptized and that we are baptized on the right side of our conversion. Both my husband and I had to get that right. We do have a choice of whom we will serve in this world and with whom we will spend eternity. We chose Jesus Christ. He is the One Who died for us, and in so doing paid the penalty for our sins and imputed His righteousness to us.

Wherever He has placed us, that is our pulpit; that is our place of missionary work. "Set your mind on things above, not things on the earth" (Colossians 3:2, NKJV). If we are surrendered to Him and doing our work for Jesus as we should be, we are pleasing Him.

None of us know when the Lord will say that our lives are over here on this earth. But Father God has always known the number of our days. Choose eternal life with Him and begin right now to live the life of royalty—being a part of His kingdom. One day soon we will live with Him in His perfect kingdom in heaven. He is the King of kings! (Philippians 1:27–30). Jesus lived, He died for our sins, He arose, and He ascended into heaven, leaving a promise behind that He is coming again for His children. Amen!

www.ingramcontent.com/pod-product-compliance
Lightning Source LLC
Chambersburg PA
CBHW031825090426
42741CB00005B/140